I0799867

IMAGES
of America

MARTIN COUNTY

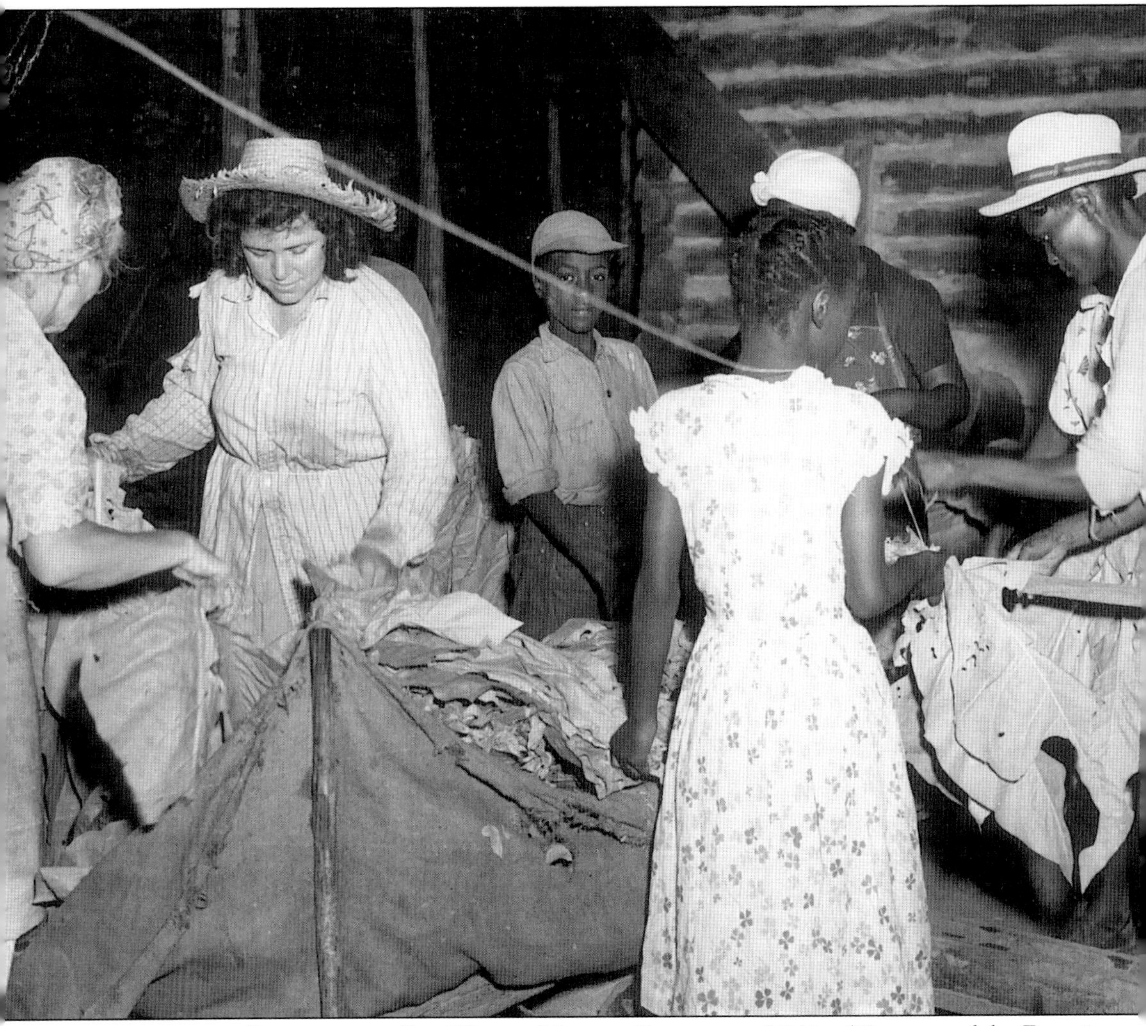

HARVESTING TOBACCO THE OLD WAY IN MARTIN COUNTY, C. 1940S. (Courtesy of the Francis Manning Room.)

IMAGES
of America

MARTIN COUNTY

Fred W. Harrison Jr.

ARCADIA
PUBLISHING

ISBN 978-0-7385-0272-4

Published by Arcadia Publishing
Charleston, South Carolina

Printed in the United States of America

Library of Congress Catalog Card Number: Applied for.

For all general information contact Arcadia Publishing at:
Telephone 843-853-2070
Fax 843-853-0044
E-Mail sales@arcadiapublishing.com
For customer service and orders:
Toll-Free 1-888-313-2665

Visit us on the Internet at www.arcadiapublishing.com

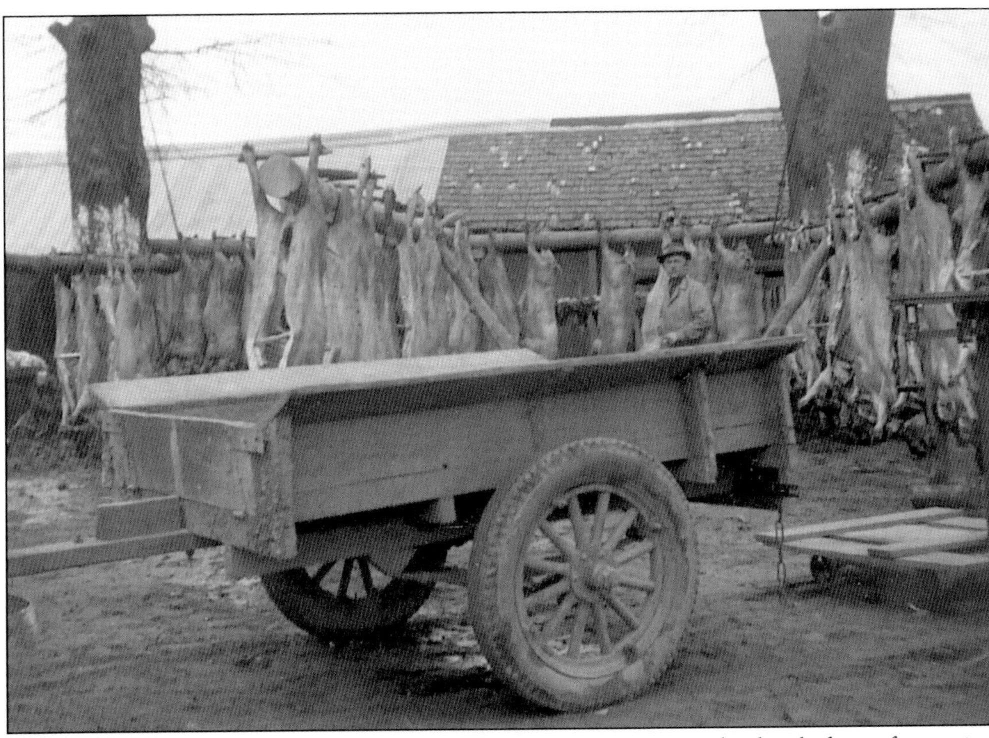

An Old-Fashioned Hog Killing in Martin County, c. 1940s. In the days before refrigeration was the norm, hog killings were often social events in farming communities. Families would assist each other in the butchering and preparation of meat for curing and storage in the smokehouse (Courtesy of the Francis Manning Room.)

Contents

ACKNOWLEDGMENTS

This book would not have been possible without the generous support of the Library Committee of the Martin County Historical Society. This group currently maintains the Francis Manning Room in the library of Martin Community College. The Manning Room is, with few exceptions, one of the finest repositories devoted to the history of a single county in the state. Established in 1984, the collection in large part derives its existence from historical papers, maps, books, pictures, etc., bequeathed to the Martin County Historical Society by the late Francis M. Manning, Williamston's newspaper editor and a county historian. Manning's close friendship with the late Warren Biggs, a longtime collector of county and regional memorabilia, was a main source of preservation for much of the history that is known about Martin County today. While Biggs collected early manuscripts and such pertaining to the county's history, Manning missed few, if any, opportunities to promote them through his newspaper, the *Enterprise*. By the time of his death, Biggs had amassed a warehouse full of materials relating to the county, leaving it to his friend Francis to sort and maintain. Manning continued to share this valuable core of items with the public through his special editions of the *Enterprise*. The Francis Manning Room was established to honor Manning for his lasting contributions to the county and to house his collection of historical materials, some of which are also housed in the East Carolina Manuscript Collection at East Carolina University.

I might add that many of the photographs found in the Manning Room are attributed to the late Eugene Rice, Martin County photographer, as well as to the Royal Photographic Center of Williamston. The Manning Room photographs provided the bulk source of images used in this publication. Accordingly, I'd like pay special tribute to Doris L. Wilson, chairman of the Library Committee of the Martin County Historical Society, for her untiring support of my endeavor. She and her wonderful group of volunteers, besides granting permission to publish these images, also spent a number of hours sorting them and advising the author on additional contacts. Also noteworthy of praise is Margaret M. Griffin, who, though not a native of Martin County, has embraced a deep appreciation of its past and likewise has been an avid promoter of its importance to the life and character of the community.

Special thanks goes to J. Earl Bailey for his technical expertise which made possible the use of several rare images found in the book and to Lynette Lundin of the Special Collections Department of Joyner Library at East Carolina University for her assistance in the reproduction of an extraordinarily rare map. Thanks is also extended to Sarah Manning Pope, who loaned her valuable collection of postcards relating to Martin County. Finally, I would like to extend my deepest appreciation to the following contributors whose pictures, stories, and words of encouragement have made this worth all the more to me: Patsy R. Miller, Ann H. McKeel, Alton Hopewell, Sallie H. Long, Chloe G. Tuttle, Clarence Pate, the family of the late Josephine R. Smith, the staff of the Martin Community College Library, Mary M. Jones Peele, Virginia B. Rodgers, Frances P. Whitley, Becky Jenkins, Mary Charles G. Coppage, Michael G. Taylor, Mary G. Dixon, Joyce T. Roberson, Alma J. Bailey, and Ila Parker.

INTRODUCTION

It seems quite possible that Ralph Lane, the governor of Sir Walter Raleigh's first colony sent to the New World, may have been the first to view the area now referred to as Martin County. According to record, Lane and his associates made an inland journey up present-day Roanoke River in 1585, in search of gold. Historians estimate that the group traveled as far as modern Williamston or Hamilton before returning to Roanoke Island, nearly starved and with little except Lane's descriptive accounts to show for their efforts. Likewise, others would continue to pass through the area in the coming years, though it would be nearly a century before any permanent settlement in the area would begin.

The 1660s marked the first visible increase of people in the region, and with that came the creation of Albemarle County in 1664. Within this original county were several precincts including Chowan, which covered present Martin County. By 1740, Bertie and Tyrrell Counties had been created from portions of Chowan. By 1760, Bertie County was divided in half to create Halifax County. It was from this portion of Halifax County and the western half of Tyrrell County that Martin County was formed in 1774. Early inhabitants of Martin County concentrated their initial settlement along the banks of the Roanoke. Most were primarily of English descent, migrating from the earliest of settlements in southeastern Virginia, and more than a few were drawn to the region by speculative opportunities associated with the land.

By the early 18th century, the local Native American population began to resent the continued encroachment of whites in the area and, on September 22, 1711, waged an all out surprise massacre on the newcomers. The event was highly destructive to settlements along the Roanoke River, and, for a time, the Tuscaroras seemed to have achieved their aim. But in the following year, a decisive battle near New Bern reduced their power significantly. In 1718, the Tuscaroras submitted to a treaty that placed them on a reservation just across the river from Williamston, in neighboring Bertie County.

Incorporated as the seat of government for Martin County in 1779, Williamston had its beginnings as a port of entry along the Roanoke as early as 1730. Vast quantities of naval stores shipped from the location earned the port its initial reference as Tar Landing. Upon incorporation, the name was changed to Williamston in honor of Martin County militia leader Col. William Williams.

In 1777, John Llewelling originated a widespread Tory conspiracy in Martin County aimed at murdering leaders of the Revolutionary War movement, including North Carolina Governor Richard Caswell. Quick action of another Martin native, Nathan Mayo, rendered the plot void. Llewelling was sentenced to hang but was secured a pardon through the efforts of his wife.

As with the South in general, a plantation-style economy began to emerge in Martin soon after 1800. By the 1830s, cotton had become a significant factor in the county's trade activities. The largest plantations to be found in Martin were mainly those along the river. As a matter of consequence, primary shipping lines on the watercourse had their origin or control based in Martin County. Slavery became a mainstay as the need for labor in the cotton fields and in the forests with naval stores production increased. In 1850, slaves in Martin totaled 3,367; there were 4,615 white inhabitants.

The Civil War and its aftermath retarded much of the growth and progress made by the county in previous years. Williamston civic and business leader Cushing Biggs Hassell estimated that there were nearly $2 million in damages to the county as a result of the conflict, an astronomical sum at the time. The towns of Williamston, Hamilton, and Jamesville were severely looted, with Hamilton and Jamesville suffering much in the way of fire. Jamesville, in fact, was all but destroyed by fire. A radical element took control of the county after the war, ousting much of Martin's earlier political leadership. Former U.S. congressman and later Confederate judge Asa Biggs found the situation unbearable and left both his home and legal practice in Williamston for a new career as a commission merchant in Norfolk, Virginia.

By the 1870s, lumbering marked a significant renewal of fortunes to some, if not all, Martin County residents. The Jamesville & Washington Railroad and Lumber Company and the Dennis Simmons Lumber Company were the chief industrial concerns in the county at this time. The latter, founded by lumber merchant Dennis Simmons, was one of the largest of its kind in the state. The former is particularly remembered for having the first railroad constructed in the county between Jamesville and Washington.

The Williamston and Tarboro Railroad, completed in 1882, became the county's second such road and fostered the growth of new towns such as Everetts, Robersonville, and Parmele. Most influenced was Robersonville, which saw its fortunes rise swiftly after the introduction of tobacco in the county during the 1890s. The first tobacco market to open in the county was in Robersonville in 1900.

Martin experienced another highlight in transportation with the opening of the Roanoke River Bridge and its causeways in 1922. A memorable flood severely damaged the bridge in August of 1940, but it was soon rebuilt and continues to be a vital link across the Roanoke River.

Like Robersonville, Williamston also emerged as a center for tobacco trade after 1900. The time was especially ripe for young entrepreneurs willing to take on the extensive business opportunities connected with tobacco. Many enterprising young men like L.B. Harrison came to Williamston, especially from the rural Griffins and Bear Grass Townships, between 1900 and 1930. With increased demand for consumer goods and services after World War II, modern Williamston was born amid a flurry of construction activities in the 1950s. New neighborhoods in the west and east portions of town and the erection of a new hospital and school facilities characterized the period. Symbolic of the competition of old and new forces along Main Street was the untimely fire that destroyed the town's picturesque city hall in December 1958.

Martin County continues today to hold on to its rich tradition of agriculture. Tobacco, though much diminished since the 1980s, continues as an important cash crop. On the same note, the county's long association with forest products is still much evidenced in the operations of the Weyerhaeuser Corporation in the lower east portion of the county. Also of continuing importance are the family histories that serve to bind the county and give it an identity that can belong only to Martin County.

Fred W. Harrison Jr.
July 26, 1999

One

WILLIAMSTON 1860–1940

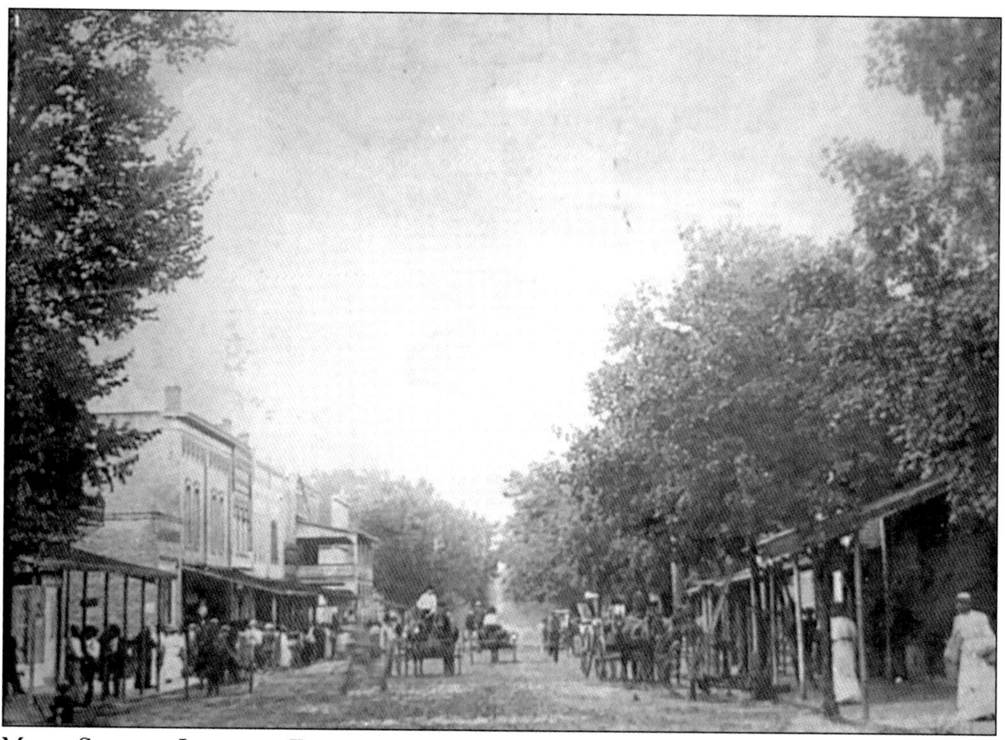

MAIN STREET, LOOKING EAST, C. 1900. Brick structures began to replace older wood frame ones along the street toward the close of the 1890s. (Courtesy of the Sarah M. Pope Collection.)

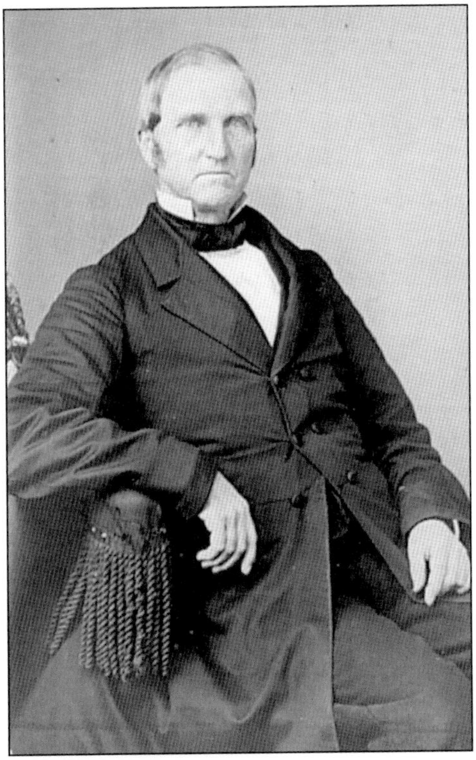

Cushing Biggs Hassell (1809–1880). A prominent business, civic, and religious leader, Hassell undoubtedly remains one of the most significant figures in 19th-century Williamston and Martin County. (Courtesy of the Francis Manning Room.)

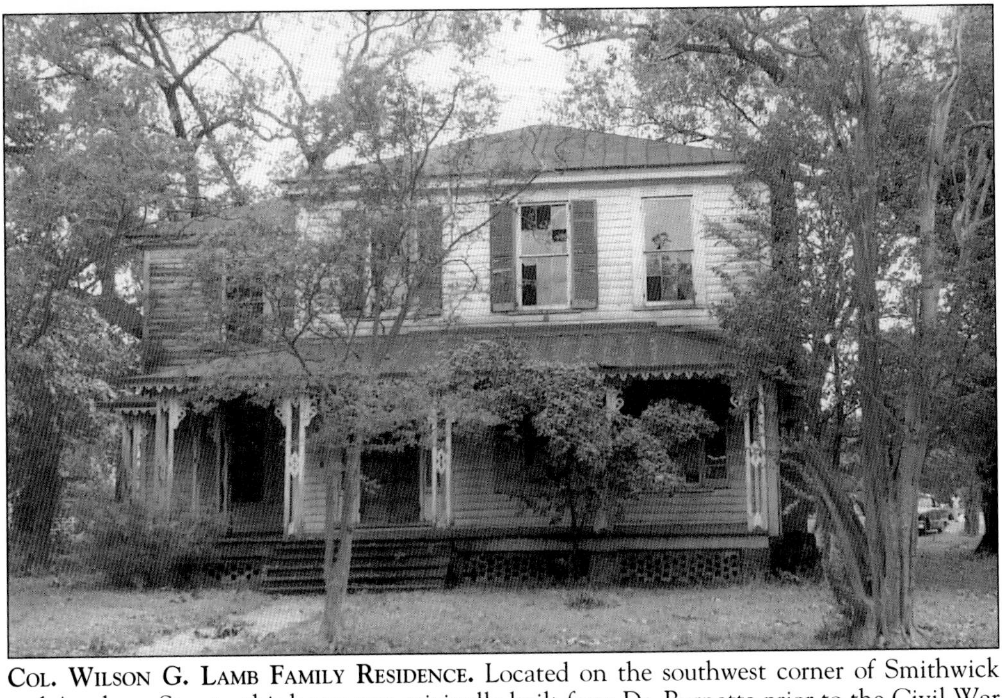

Col. Wilson G. Lamb Family Residence. Located on the southwest corner of Smithwick and Academy Streets, this house was originally built for a Dr. Burnette prior to the Civil War and was purchased some years later by the Lamb family. This photo was taken in 1960, shortly before the house was demolished. (Courtesy of the Francis Manning Room.)

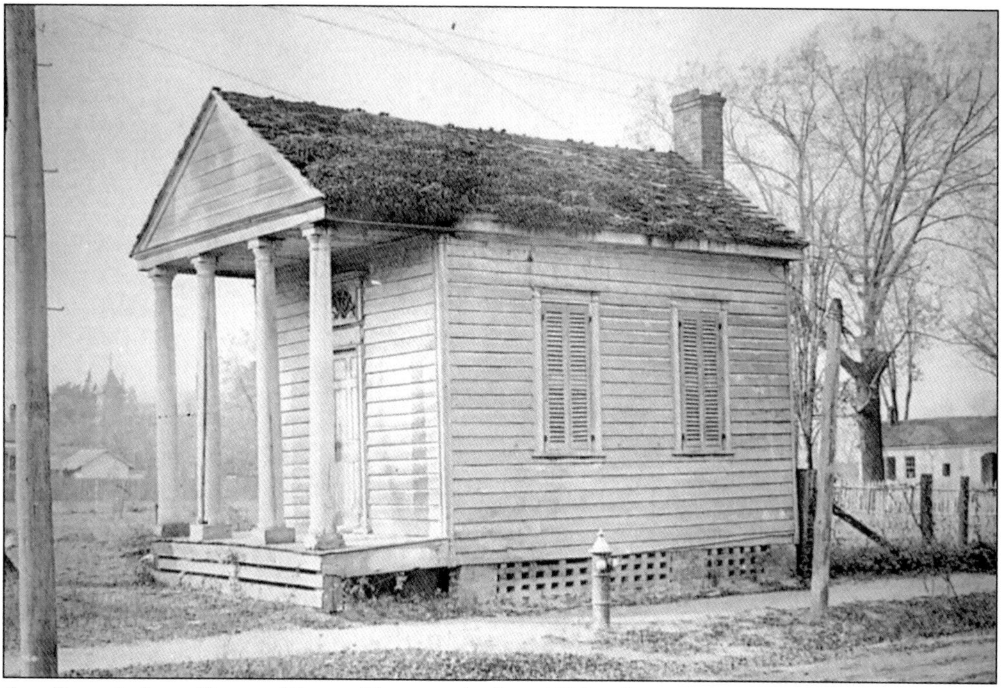

ASA BIGGS'S LAW OFFICE. Pictured here in the late 1920s, this structure stood on the northwest corner of Church and Smithwick Streets (opposite the Asa Biggs home) from about 1830 until it was torn down in 1930. A brick residence was built on the same spot in 1939. (Courtesy of the Francis Manning Room.)

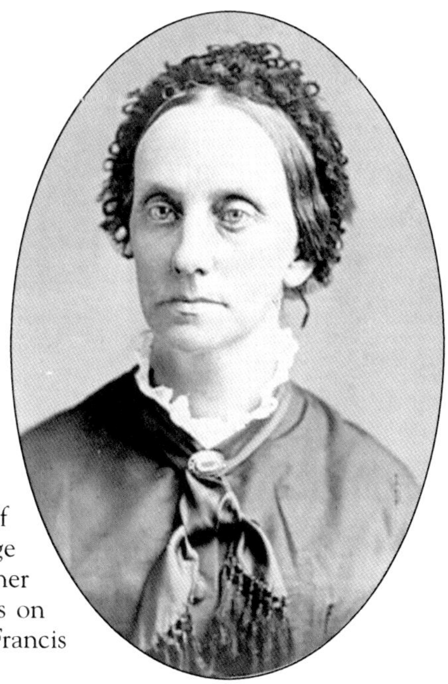

MARTHA JEWETT HASSELL. The second wife of Cushing Biggs Hassell, Martha's Northern heritage helped her to persuade Union troops against burning her husband's home and property in one of several raids on Williamston during the Civil War. (Courtesy of the Francis Manning Room.)

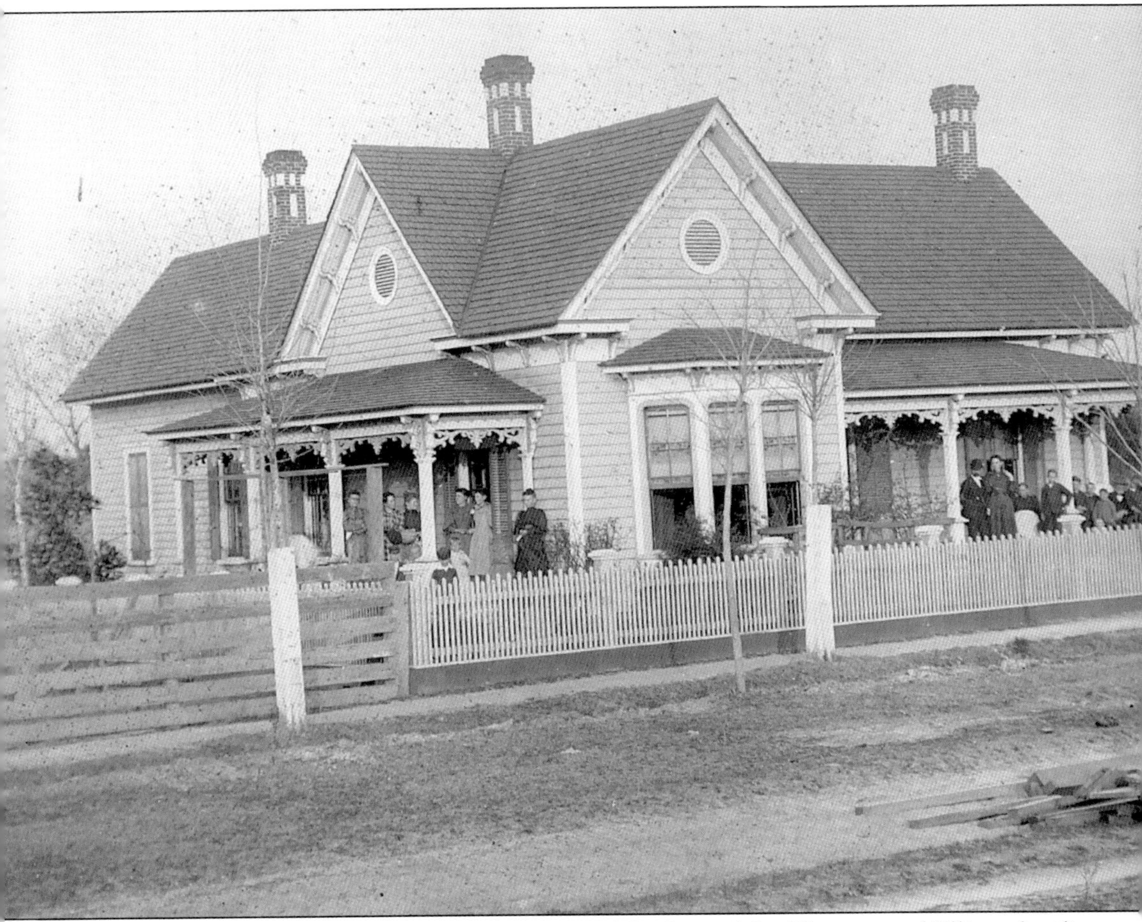

A Scene from New Town, March 28, 1895. Members of the Thrower and Ellison families gather in front of this house located near the northeast corner of South Watts and Hatton Streets. New Town began as Williamston's first solely residential development in the 1840s. (Courtesy of the Francis Manning Room.)

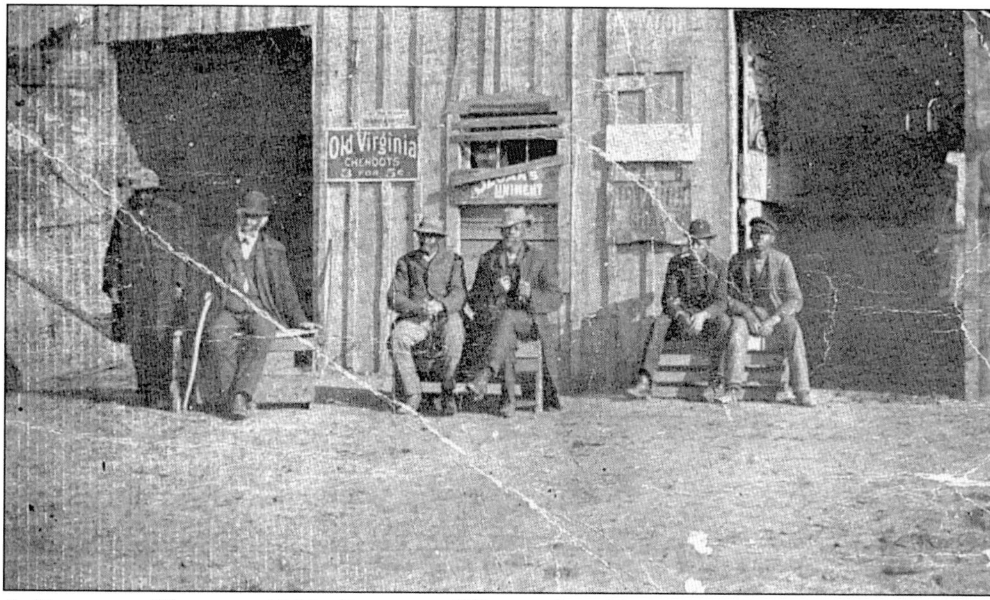

A Postcard View, c. 1900, Entitled "Uncle Gus Taking a Sun Bath." During the Reconstruction period, Augustus Johnson, pictured at far left, became the first elected African-American town commissioner in Williamston. (Courtesy of the Francis Manning Room.)

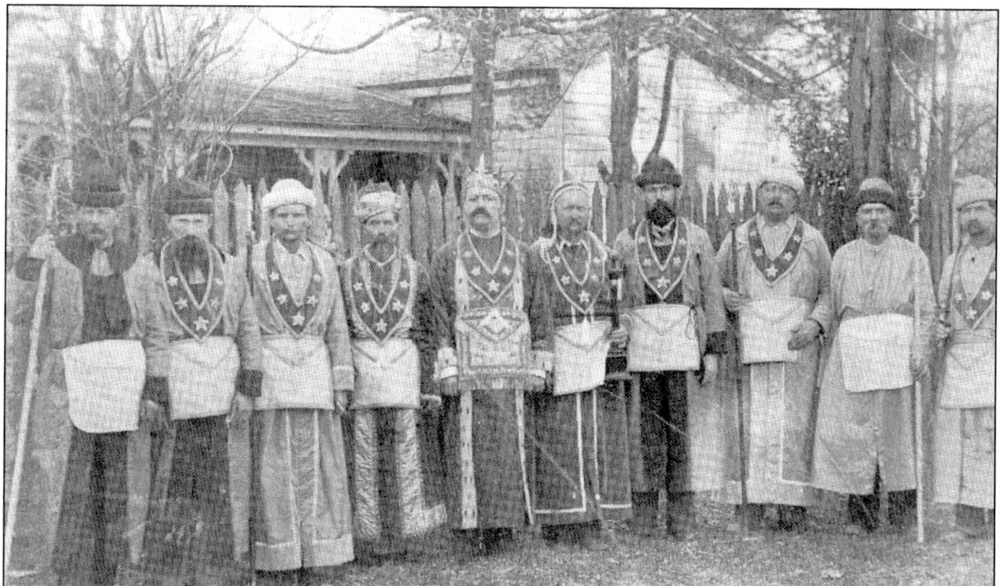

Williamston Masons, c. 1893. Pictured from left to right (and followed by each individual's professional occupation and position within the Masons) are as follows: Alec H. Smith (lawyer, steward), Samuel R. Biggs (county treasurer, secretary), James A. Teel (register of deeds, senior deacon), John H. Hatton (blacksmith, senior warden), Harry W. Stubbs (state legislator, master), Eli Gurganus (merchant and peanut broker, junior warden), Dr. W.H. Harrell (physician, treasurer), James D. Leggett (merchant and farmer, junior deacon), Richard Clary (police officer, steward), and William H. Bennett (register of deeds, tyler). (Courtesy of the Francis Manning Room.)

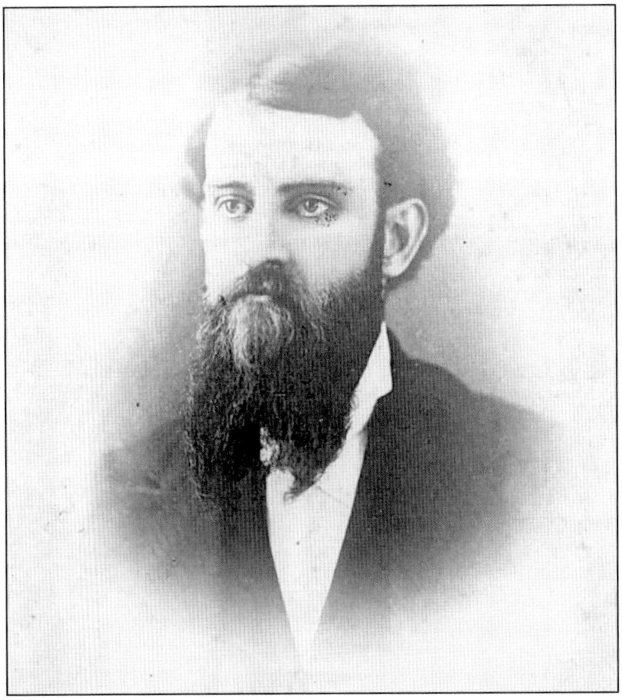

DR. ALONZO HASSELL. The son of Cushing B. Hassell, Alonzo graduated from the University of Maryland Medical College in 1870 and maintained a medical practice in Williamston until his death in 1888. (Courtesy of the Francis Manning Room.)

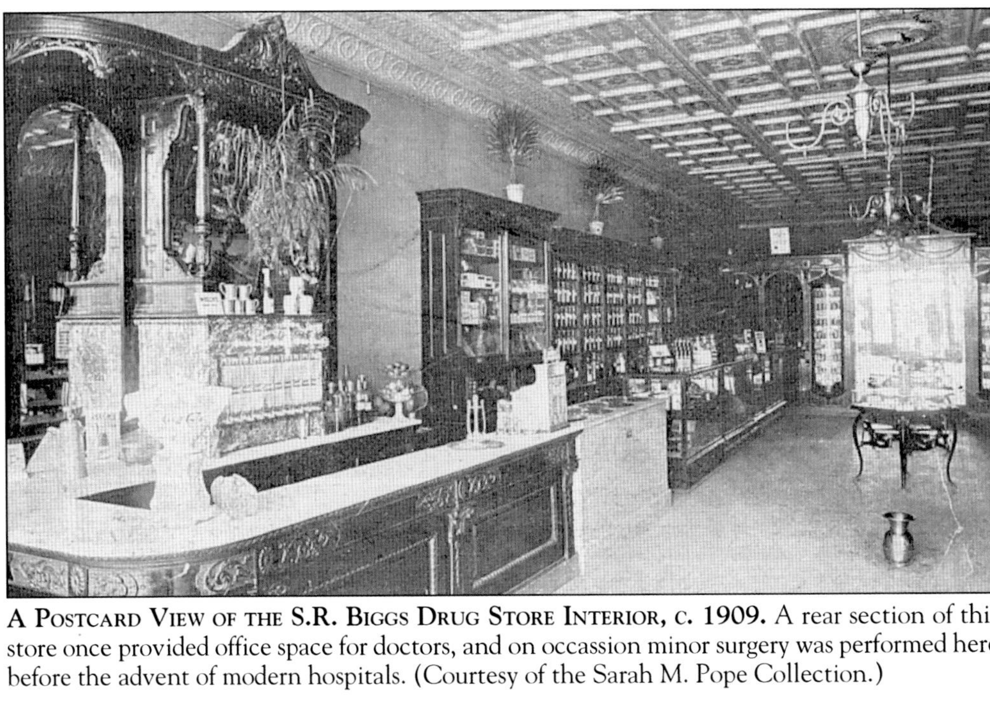

A POSTCARD VIEW OF THE S.R. BIGGS DRUG STORE INTERIOR, C. 1909. A rear section of this store once provided office space for doctors, and on occassion minor surgery was performed here before the advent of modern hospitals. (Courtesy of the Sarah M. Pope Collection.)

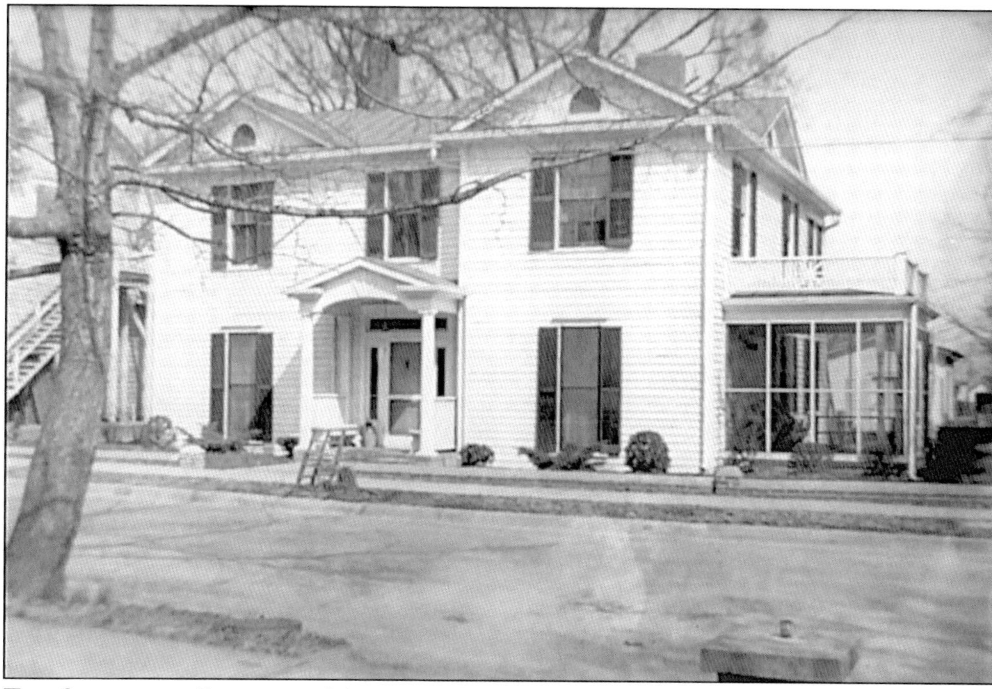

The Southeast Corner of Main and South Biggs Streets. This home is believed to have been once owned by members of the Carstarphen family. The present Martin County Courthouse now sits on this property. (Courtesy of the Francis Manning Room.)

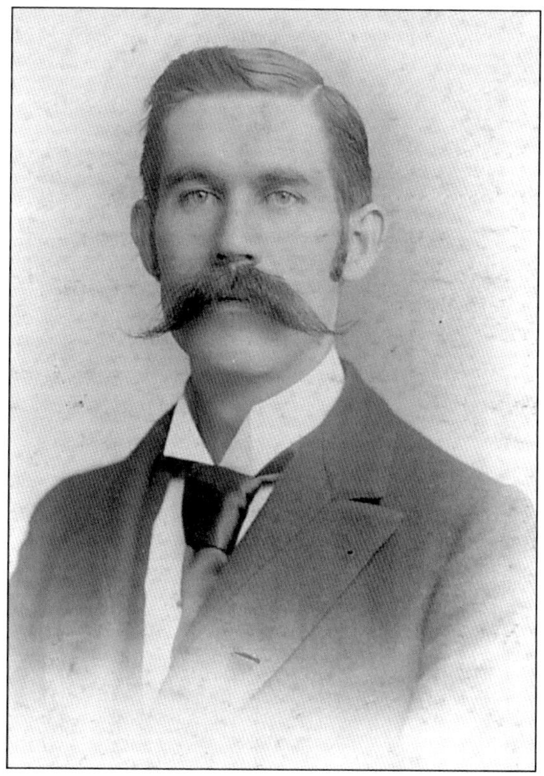

Dr. W.H. Harrell. Dr. Harrell practiced medicine in Williamston from 1885 until his death in 1905. (Courtesy of the Francis Manning Room.)

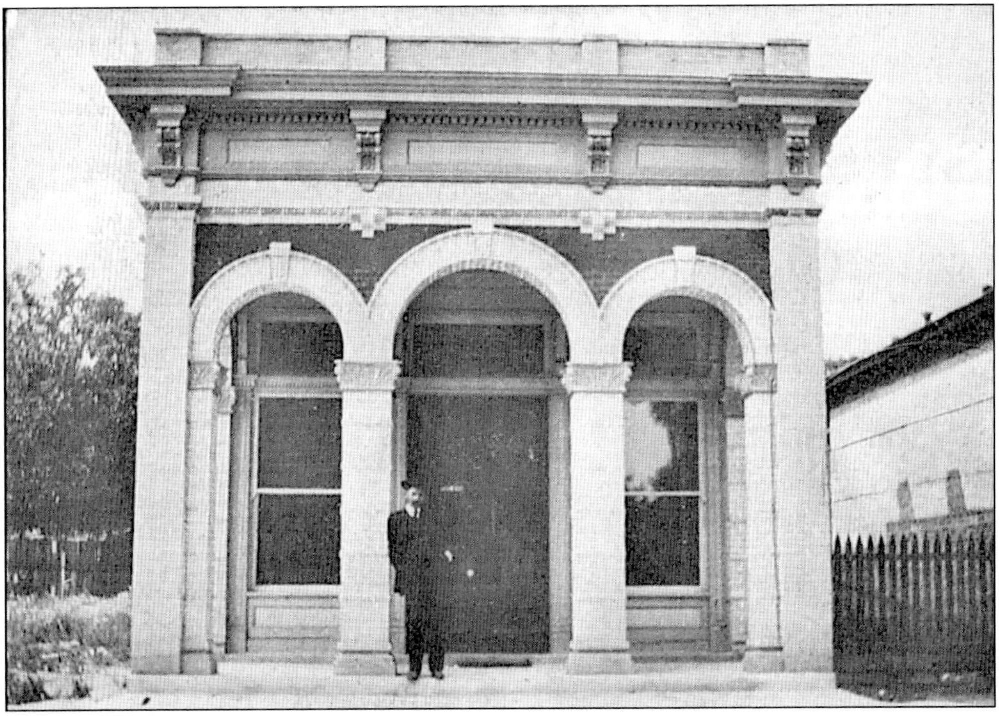

THE WHEELER MARTIN LAW OFFICE. This *c.* 1910 postcard shows the Wheeler Martin Law Office next to the old city hall on Main Street. (Courtesy of the Sarah M. Pope Collection.)

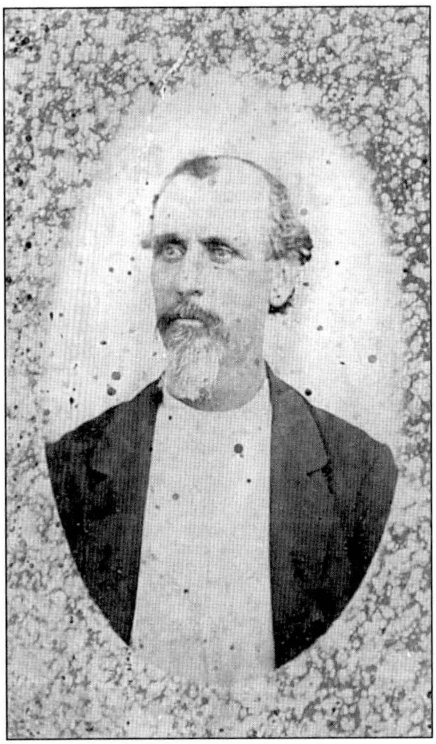

WILLIAM JONATHAN HARDISON. A popular Martin County sheriff from 1874 to 1896, Hardison was originally from Beaufort County. (Courtesy of the Francis Manning Room.)

CONDENSED STATEMENT OF CONDITION

BANK OF MARTIN COUNTY

November 17, 1916

Resources		Liabilities	
Loans and Discounts	$302,492.93	Capital Stock	$ 15.000.00
Stocks and Bonds	16,280 75	Surplus and Profits	31,150.91
Furniture and Fixtures	3,140.00	Deposits	327,580.01
Real Estate	1,750.00	Bills Payable	47,000 00
Cash and in Banks	97,067.24		
	$420.730.92		$420,730.92

Deposits Compared

November 17, 1915	$178,451.04
November 17, 1916	***327,580.01***

Accounts Solicited - Large or Small - Ample Facilities to Meet all Requirements

Four Per Cent on Time Deposits

A 1916 STATEMENT FROM THE BANK OF MARTIN COUNTY. (Courtesy of the Francis Manning Room.)

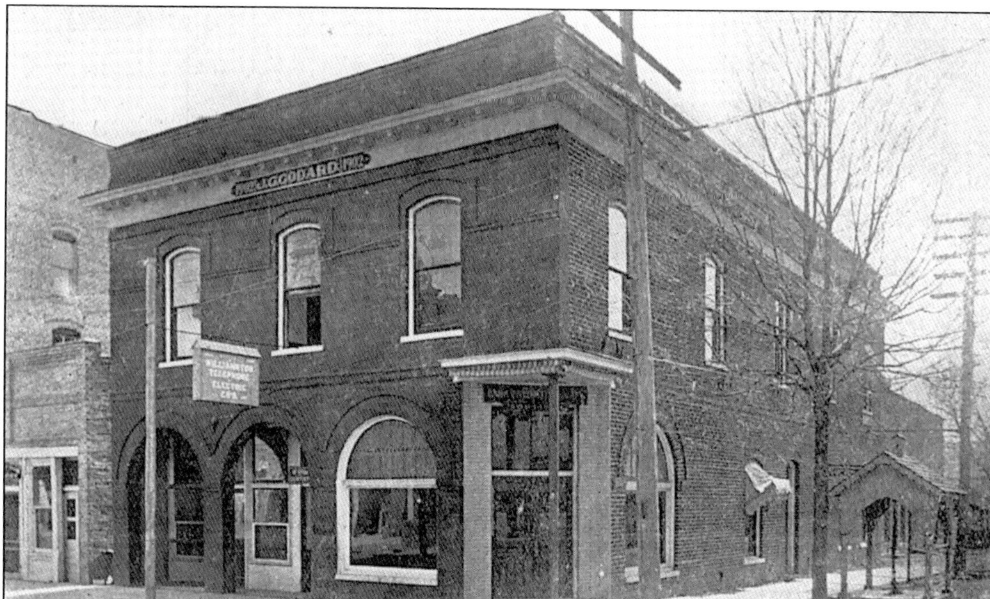

A 1910 POSTCARD VIEW OF THE BANK OF MARTIN COUNTY. Joseph G. Goddard built this office building on the corner of Main and Smithwick Streets in 1899 primarily to house the Bank of Martin County. It began operations on January 22, 1900. Additionally, the location served as headquarters for the town's first telephone and electric company, which was owned by W.C. Manning. (Courtesy of the Sarah M. Pope Collection.)

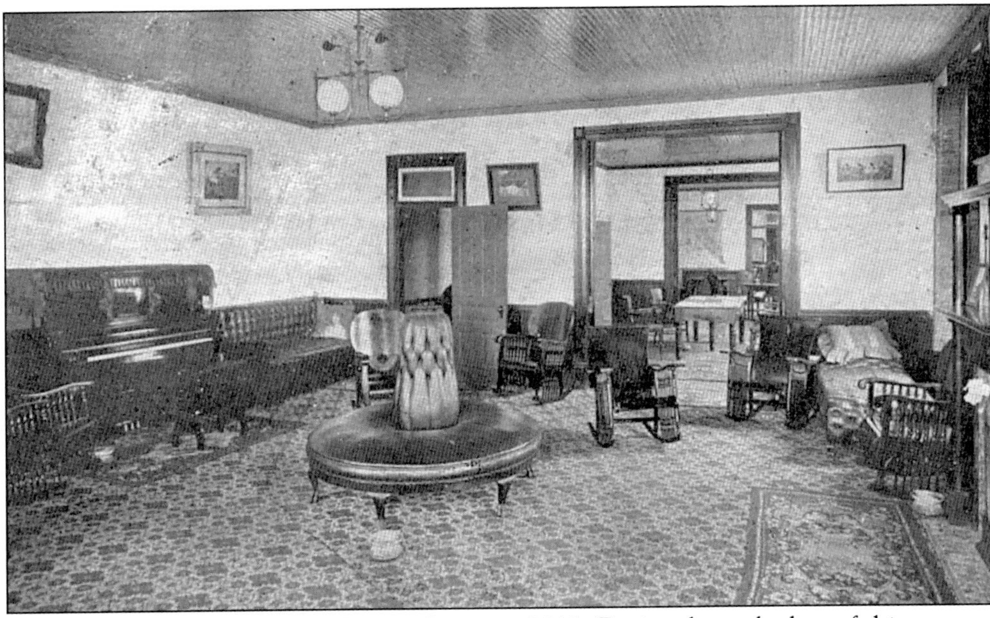

A Postcard View Inside the Lotus Club, c. 1910. During the early days of this century, the Lotus Club served as a popular downtown gathering spot for Williamston's social elite. (Courtesy of the Sarah M. Pope Collection.)

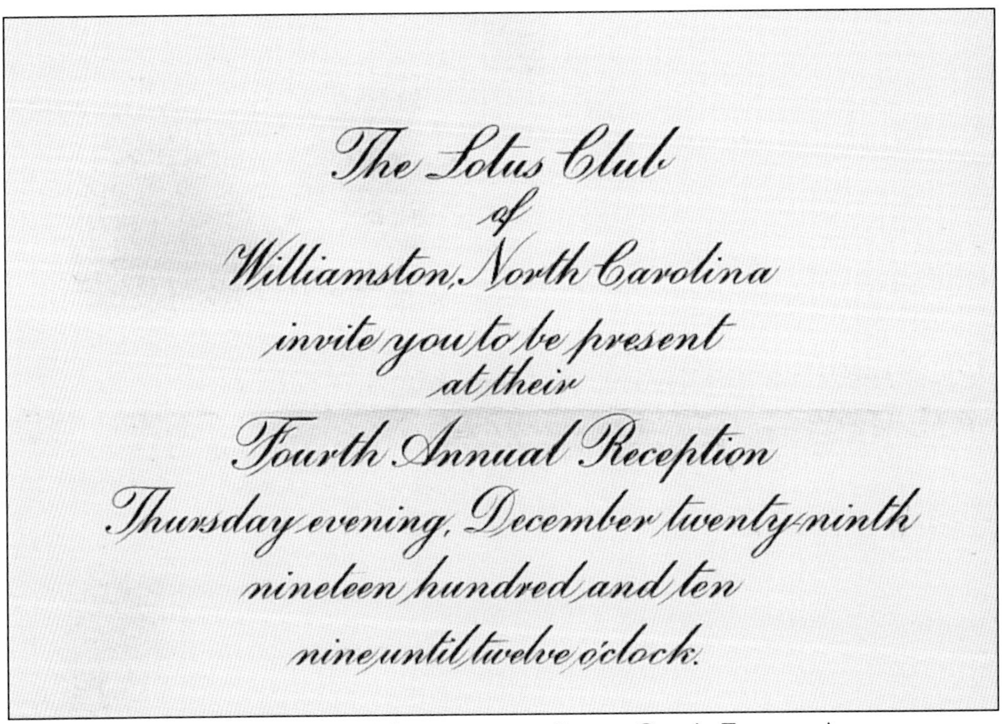

The Lotus Club
of
Williamston, North Carolina
invite you to be present
at their
Fourth Annual Reception
Thursday evening, December twenty-ninth
nineteen hundred and ten
nine until twelve o'clock.

An Invitation to a Reception Honoring the Lotus Club's Fourth Anniversary in 1910. The club was incorporated as a literary and social club on July 28, 1906. (Courtesy of the Francis Manning Room.)

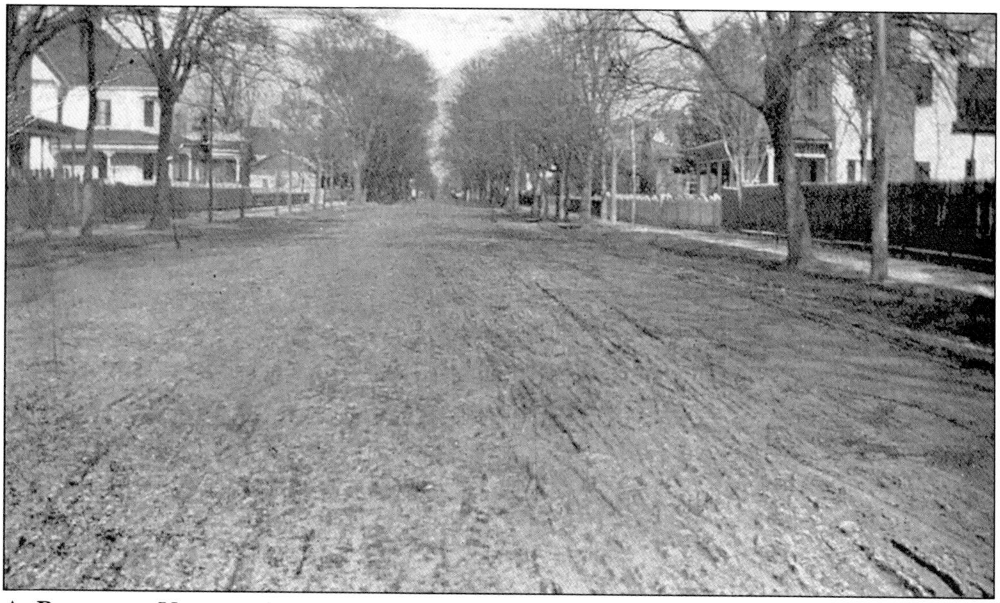

A POSTCARD VIEW OF MAIN STREET, LOOKING EAST TOWARDS THE BUSINESS DISTRICT, c. 1910. (Courtesy of the Sarah M. Pope Collection.)

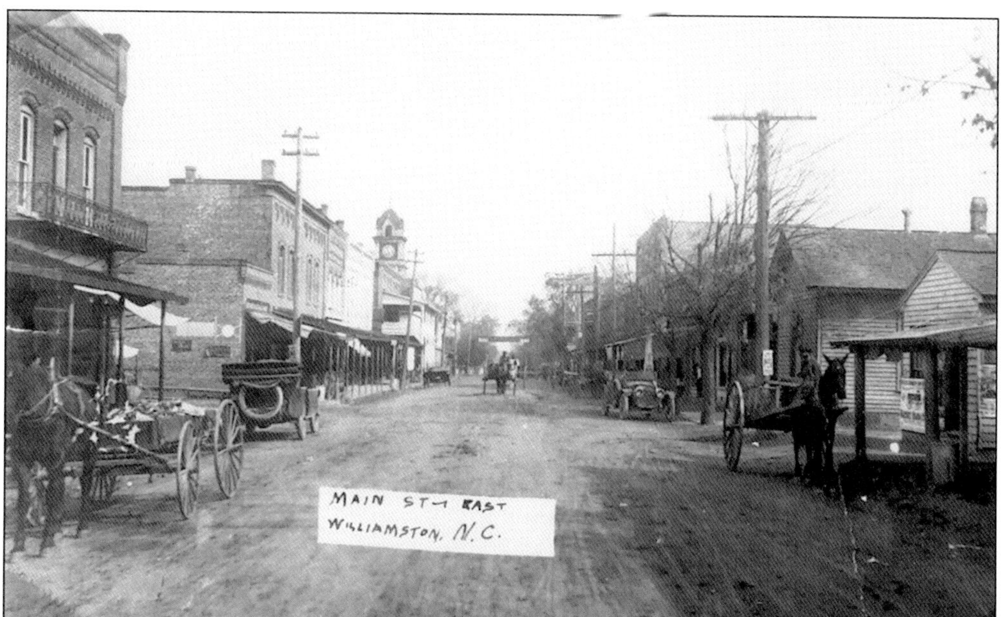

THE MAIN STREET BUSINESS DISTRICT, c. 1917. (Courtesy of the Sarah M. Pope Collection.)

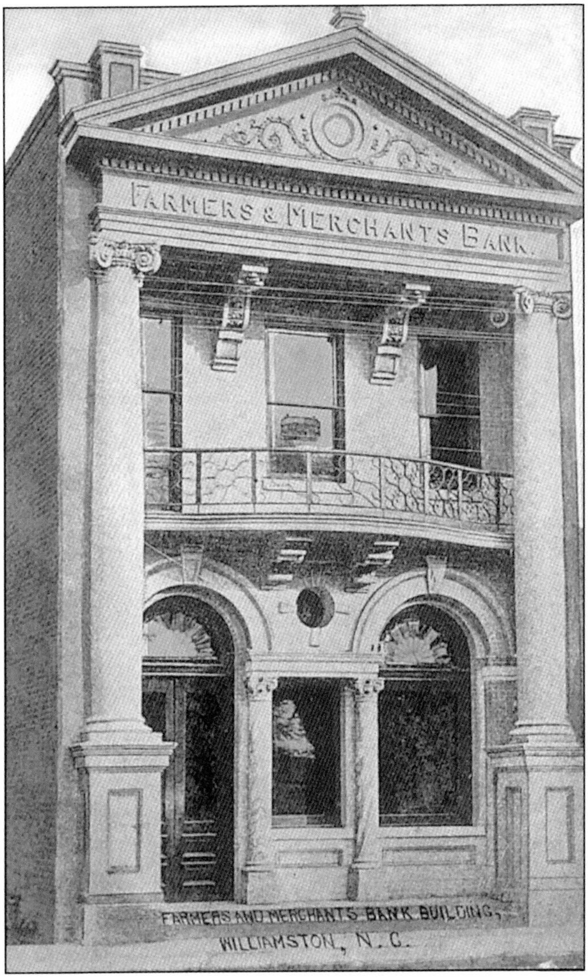

The Farmers and Merchants Bank. Opened for business on June 1, 1905, the Farmers and Merchants Bank was the only bank in the county to make it through the dark days of the Great Depression. Bank president Dr. John D. Biggs surrendered the better part of a personal fortune (inherited mainly from his family's interest in the Dennis Simmons Lumber Co.) in order to save depositors' holdings. (Courtesy of the Sarah M. Pope Collection.)

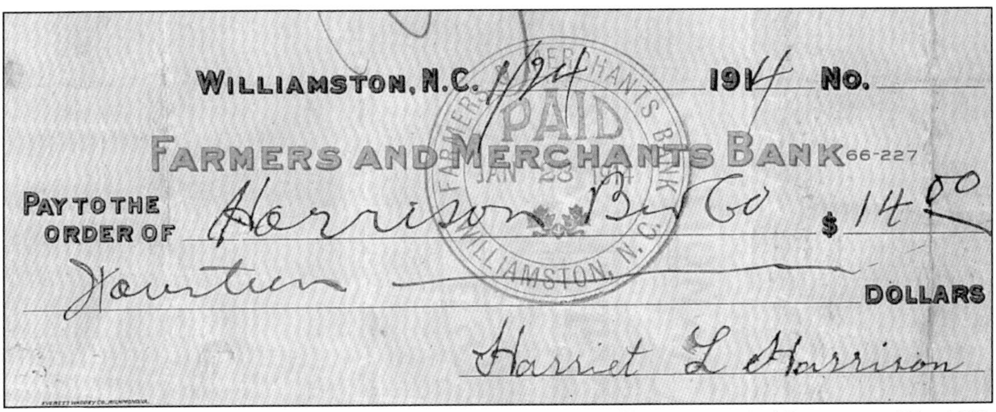

A Canceled Check from the Farmers and Merchants Bank, 1914. (Courtesy of Fred W. Harrison Jr.)

WILLIAMSTON FIRST METHODIST CHURCH, c. 1915. Early residents often recall being able to see the tallest spire of this building from as far away as the river wharf. Both spires were removed in the late 1940s or early 1950s. (Courtesy of Ann H. McKeel.)

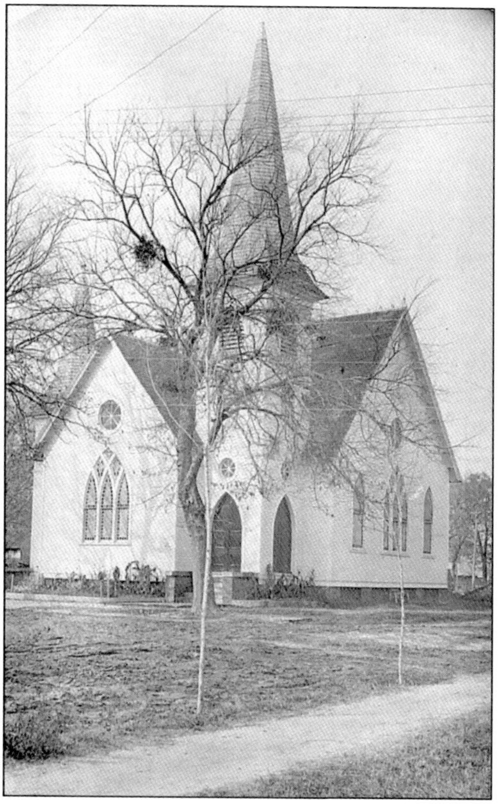

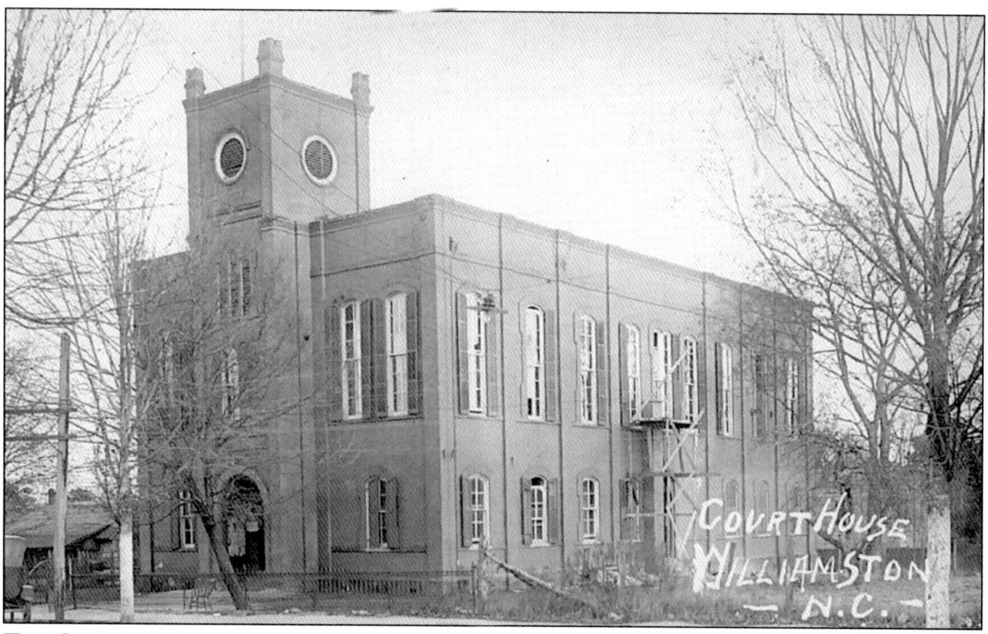

THE OLD MARTIN COUNTY COURTHOUSE, c. 1915. (Courtesy of Ann H. McKeel.)

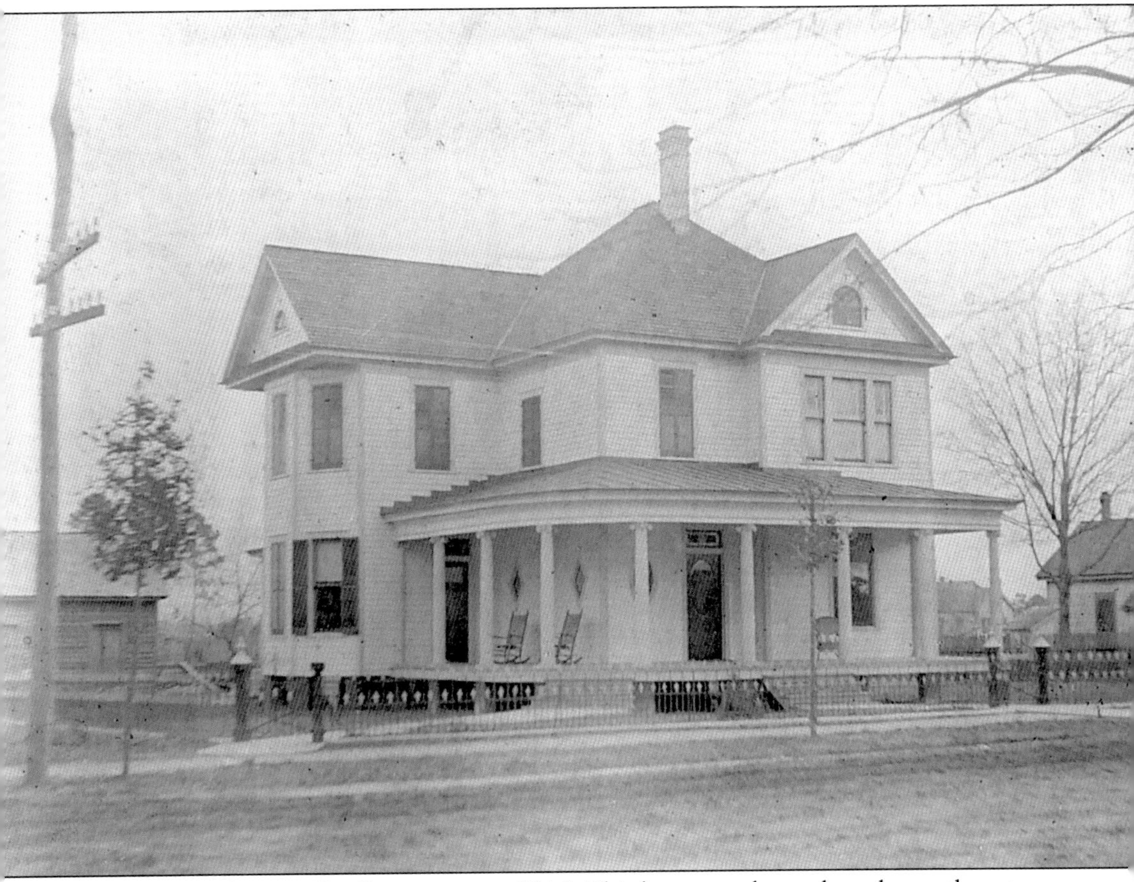

The C.H. Godwin Sr. Residence, c. 1916. This home was located on the southwest corner of West Main and Pearl Streets until it was demolished in the early 1970s. (Courtesy of Mary Charles G. Coppage.)

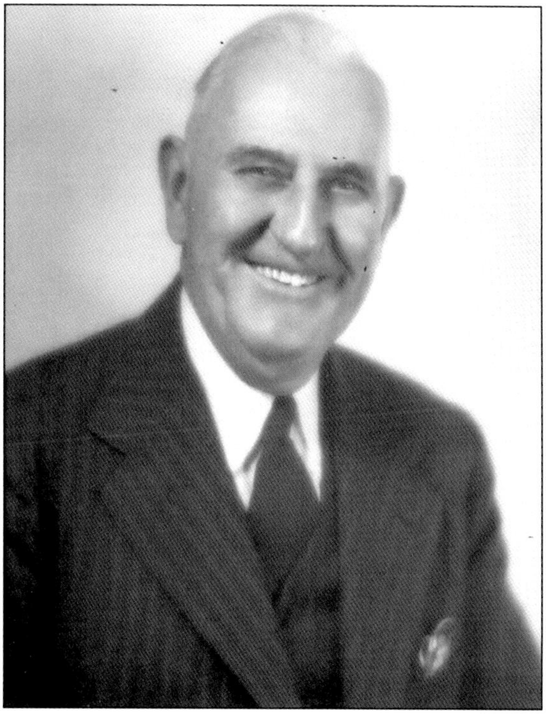

CHARLES HUDGINS GODWIN SR. (1881–1967). (Courtesy of Mary Charles G. Coppage.)

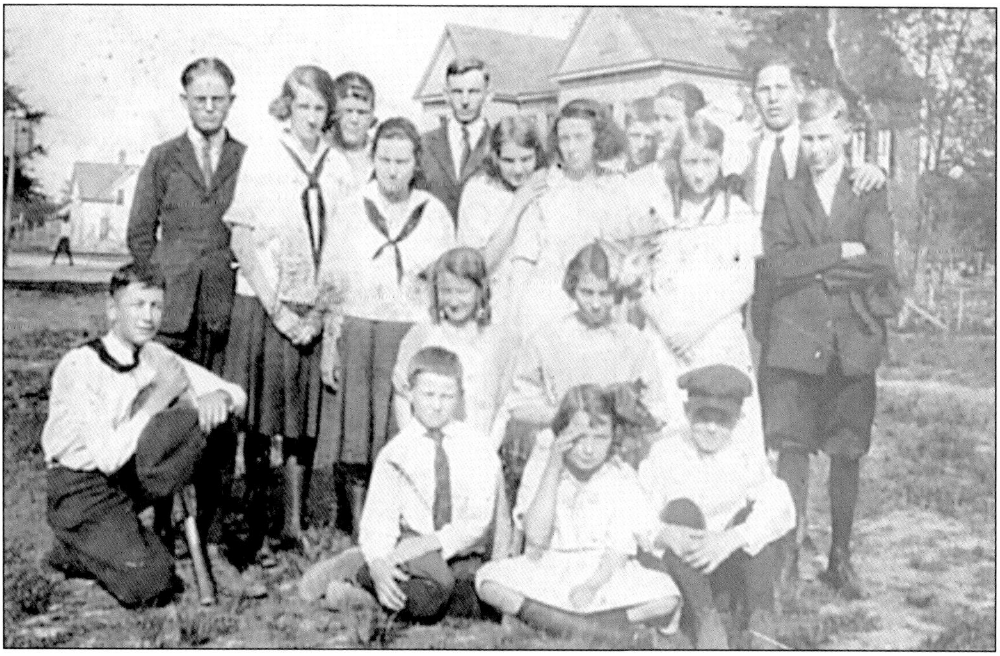

THE WILLIAMSTON HIGH SCHOOL CLASS OF 1926. Pictured, from left to right, are as follows: (front row) Cecil Taylor, Lucille Hassell, and Eli Barnhill; (middle row) Lon Hassell, Elizabeth Gurganus, and Trulah Ward Page; (back row) Briscoe Rogers, Evelyn Harrison, Ruth Manning, Nina Jones, Louis Lafayette Steffey (faculty), Margaret Joyner, Martha Leggett, James Herbert Ward, Sam Brown, Mary Melissa Andrews, Ira Harrison, and Bruce Whitley. (Courtesy of the Francis Manning Room.)

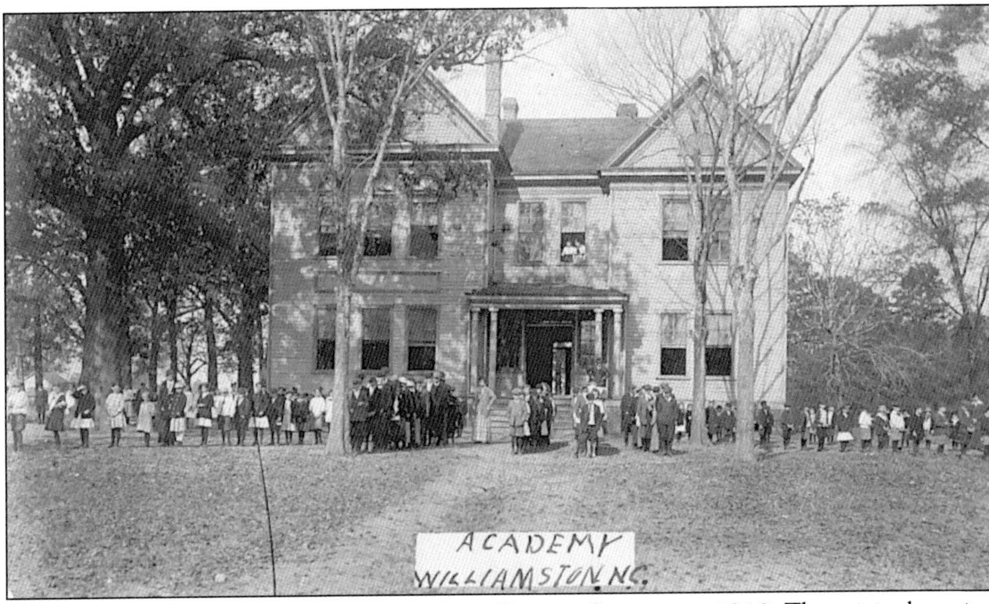

WILLIAMSTON ACADEMY, LATER WILLIAMSTON GRADED SCHOOL, C. 1910. The original portion of this building was constructed in 1817 and enlarged and remodeled near the turn of this century. It was moved in 1917 to accommodate a brick structure on the same site known as the Church Street School and was later demolished. (Courtesy of Fred W. Harrison Jr.)

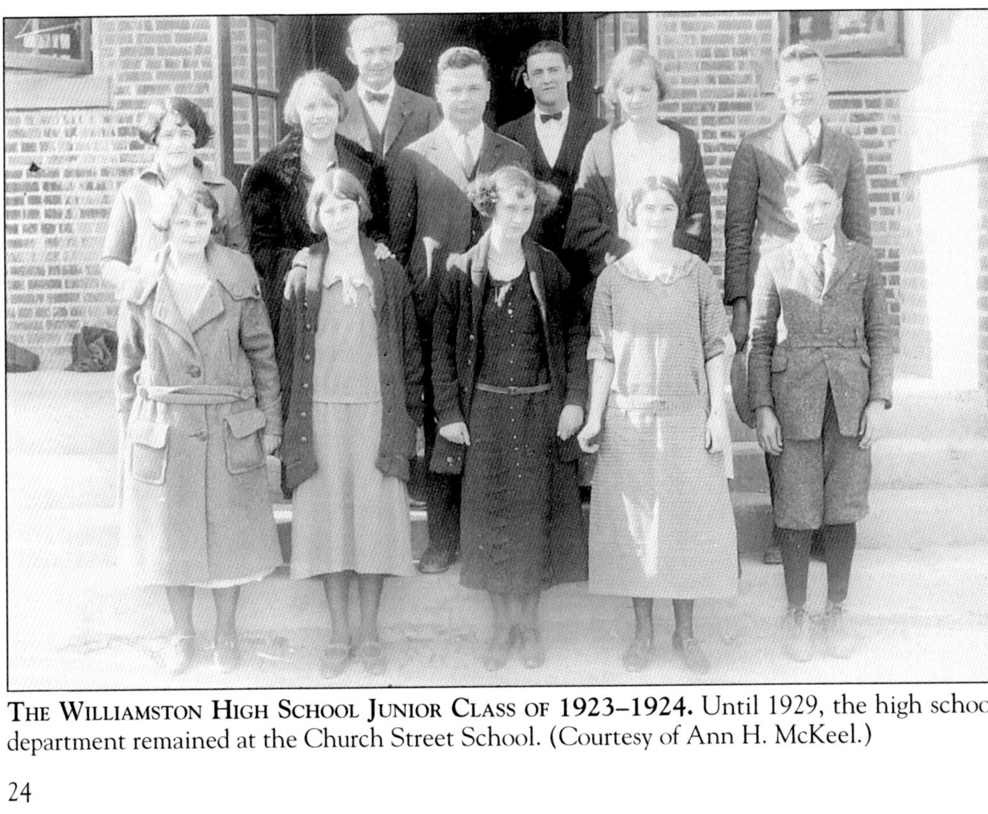

THE WILLIAMSTON HIGH SCHOOL JUNIOR CLASS OF 1923–1924. Until 1929, the high school department remained at the Church Street School. (Courtesy of Ann H. McKeel.)

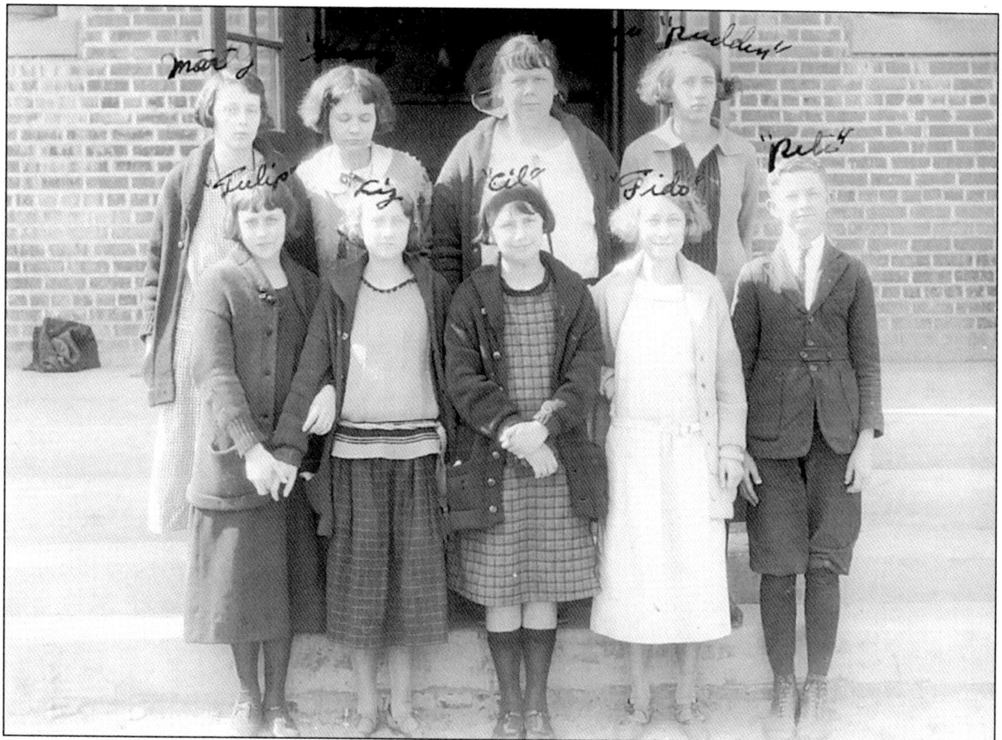

The Williamston High School Sophomore Class of 1923–1924. (Courtesy of Ann H. McKeel.)

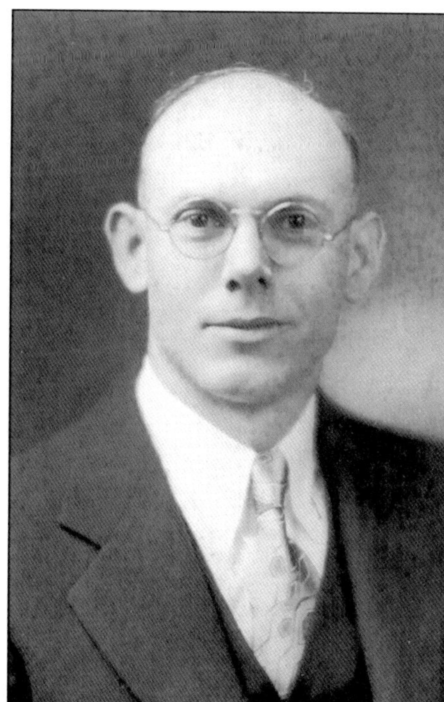

J. Sam Getsinger, c. 1925. A South Haughton Street resident, Getsinger served as the register of deeds of Martin County from 1924 to 1967, one of the longest tenures ever recorded for a register in the state. (Courtesy of Fred W. Harrison Jr.)

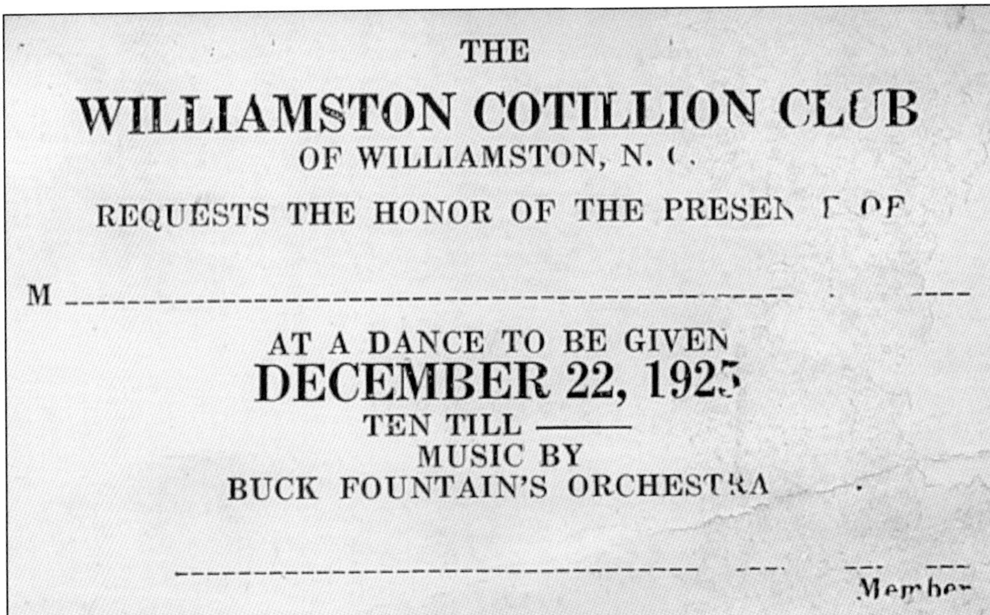

THE

WILLIAMSTON COTILLION CLUB

OF WILLIAMSTON, N. C.

REQUESTS THE HONOR OF THE PRESEN[illegible] OF

M ________________________________

AT A DANCE TO BE GIVEN

DECEMBER 22, 1925

TEN TILL ——

MUSIC BY

BUCK FOUNTAIN'S ORCHESTRA

____

Member

A Williamston Cotillion Club Ticket. (Courtesy of Margaret M. Griffin.)

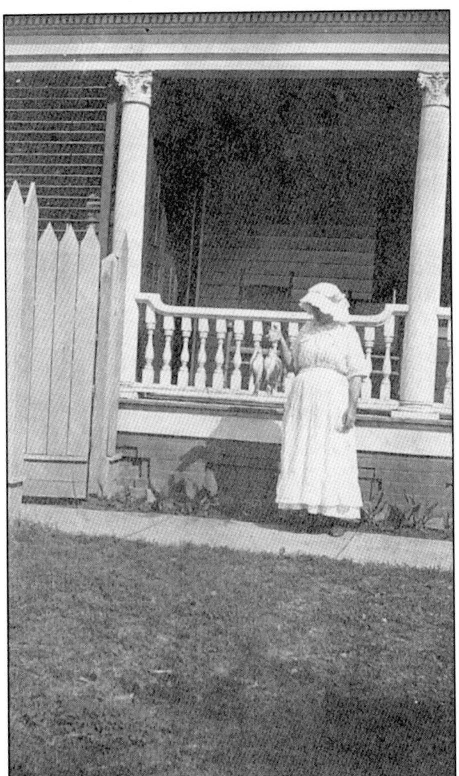

Miss Jane, c. 1925. Miss Jane served as a housekeeper to Mr. and Mrs. J.G. Staton at their home on the corner of Main and South Haughton Streets. Miss Jane is shown here with fish probably caught by Mr. Staton. (Courtesy of Fred W. Harrison Jr.)

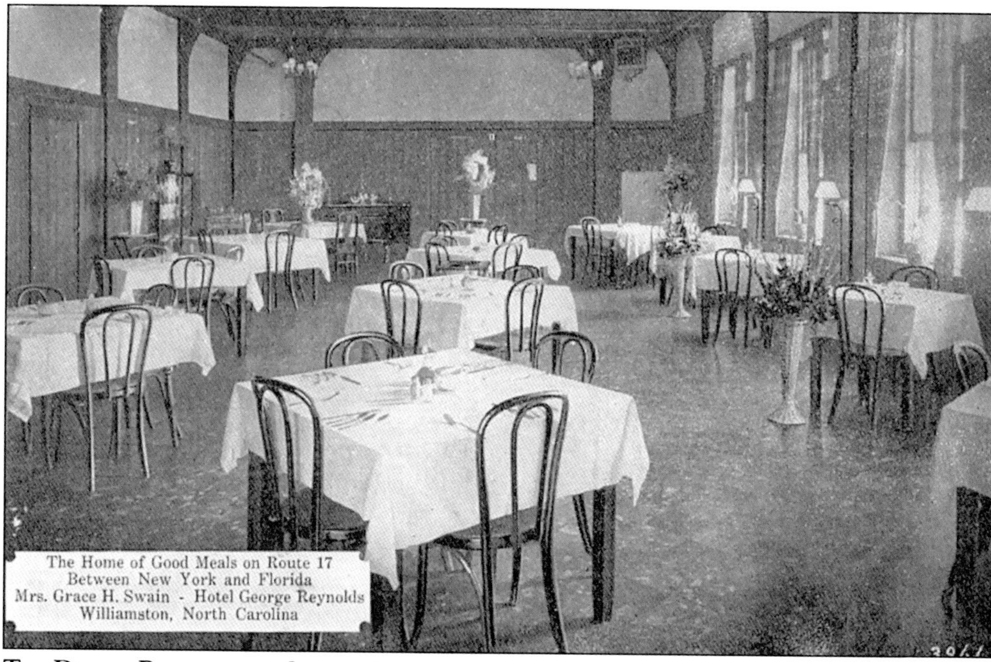

THE DINING ROOM OF THE GEORGE REYNOLDS HOTEL, c. 1935. This hotel, which was originally begun in 1896 as the Roanoke Hotel, served Williamston travelers continuously until its closing in 1954. (Courtesy of the Sarah M. Pope Collection.)

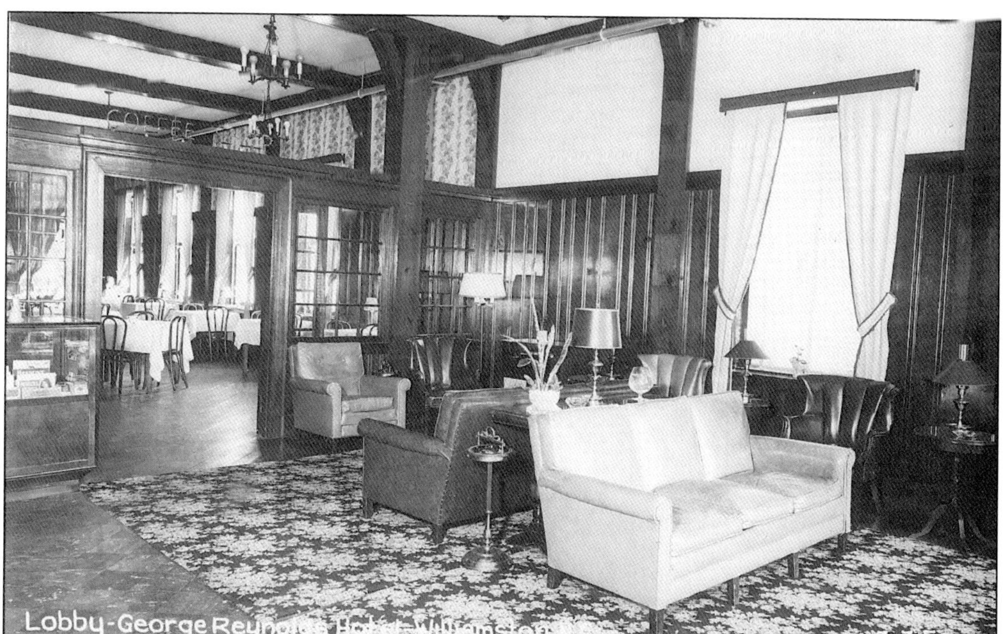

THE LOBBY OF THE GEORGE REYNOLDS HOTEL, c. 1935. (Courtesy of the Sarah M. Pope Collection.)

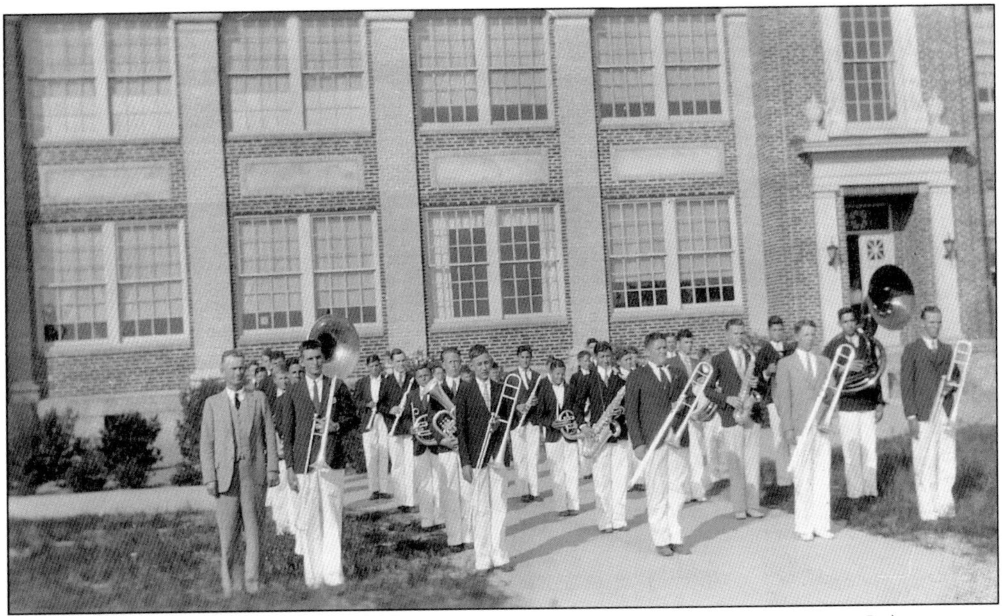

The Williamston High School Band, c. 1935. (Courtesy of Fred W. Harrison Jr.)

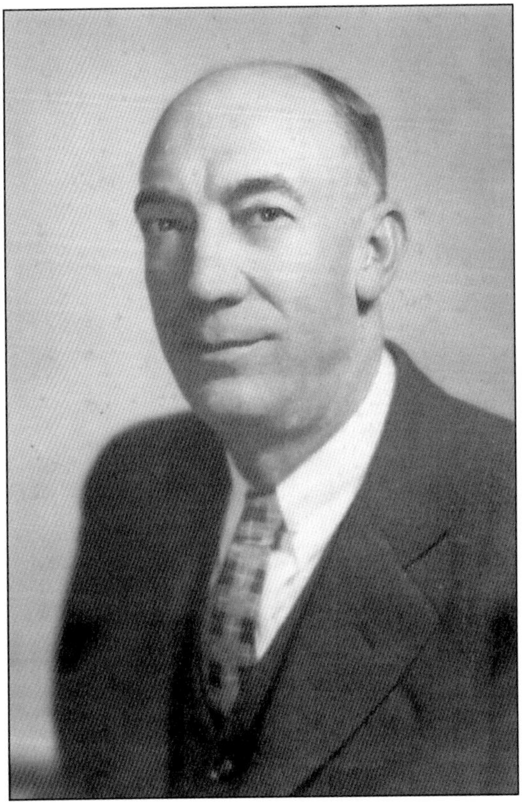

Lovett Biggs Harrison (1876–1938). One of several brothers who came to Williamston from the Bear Grass community in the late 1890s and became leading businessmen in Williamston during the first quarter of this century, L.B. Harrison was a senior partner in the Harrison Brothers firm, which operated from about 1901 until his death in 1938. (Courtesy of Ann H. McKeel.)

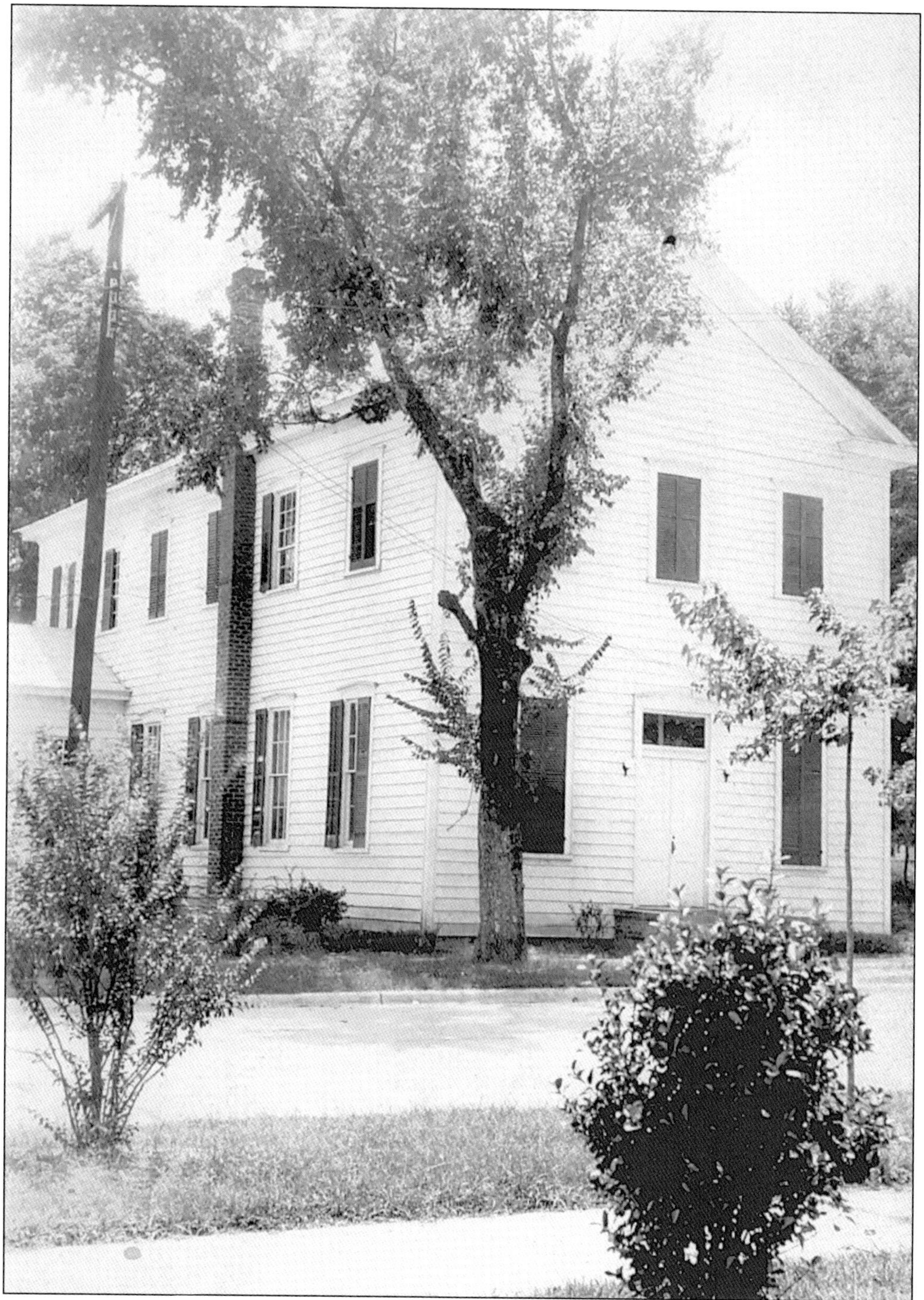

The Skewarkee Masonic Lodge, c. 1935. Constructed in 1828, this building was enlarged with a second story in the 1890s and the entrance was moved from its original location on Smithwick Street to Church Street. The lodge was acquired by the Williamston Woman's Club in the late 1950s when the Masons moved to a new location, and it was demolished some years later. (Courtesy of the Francis Manning Room.)

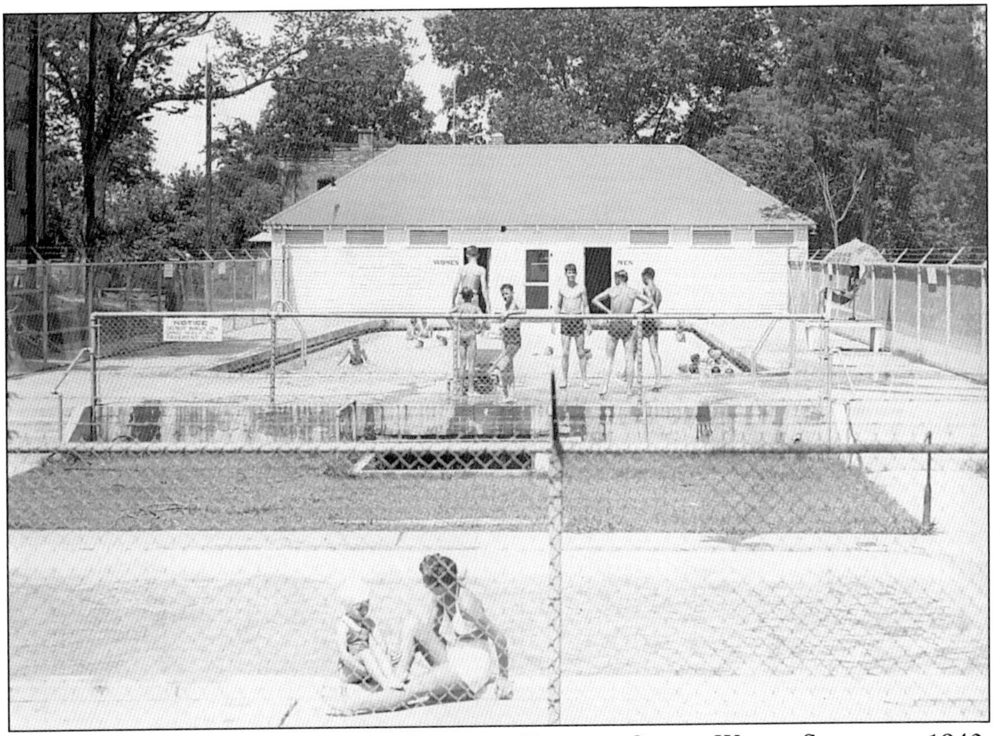

The Old Williamston Municipal Swimming Pool on South Watts Street, c. 1940. (Courtesy of the Francis Manning Room.)

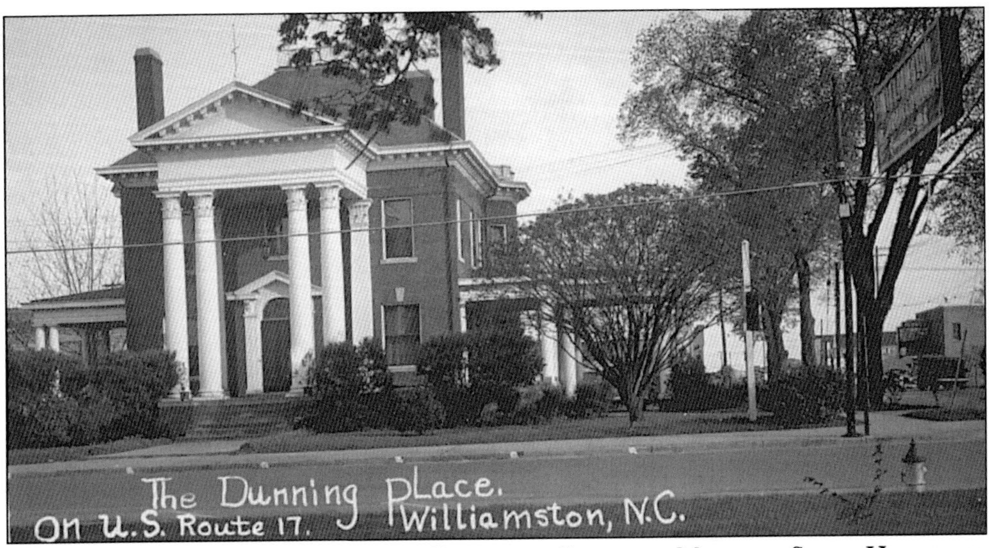

The Archer R. Dunning Home on the Southeast Corner of Main and South Haughton Streets, c. 1940. An attorney, A.R. Dunning served as the mayor of Robersonville before moving to Williamston about 1912. He built this home shortly thereafter and lived here until his death in 1932. His wife, Mary Alice Grimes Dunning, maintained the home as a boarding house until her death. The structure was finally torn down around 1970 and replaced by Wachovia Bank. (Courtesy of the Sarah M. Pope Collection.)

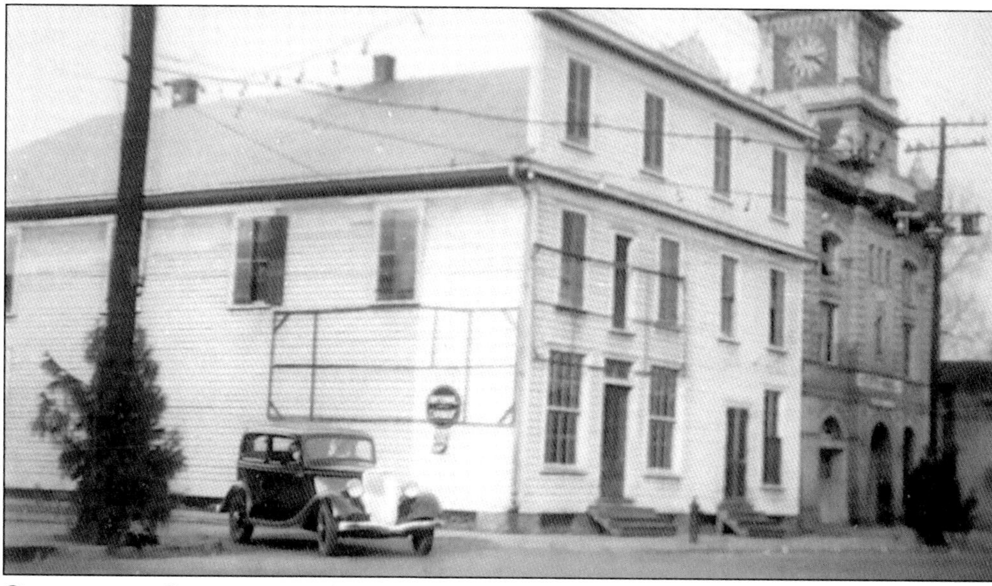

CARSTARPHEN STORE ON THE NORTHEAST CORNER OF MAIN AND SMITHWICK STREETS. This store was a landmark mercantile establishment in Williamston for many years. Built in 1872, it was considered at one time the most substantial wooden structure ever built downtown. When the building was torn down in 1934, much of the lumber was reused in building the first Williamston High School gym. (Courtesy of the Sarah M. Pope Collection.)

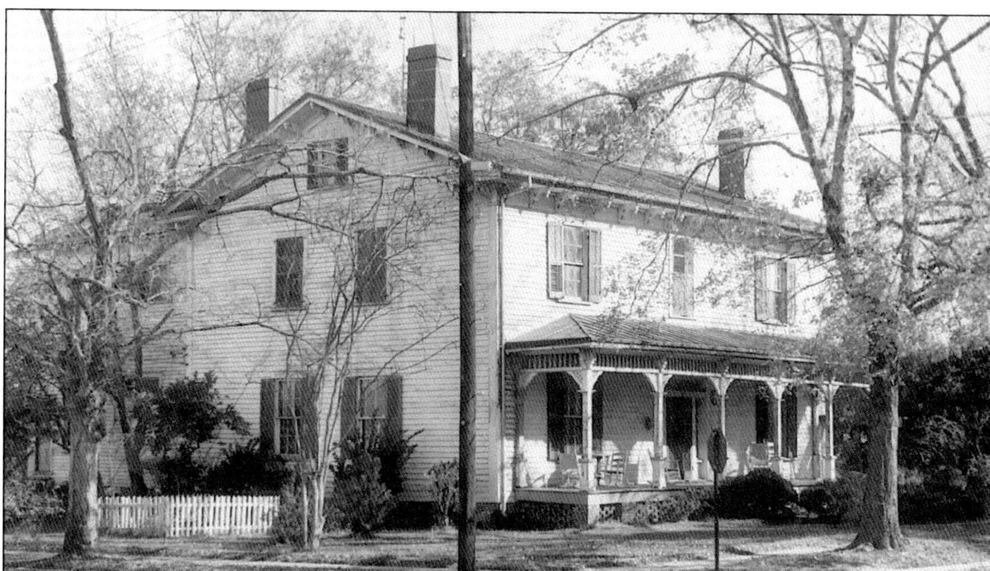

THE JOHN DAWSON BIGGS SR. RESIDENCE. Located on the corner of Ray and South Biggs Streets, this house was originally built in late 1840s for Martin County Sheriff A.S. Mooring. John Dawson Biggs was a merchant and partner in the Dennis Simmons Lumber Co. and, next to Dennis Simmons, was considered one of the wealthiest men in town. Biggs's wife, Fannie Alexander Biggs, lived here until her death, *c.* 1941. Boasting exceptional interior features, the house was salvaged for materials and torn down in the early 1980s. (Courtesy of the Francis Manning Room.)

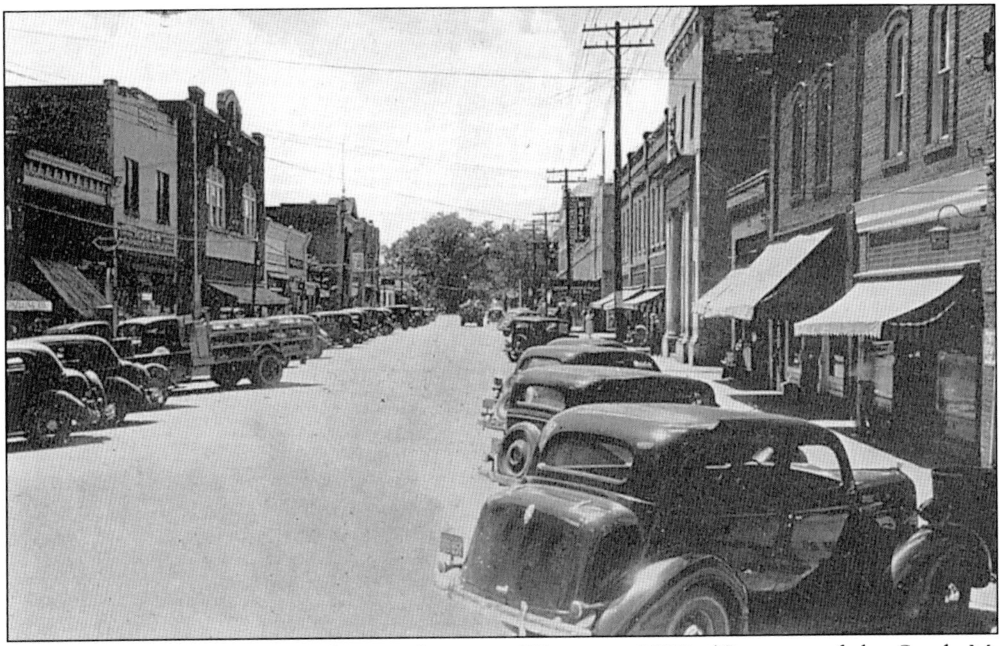

A Postcard View of Main Street Looking West, c. 1938. (Courtesy of the Sarah M. Pope Collection.)

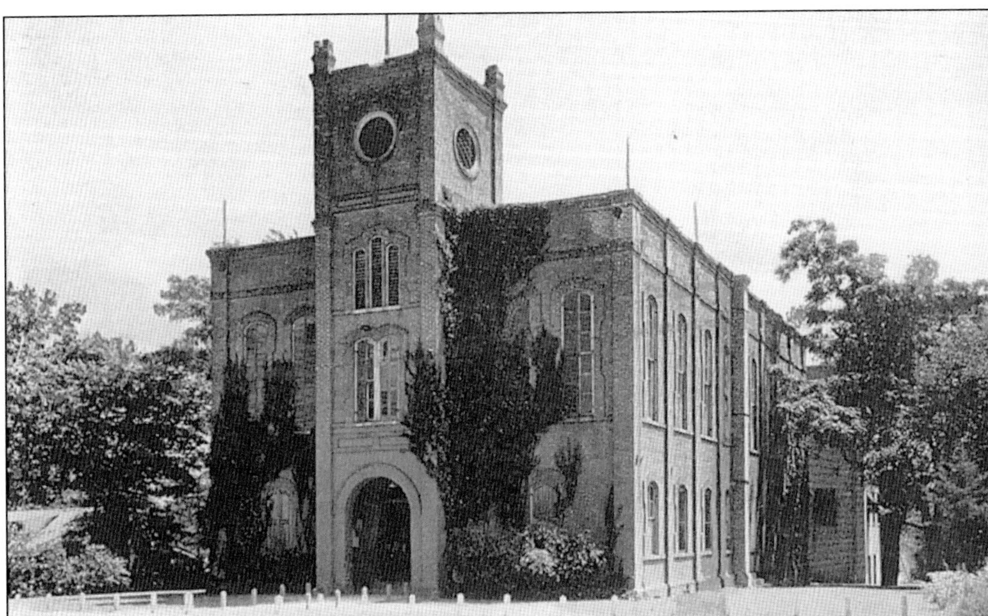

A Postcard View of the Old Martin County Courthouse, c. 1940. (Courtesy of the Sarah M. Pope Collection.)

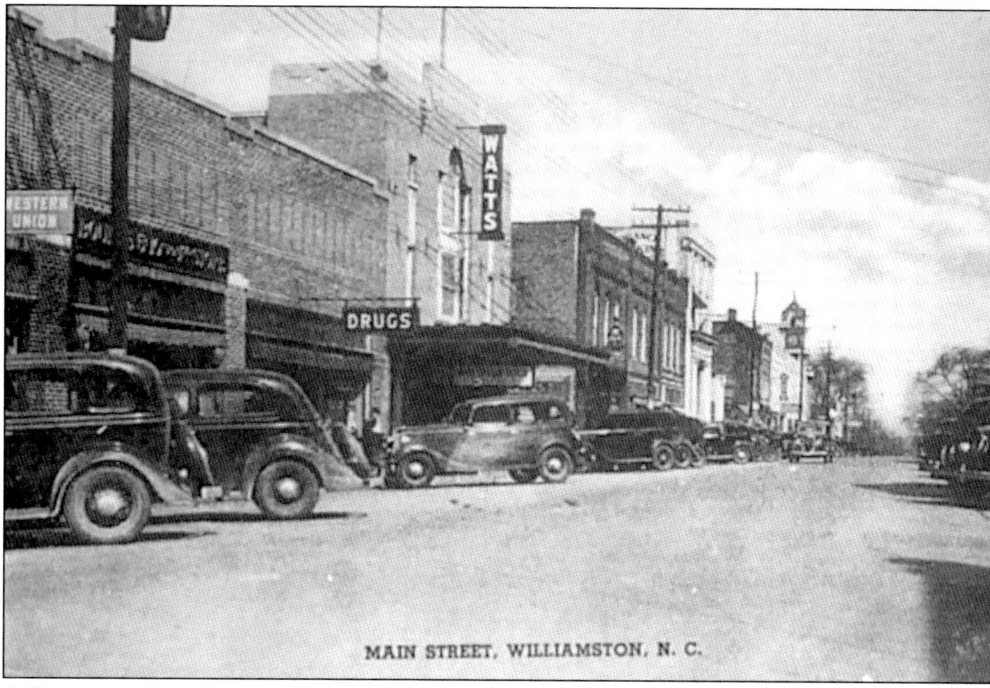

A Postcard View of the North Side of Main Street, c. 1938. (Courtesy of the Sarah M. Pope Collection.)

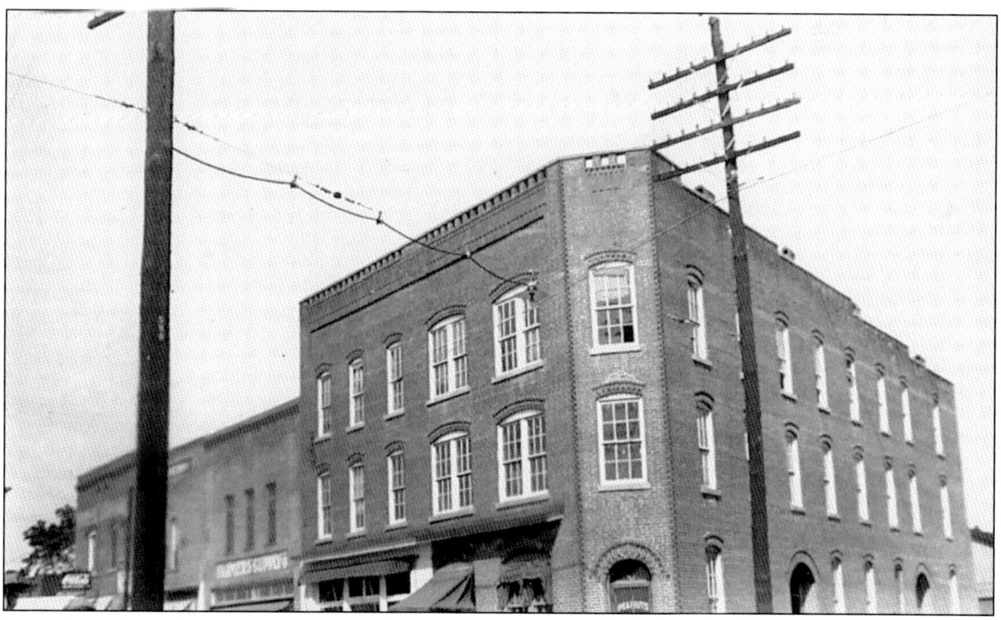

The Flat Iron Building on the Graball Section of North Washington Street, 1937. (Courtesy of the Francis Manning Room.)

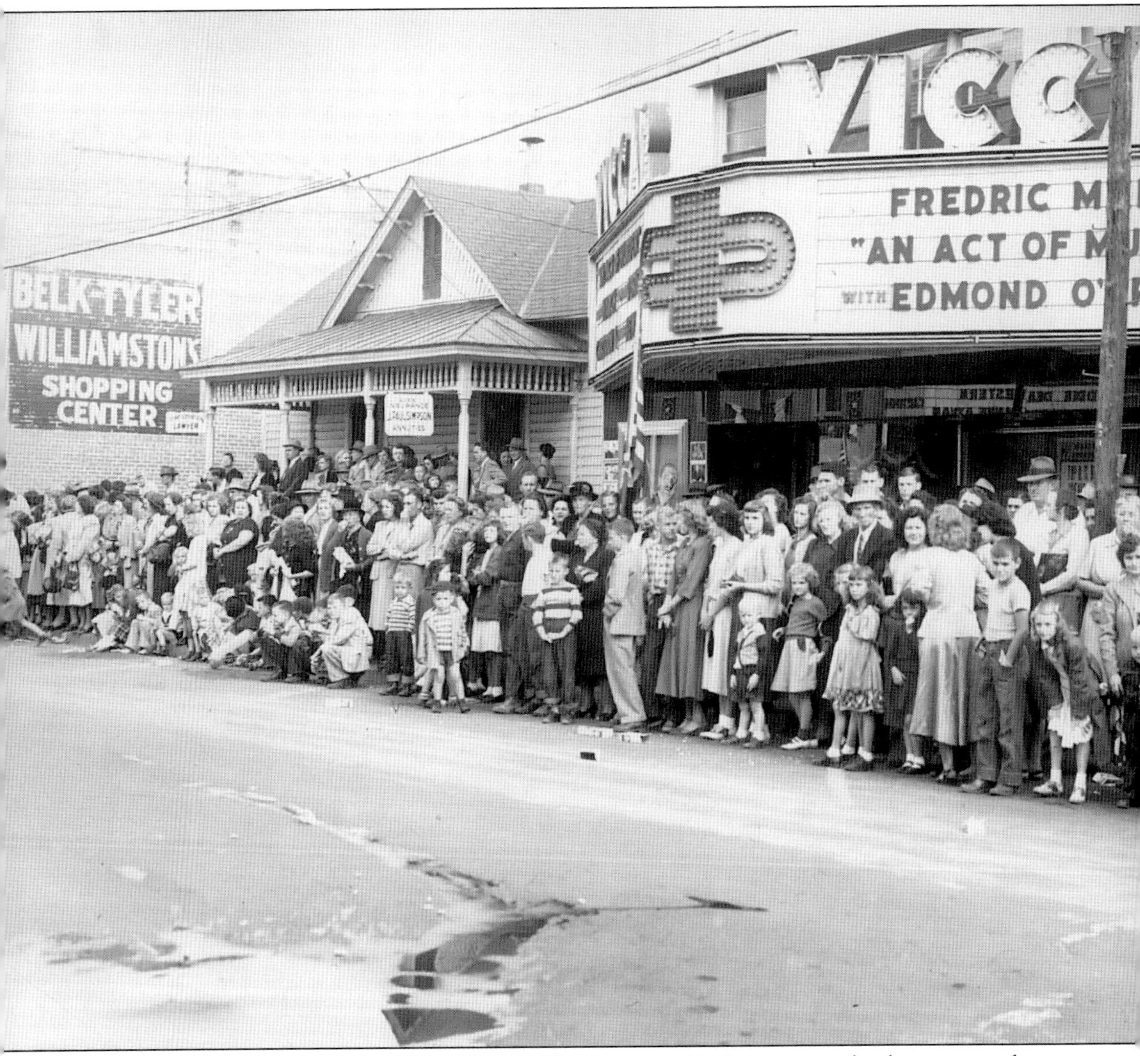

A Main Street Parade Scene, 1949. Harvest and Christmas parades began to take on a more familiar appearance on the Main Street scene after World War II. They initially began as promotional events for commercial activity downtown but have since become annual rituals for community pride. (Courtesy of Francis Manning Room.)

Two

WILLIAMSTON
1941–1970

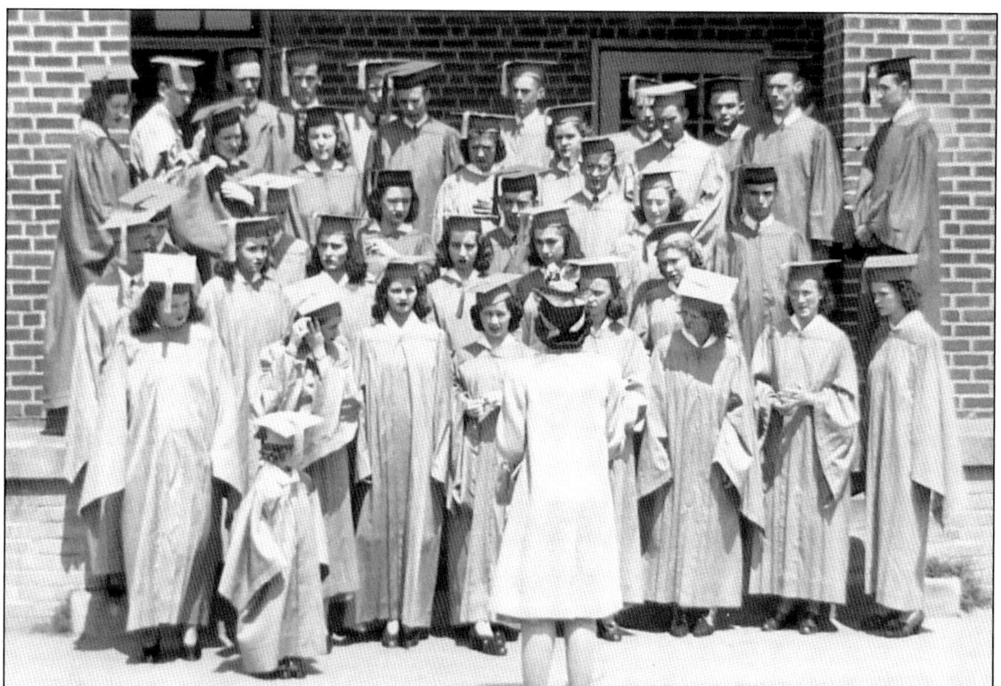

WILLIAMSTON HIGH SCHOOL GRADUATING CLASS OF 1941. (Courtesy of Francis Manning Room.)

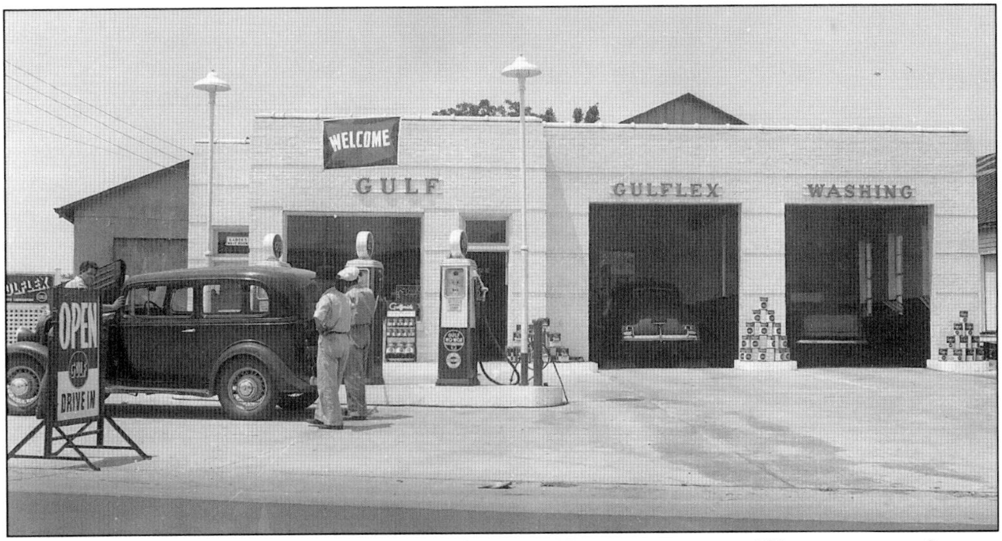

Opening of Gulf Service Station, South Haughton and Washington Street Intersection , May 24, 1941. (Courtesy of Francis Manning Room.)

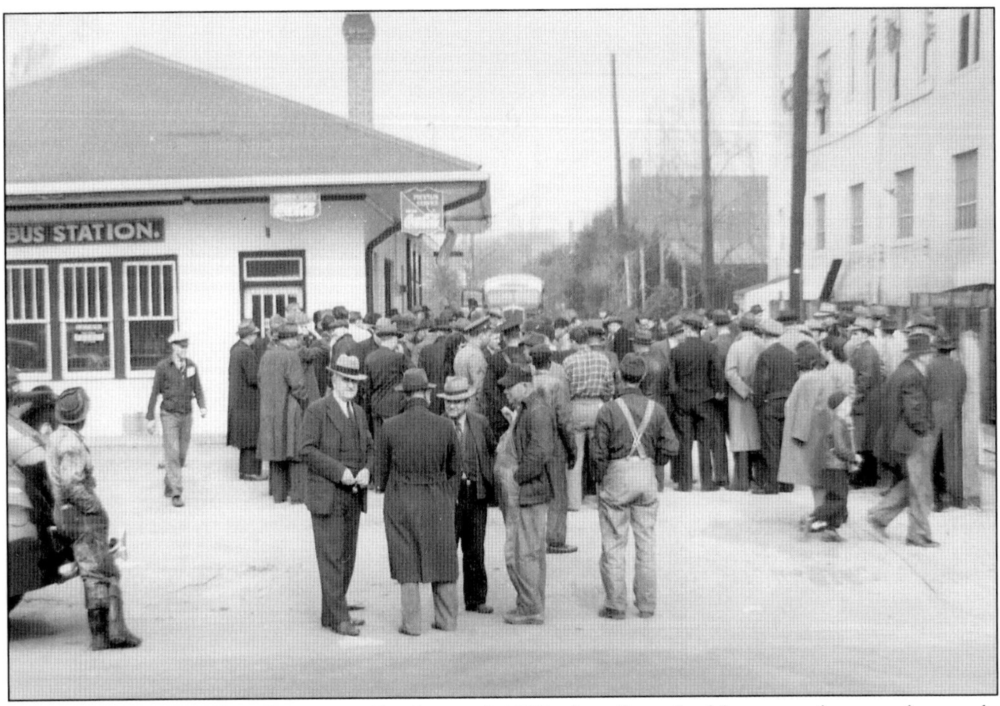

Old Williamston Bus Station. By the mid-1930s, bus lines had become the popular mode of transportation for long-distance trips. Activity at the Williamston station during World War II was especially heavy as local men began reporting for service. (Courtesy of the Francis Manning Room.)

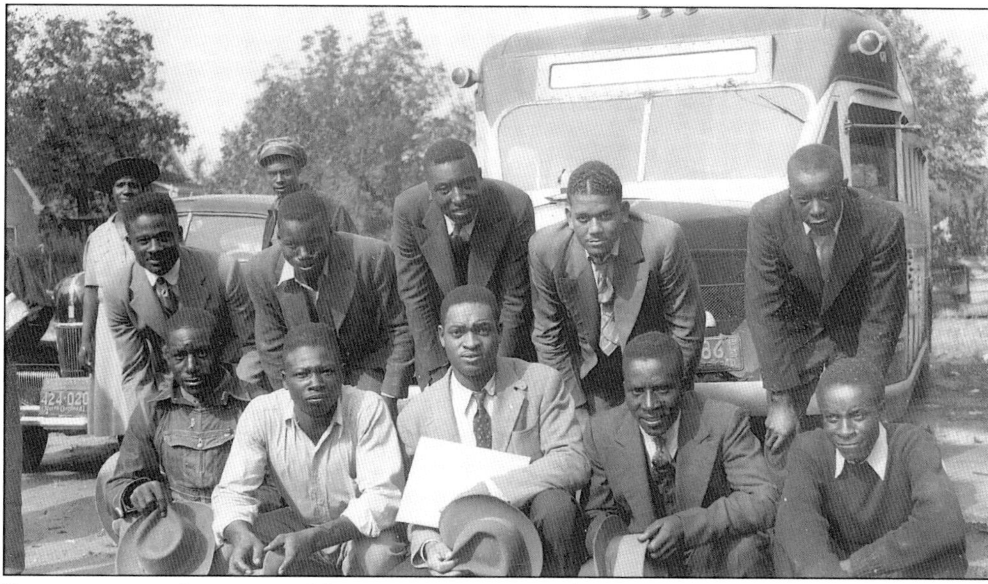

Reporting for Service on November 21, 1941. The men pictured, from left to right, are as follows: (front row) Richard Hyman, Milton Rollins, James Norris Cherry, Willie Grover Eason, and Shelbert Ore; (back row) Woodrow Narrow, Milton Roberson, Eddie Lee Smith, Edmond Pierce, and Jeremiah Brown. (Courtesy of the Francis Manning Room.)

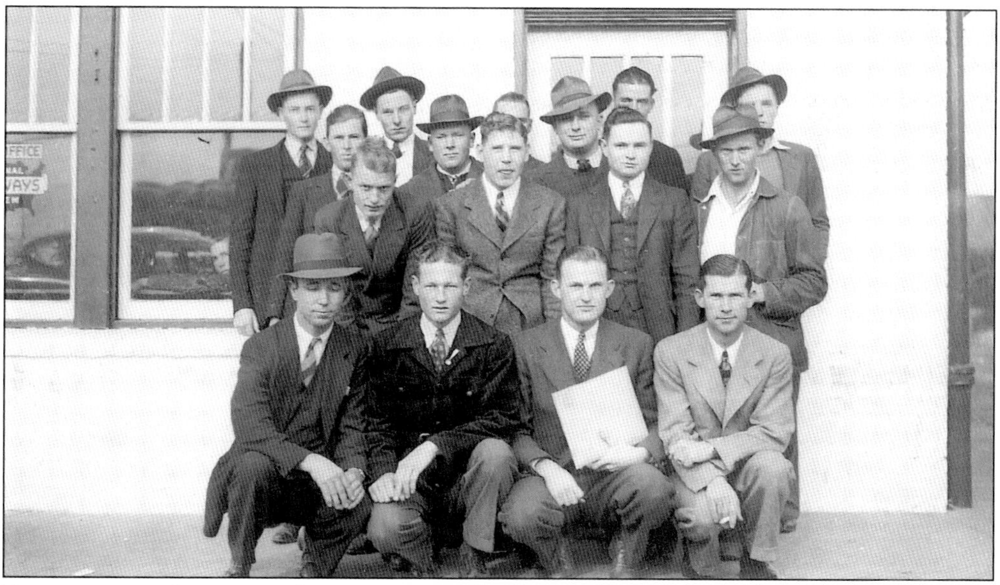

Reporting for Service on January 31, 1941. Pictured from left to right are as follows: (front row) Jesse Roberson, Charles Elbert Bullock, Marvin Theodore Roberson, and Julian Albert Roebuck; (second row) Claude Elmer Jenkins, Hildreath Rogerson, Joseph Elmer Griffin, and Robert Claborn Harris; (third row) John Davis Warren, Dennis Harding Whichard, and Heber Taylor; (back row) James Oliver Wynn, Paul Cleveland Vanlandingham, Grover Raymond Moore, Nathan Hedrick Mobley, and View Victor Nicholson. (Courtesy of the Francis Manning Room.)

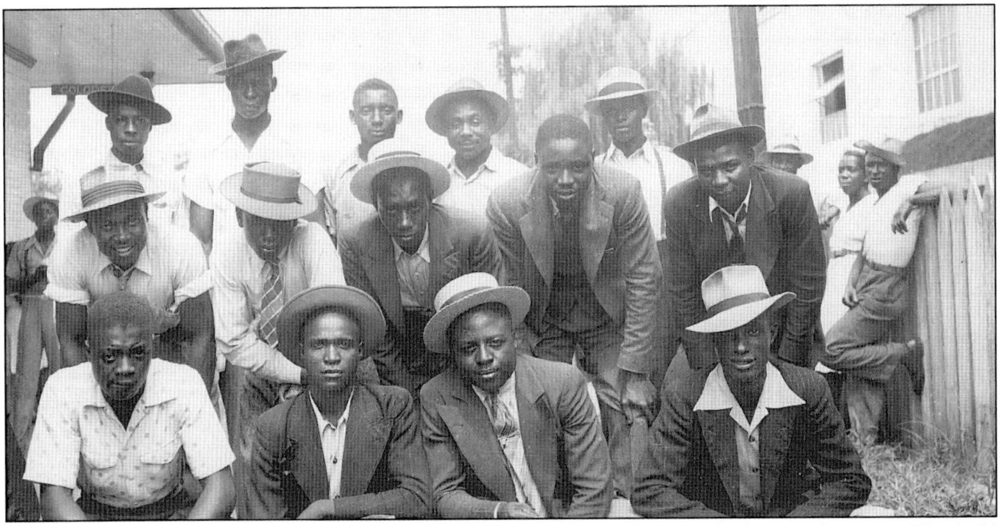

Reporting for Service on September 5, 1941. Pictured, from left to right, are Clayfield Williams, Columbus James Rodgers, Nathaniel Dunn, William Junior Spruill, William Samuel Nabry, Harry Clinton Norfleet, Lenwood Outerbridge, Vernon Lee Staton, James Willis Lloyd, William Edgar Rose, William Thomas Gray, George Washington Joyner, Charlie Clarence Ormond, and Johnny Peel. (Courtesy of the Francis Manning Room.)

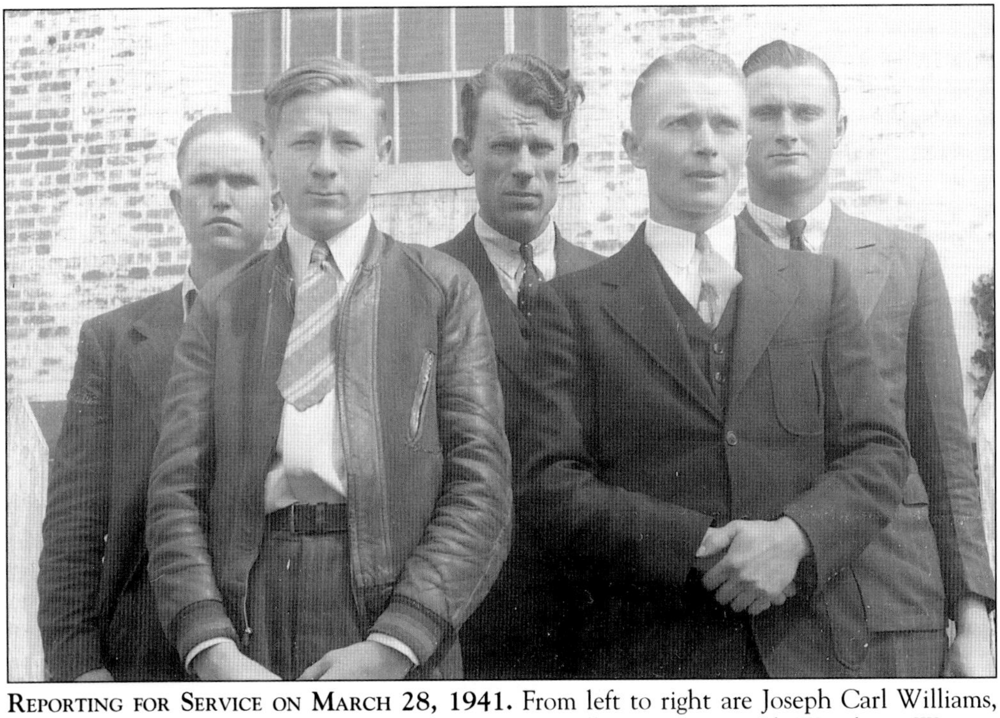

Reporting for Service on March 28, 1941. From left to right are Joseph Carl Williams, Joseph Gurganus, Lance Dutton Hardy, Douglas Albert Currie, and Woodrow Wynne. (Courtesy of the Francis Manning Room.)

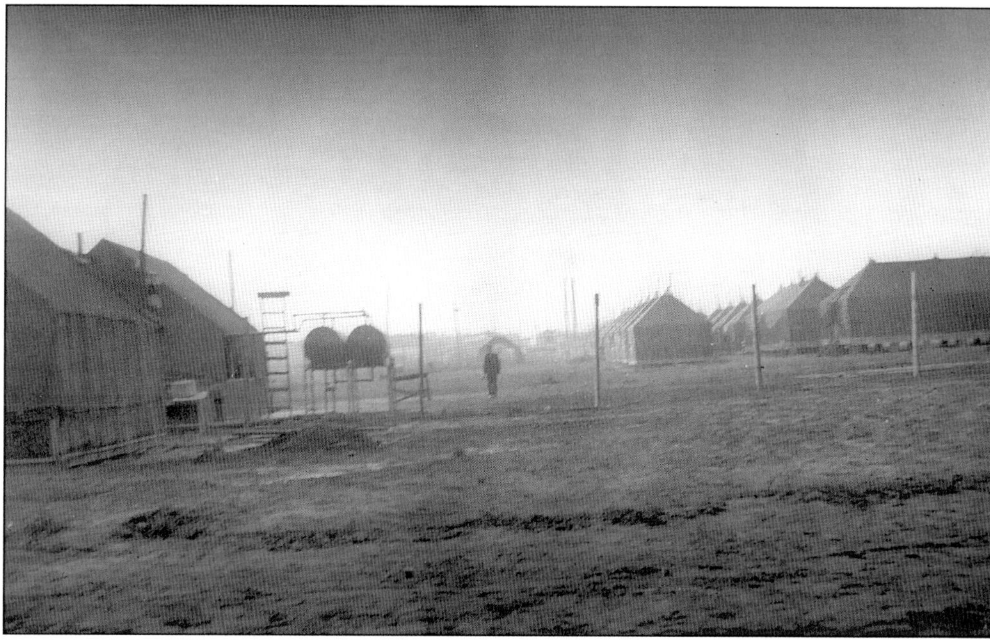

A View of the Williamston Prisoner of War Camp, c. 1944. This temporary stockade held both German and Italian prisoners of war during World War II. Prison labor from the camp was used at the nearby Standard Fertilizer Company and on farms throughout the county. (Courtesy of the Francis Manning Room.)

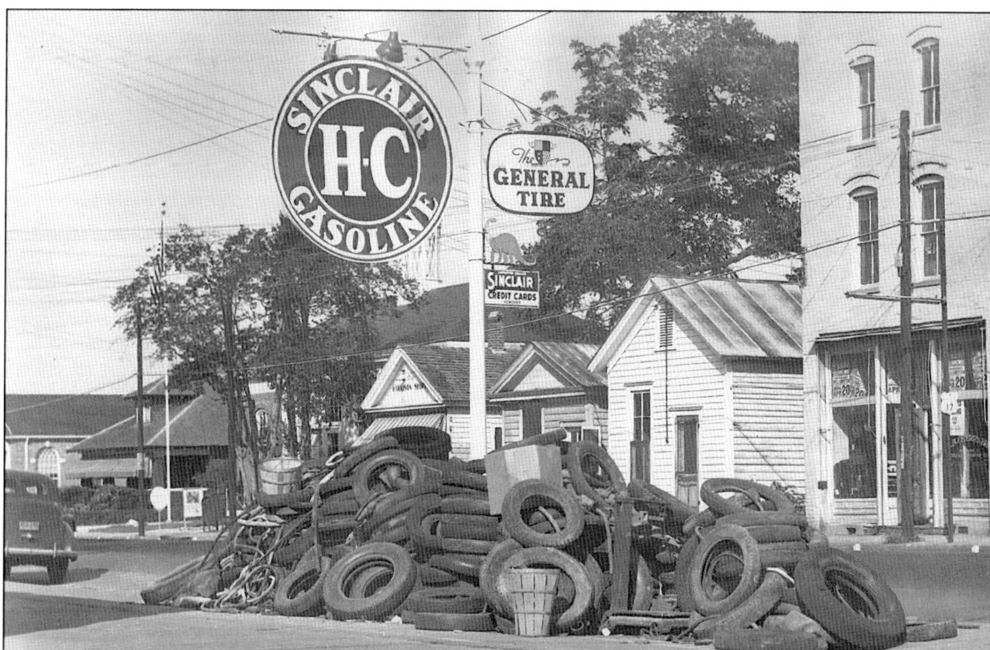

Collecting Rubber for the War Effort. This collection point is at the Sinclair Station, at the corner of Main and Smithwick Streets. (Courtesy of the Francis Manning Room.)

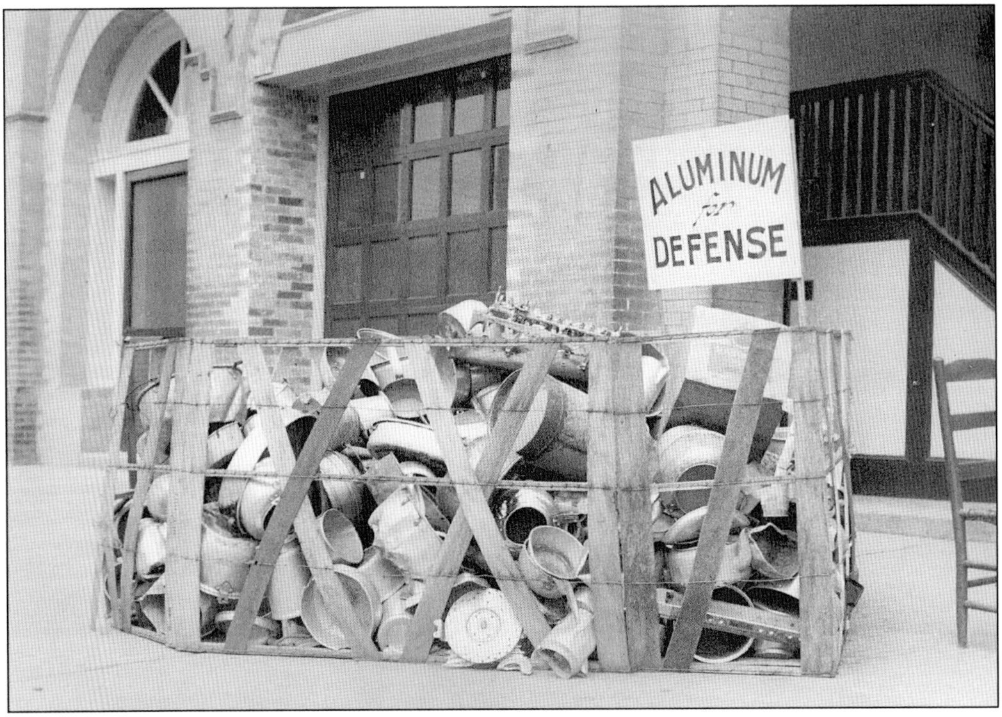

AN ALUMINUM DRIVE COLLECTION POINT IN FRONT OF CITY HALL, C. EARLY 1940S. (Courtesy of the Francis Manning Room.)

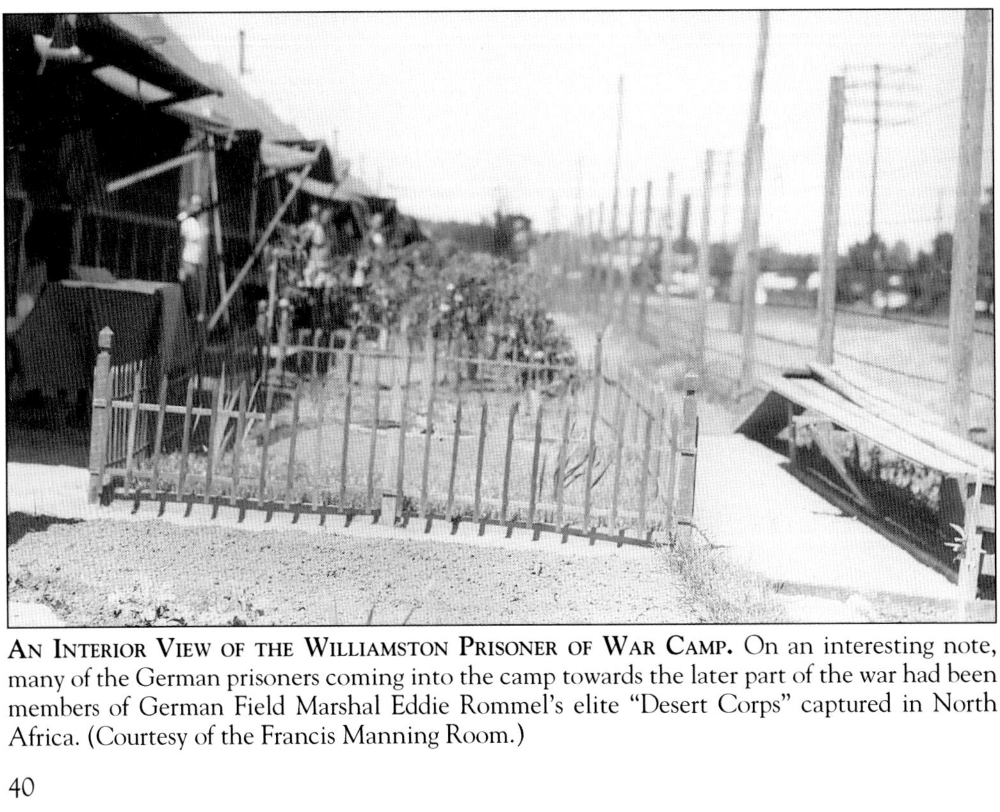
AN INTERIOR VIEW OF THE WILLIAMSTON PRISONER OF WAR CAMP. On an interesting note, many of the German prisoners coming into the camp towards the later part of the war had been members of German Field Marshal Eddie Rommel's elite "Desert Corps" captured in North Africa. (Courtesy of the Francis Manning Room.)

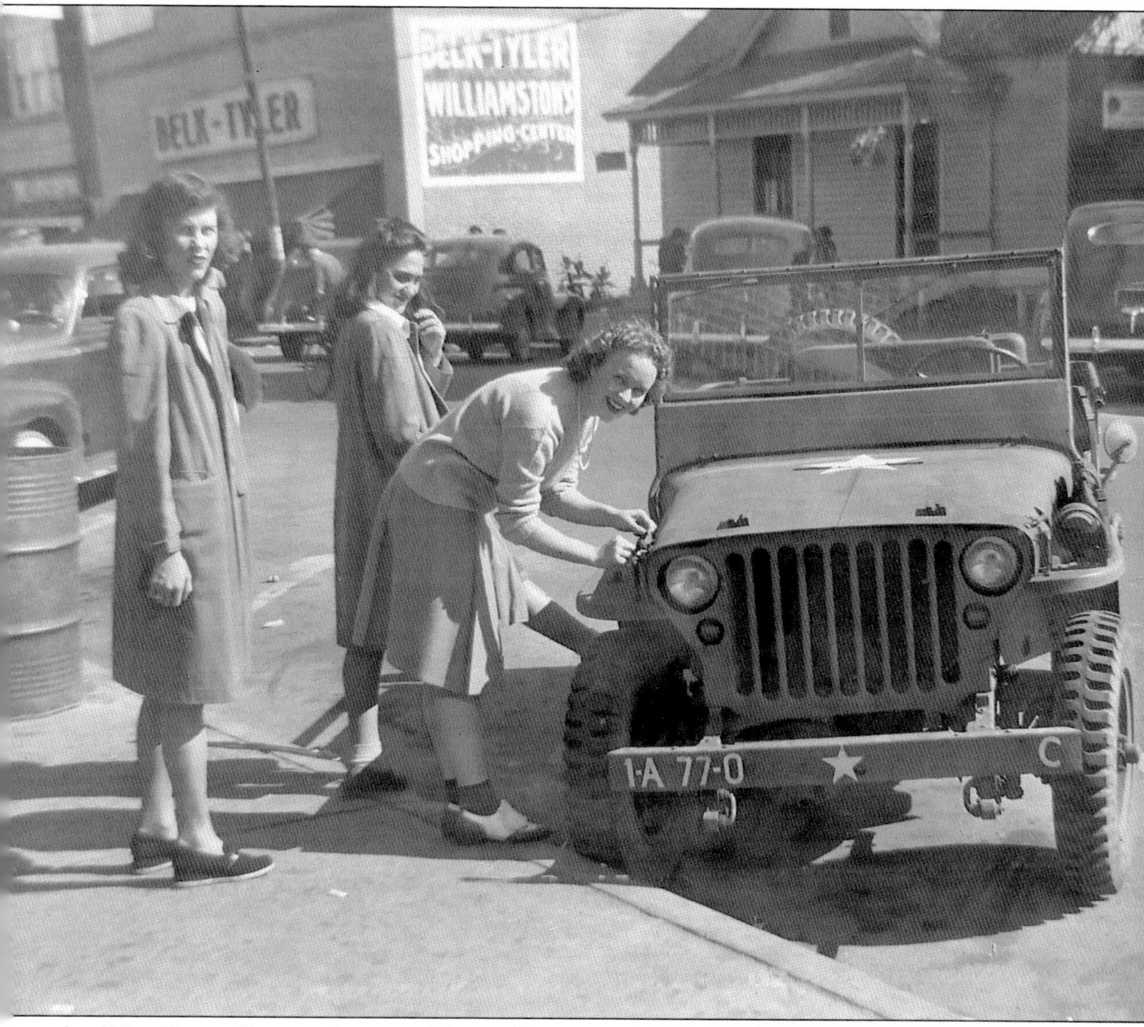

A War-Time Scene Along Main Street, c. 1944. (Courtesy of the Francis Manning Room.)

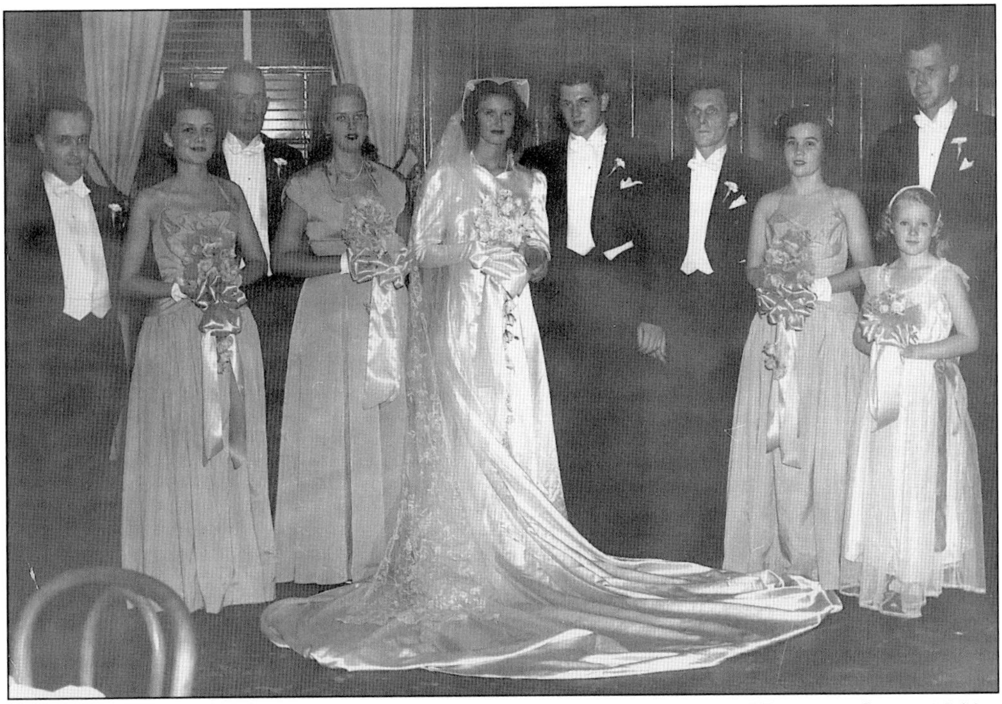

The Jones-Duetsch Wedding Reception at the George Reynolds Hotel, c. Late 1940s. Pictured from left to right are Alfred H. Ryder, Evelyn Griffin Garner, Oscar Jones, Anne Duetsch, Lucille Jones Duetsch (bride), Edward G. Duetsch (groom), Robert Duetsch, Frances Thomas Langley, Bonnie Jones Cook, and James W. Jones. (Courtesy of Fred W. Harrison, Jr.)

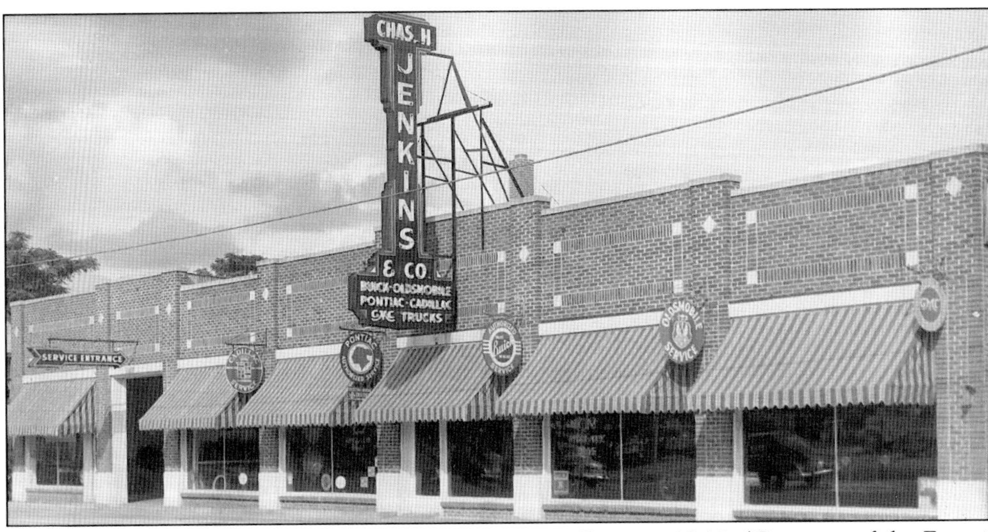

Charles H. Jenkins & Co. on South Washington Street, 1949. (Courtesy of the Francis Manning Room.)

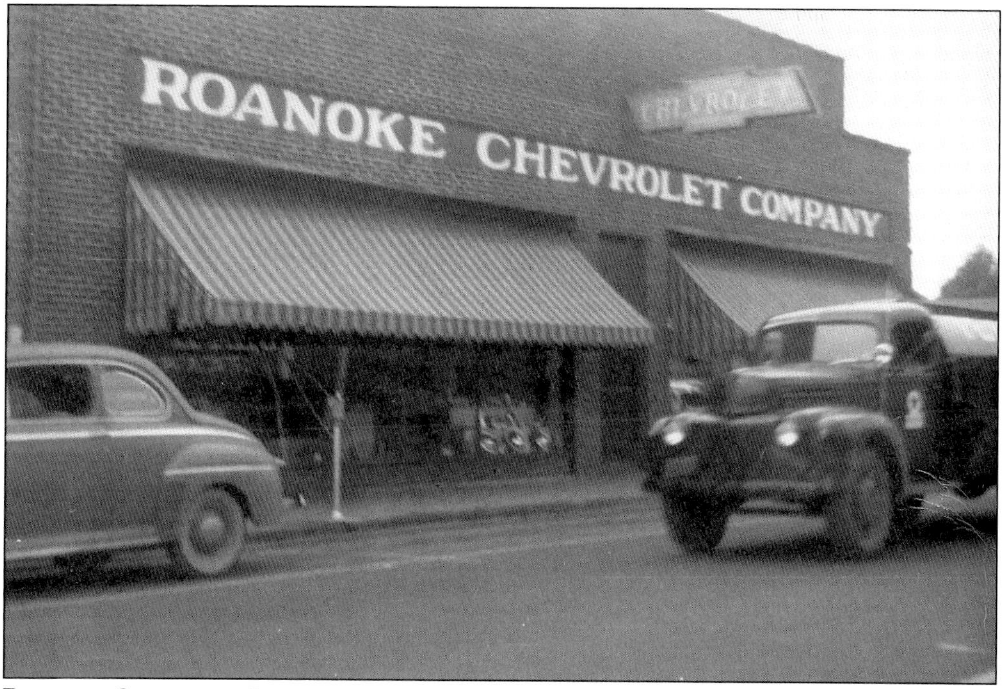

ROANOKE CHEVROLET CO., C. LATE 1940S. Shown here on the northern end of Washington Street, this business moved to the corner of Sycamore and South Washington Streets some years later. (Courtesy of Alma J. Bailey.)

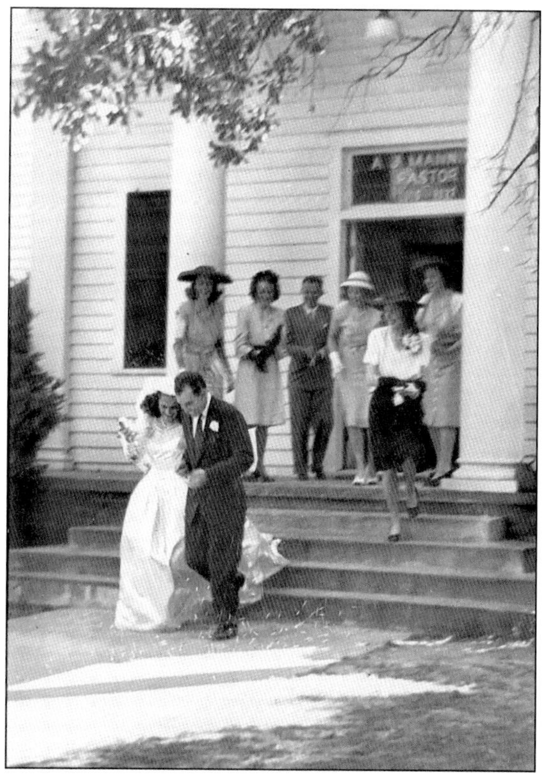

A 1940S WEDDING PARTY AT THE OLD FIRST CHRISTIAN CHURCH. Then located on South Smithwick Street, this wood-frame structure was replaced in the mid-1950s by a larger, brick building located on the corner of North Smithwick and Liberty Streets. (Courtesy of the Francis Manning Room.)

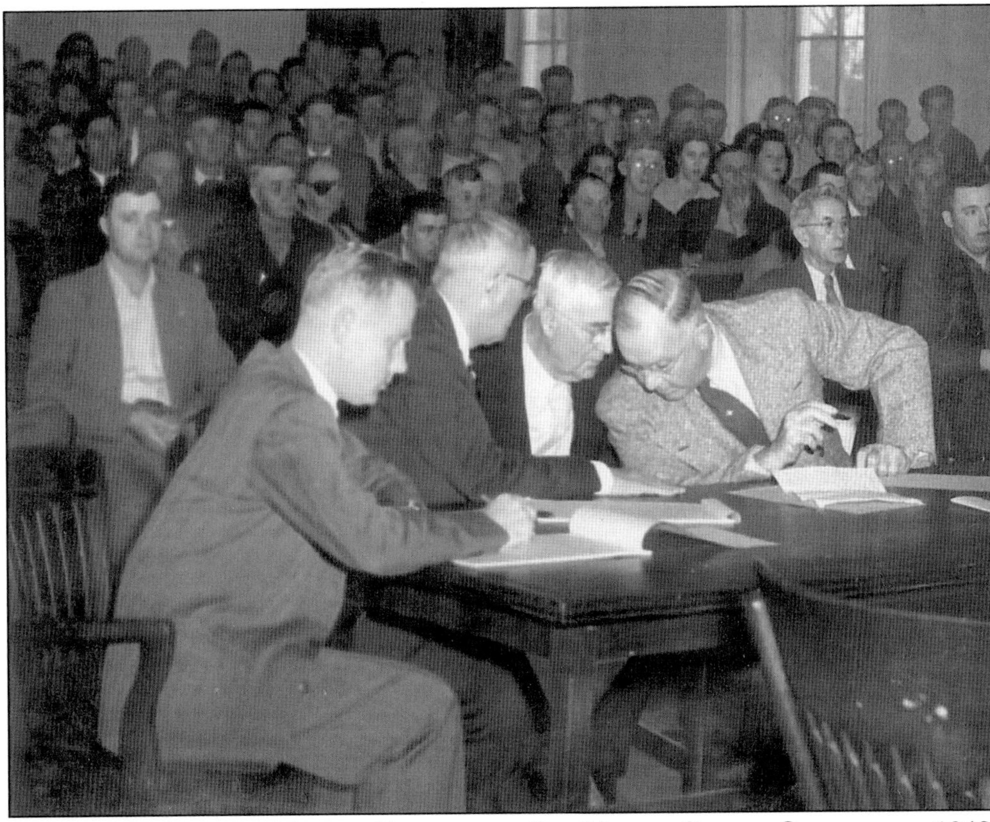

The John R. Coltrain Murder Trial in the Old Martin County Courthouse, 1949. The two men at the table at left are Edgar J. Gurganus and B.A. Critcher, senior law partners. (Courtesy of the Francis Manning Room.)

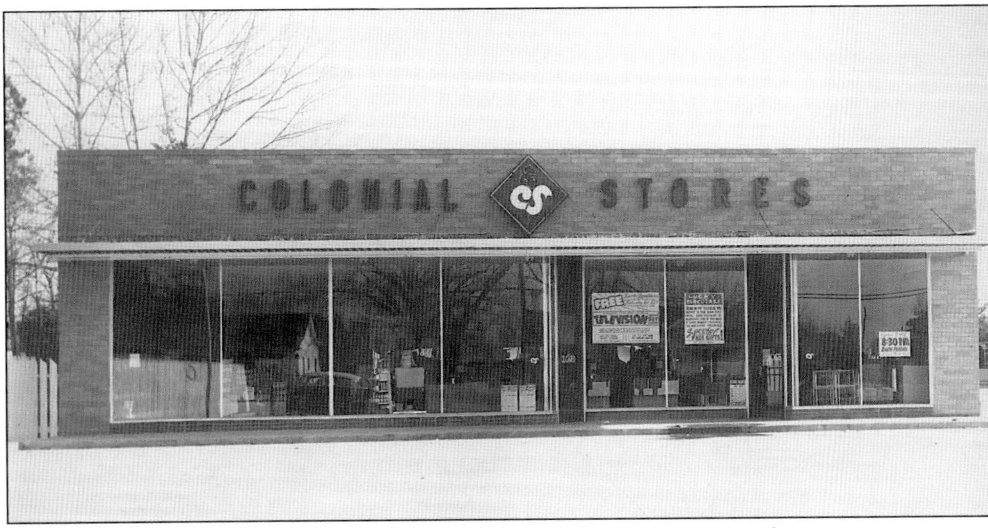

Colonial Stores. One of the first large-scale grocery chains to make its appearance in Williamston was Colonial Stores, shown here on the corner of West Main and Elm in the 1950s. (Courtesy of the Francis Manning Room.)

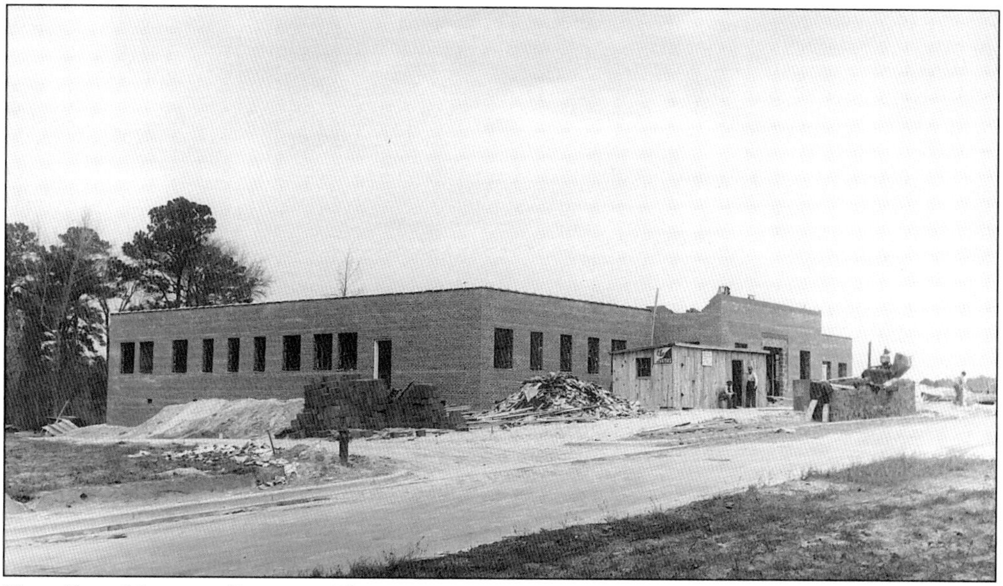

THE OLD MARTIN GENERAL HOSPITAL UNDER CONSTRUCTION, 1950. During the 1950s, Williamston saw one of its greatest periods of building construction. Increased employment and educational opportunities heightened the demand for more housing and better public facilities. Initially a private concern, the hospital (shown here on Liberty Street) was purchased by the county in the early 1960s. (Courtesy of the Francis Manning Room.)

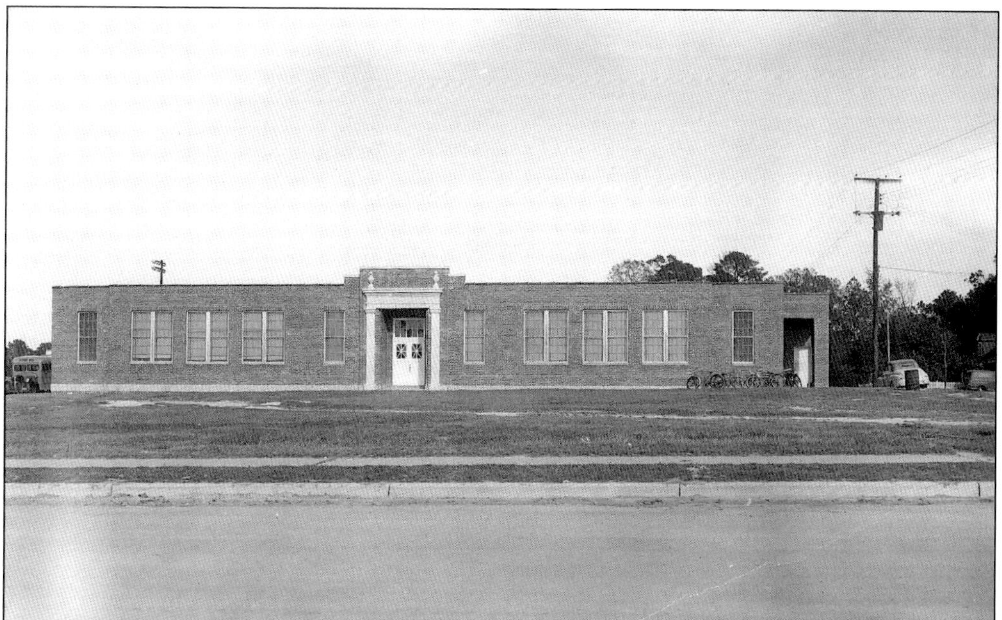

A CLASSROOM ADDITION TO THE WILLIAMSTON HIGH SCHOOL CAMPUS, C. 1950. Not long after its construction, this building was again enlarged with a second story and a rear annex, which housed a cafeteria, band room, and vocational classrooms. (Courtesy of the Francis Manning Room.)

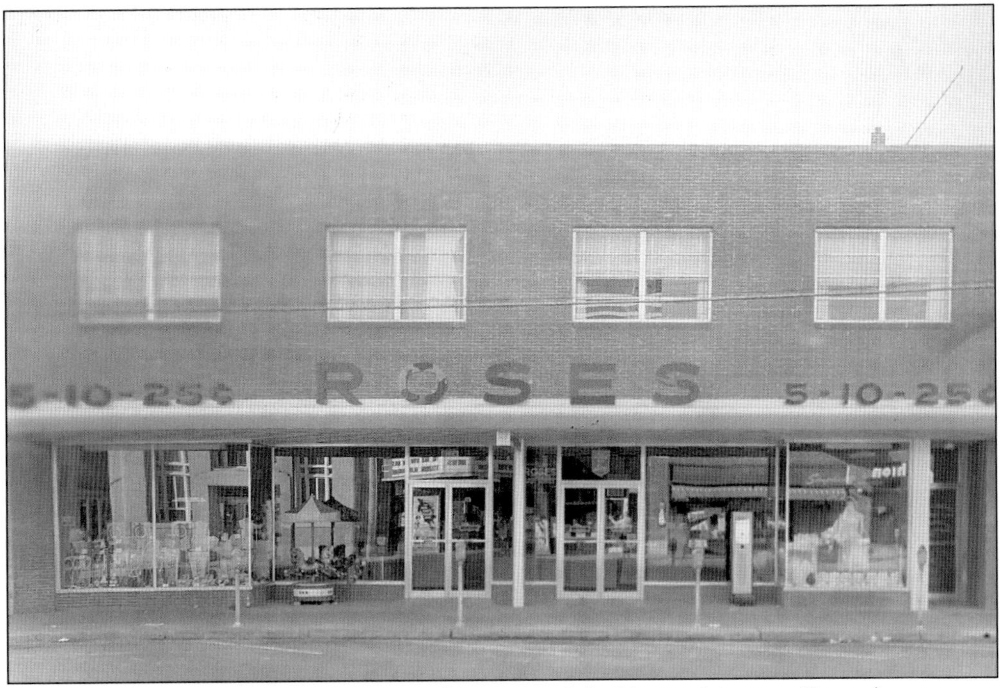

Roses Store on Main Street, c. 1958. (Courtesy of the Francis Manning Room.)

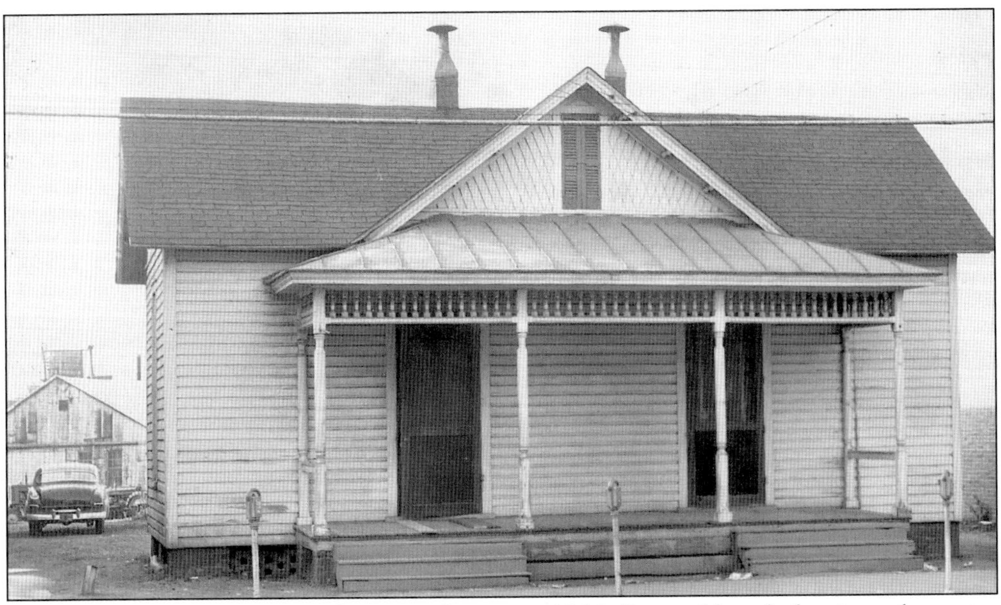

The Dennis Simmons Lumber Company Office, c. 1950. Pictured here before its replacement by Roses Store, this building served as the headquarters for the Dennis Simmons Lumber Company until its closing in 1919. The Simmons Company was one of the largest of its kind in the state during the later half of the 19th century, when Williamston was widely recognized as a "sawmill and shingle metropolis." It is noted that Simmons Company shingles were used in the first restoration of George Washington's Mt. Vernon home in the late 1850s. (Courtesy of the Francis Manning Room.)

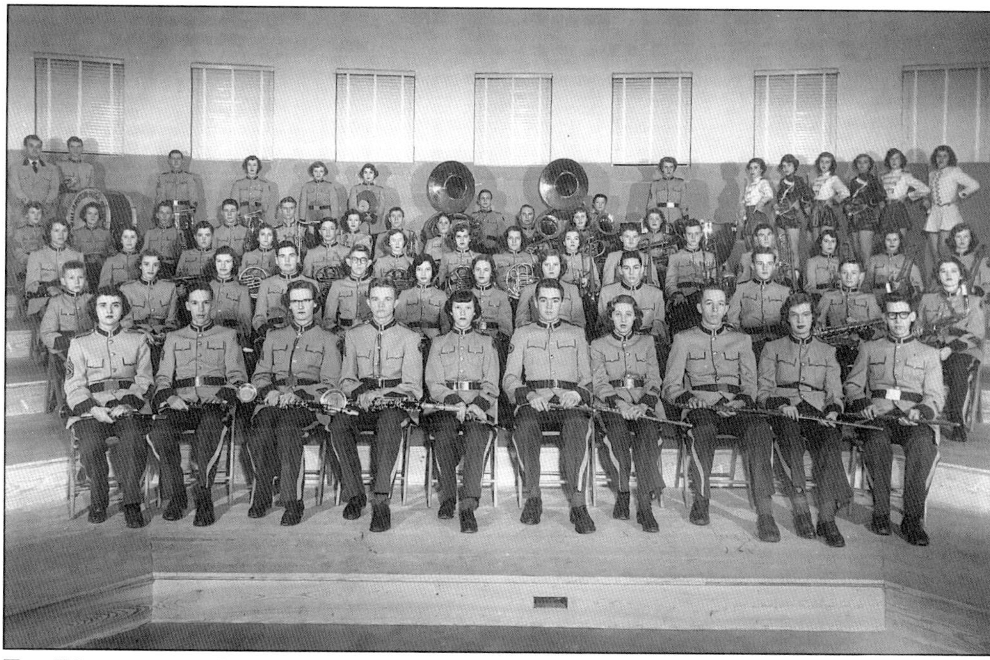

THE WILLIAMSTON HIGH SCHOOL BAND OF 1954–1955. (Courtesy of Fred W. Harrison Jr.)

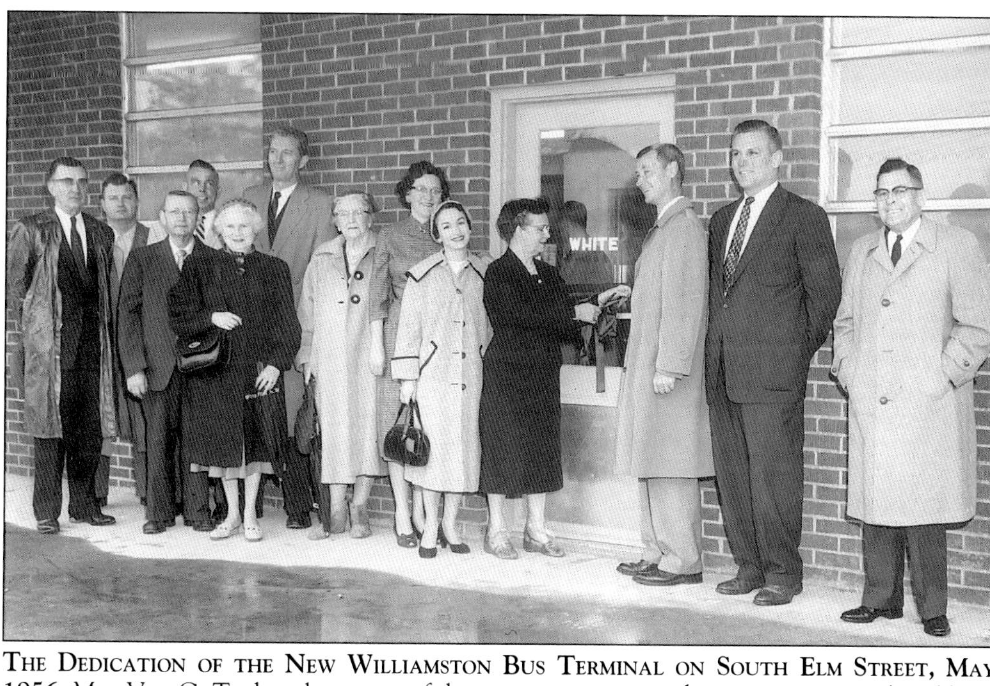

THE DEDICATION OF THE NEW WILLIAMSTON BUS TERMINAL ON SOUTH ELM STREET, MAY 1956. Mrs. Van G. Taylor, the owner of the property, is pictured at center cutting the ribbon. (Courtesy of the Francis Manning Room.)

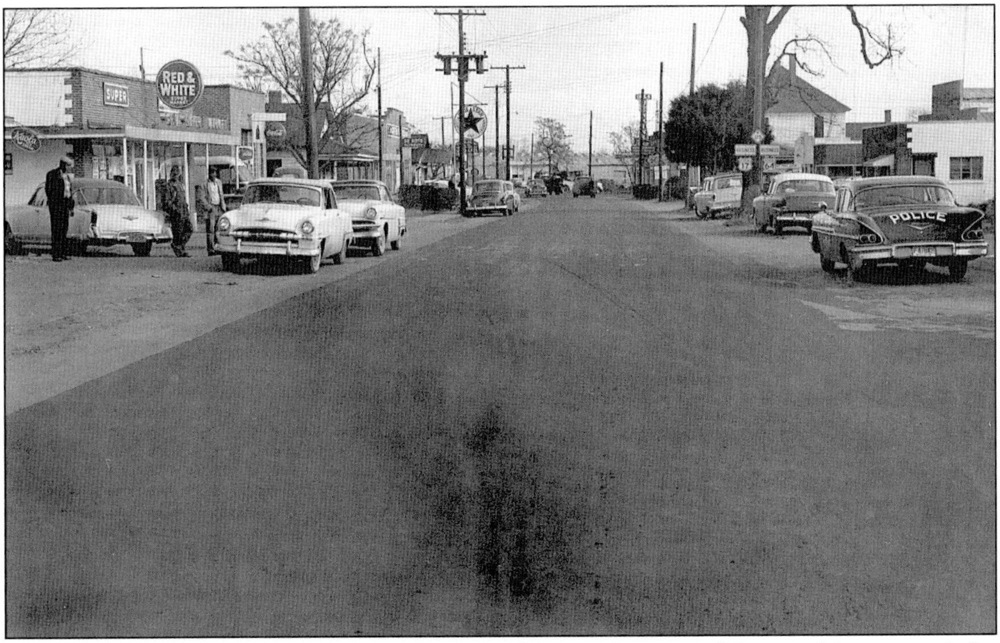

A MID-1950S VIEW OF SOUTH WASHINGTON STREET, LOOKING NORTH. (Courtesy of the Francis Manning Room.)

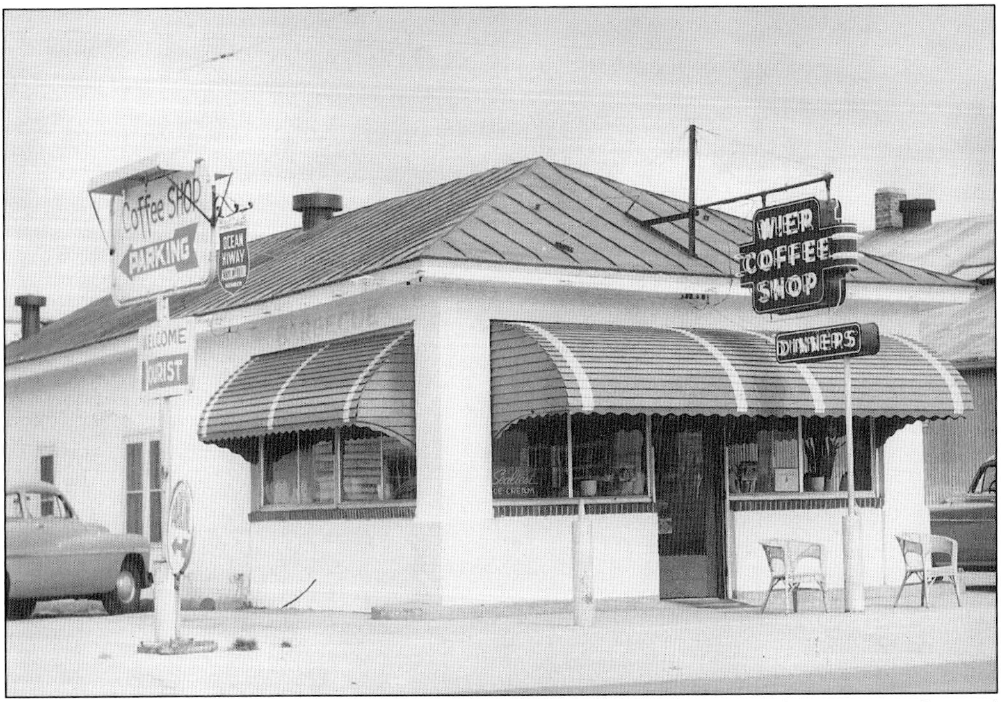

THE WIER COFFEE SHOP ON SOUTH WASHINGTON STREET, C. 1955. This business was located on the site where the Williamston Fire Department stands today. (Courtesy of the Francis Manning Room.)

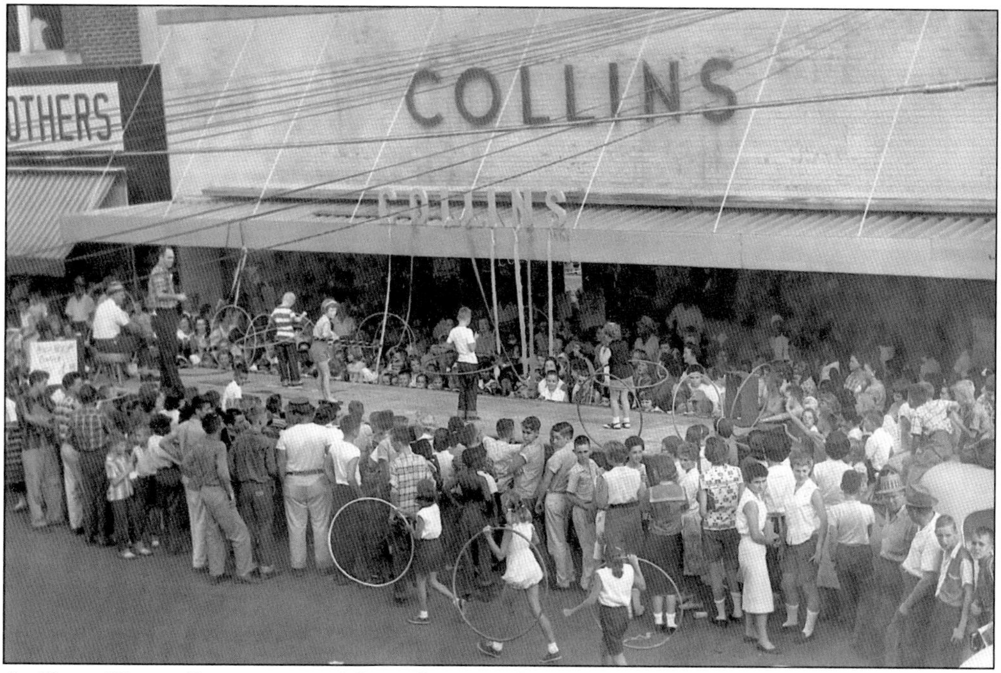

A Hula-Hoop Contest on Main Street, September 1958. (Courtesy of the Francis Manning Room.)

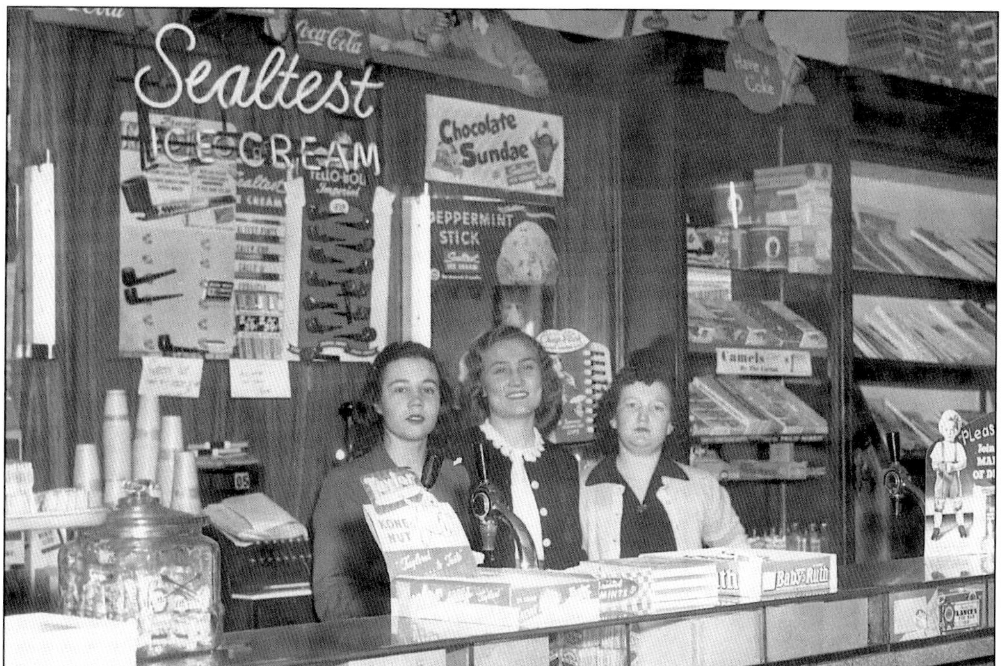

The Davis Pharmacy on Main Street, c. 1950s. (Courtesy of the Francis Manning Room.)

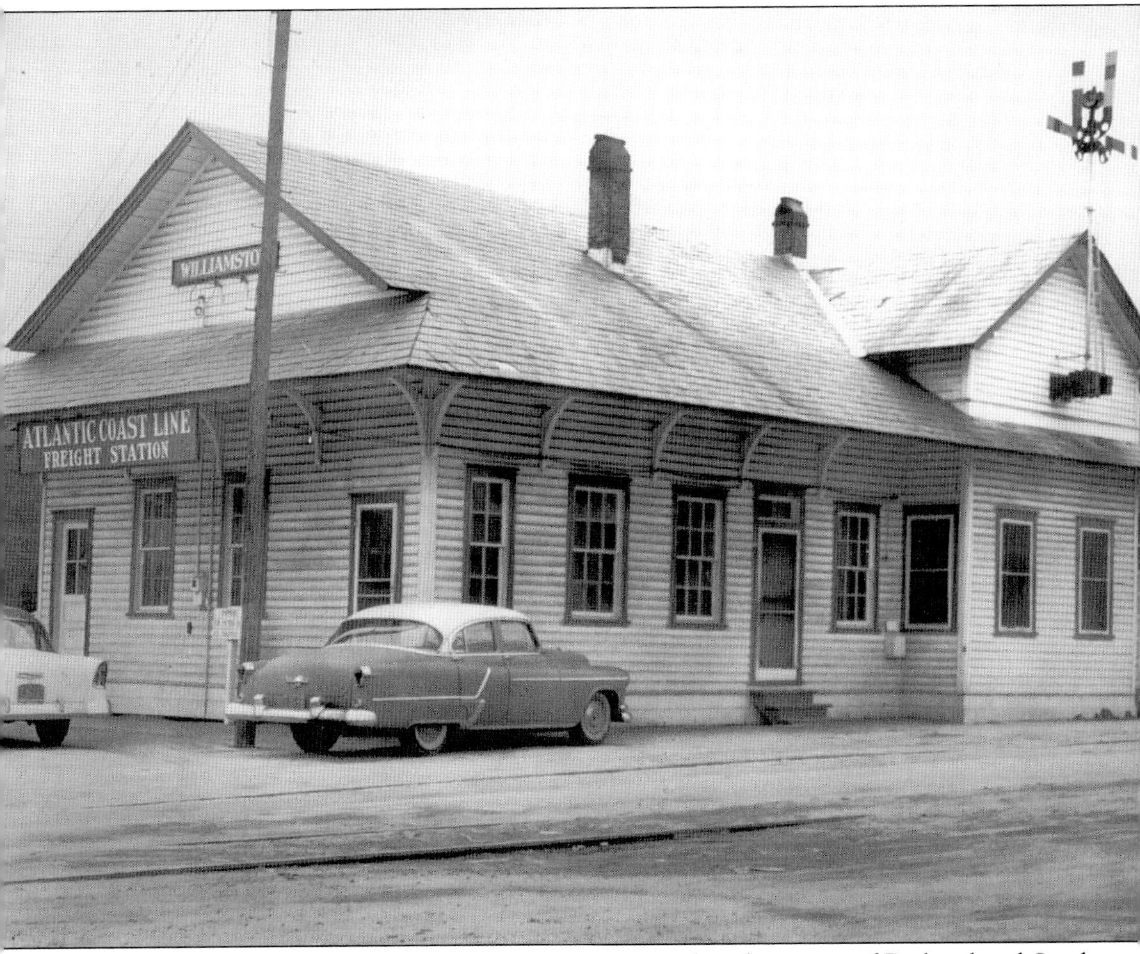

The Williamston Railroad Depot, c. 1956. Located at the corner of Railroad and South Haughton Streets, this structure was destroyed by fire in 1979. (Courtesy of J. Earl Bailey.)

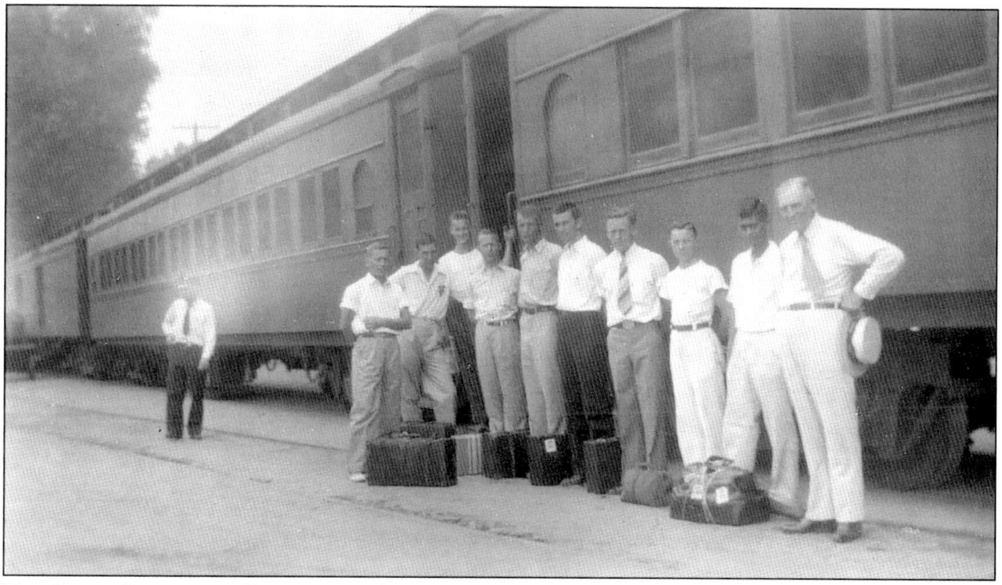

The Last Scheduled Passenger Train Service in Williamston. The group shown here is waiting to board the last scheduled passenger train to run through Williamston, which came in 1938. (Courtesy of the Francis Manning Room.)

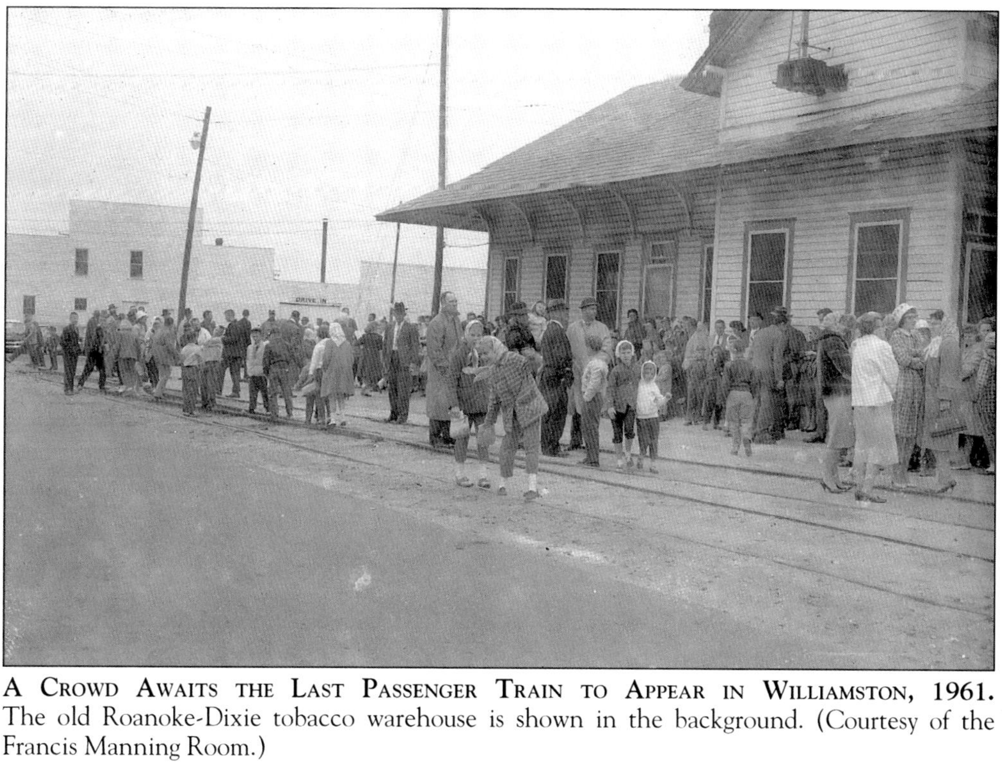

A Crowd Awaits the Last Passenger Train to Appear in Williamston, 1961. The old Roanoke-Dixie tobacco warehouse is shown in the background. (Courtesy of the Francis Manning Room.)

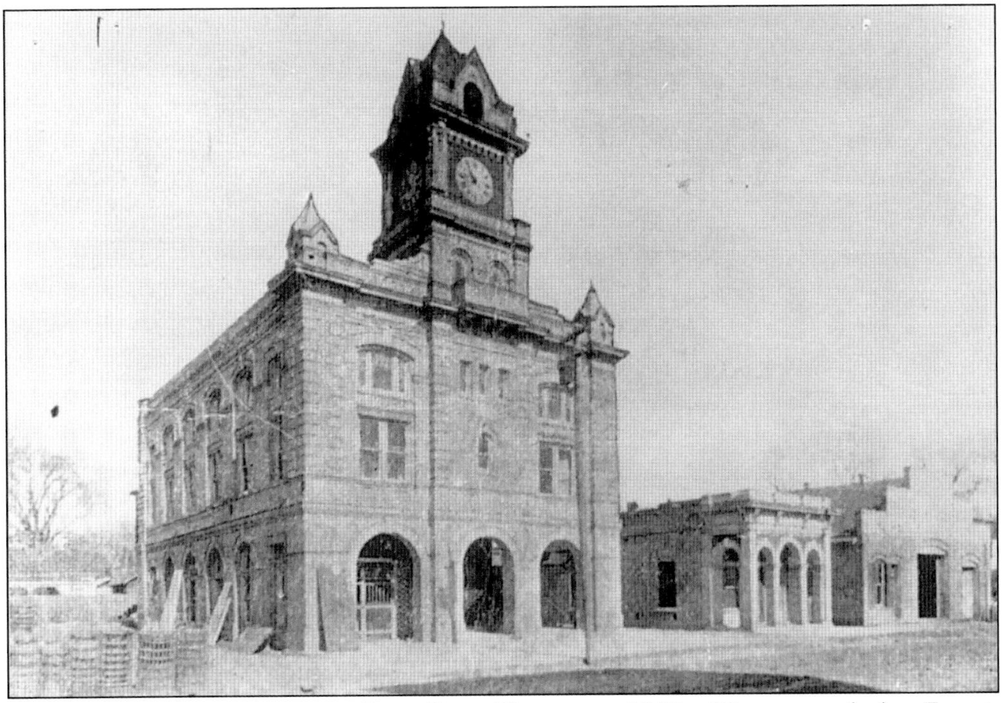

A POSTCARD VIEW OF THE OLD CITY HALL, C. 1910. (Courtesy of the Francis Manning Room.)

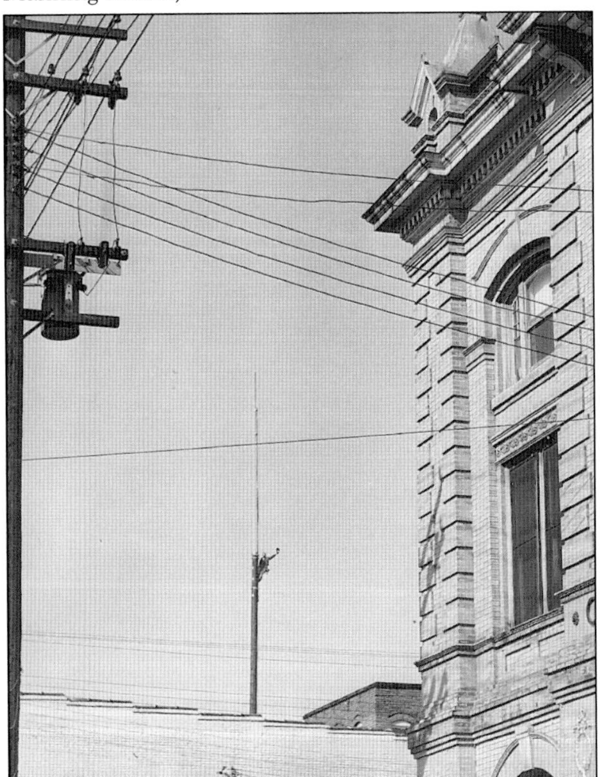

JOHN ASHLEY HARDISON ON THE NEW RADIO TOWER FOR VIRGINIA ELECTRIC POWER, 1949. (Courtesy of the Francis Manning Room.)

The December 1958 City Hall Fire. This 1907 landmark was replaced with a new structure in 1961. (Courtesy of the Francis Manning Room.)

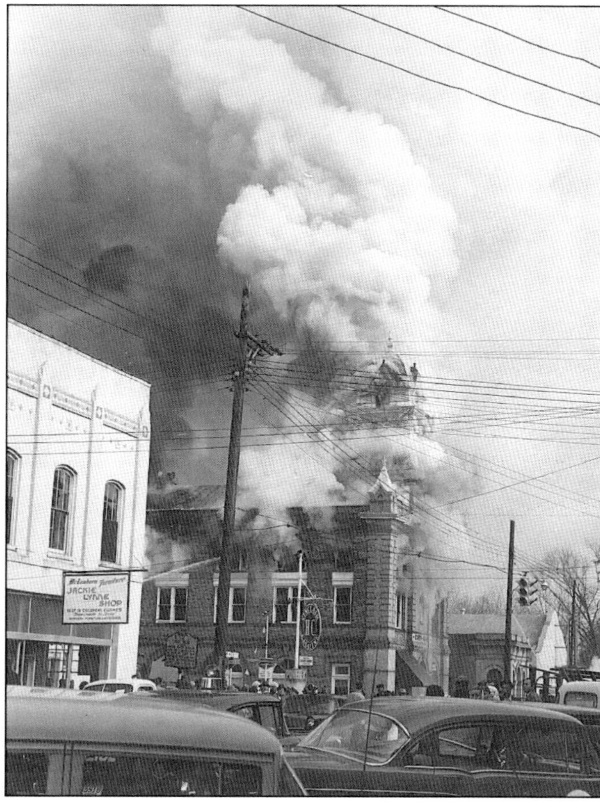

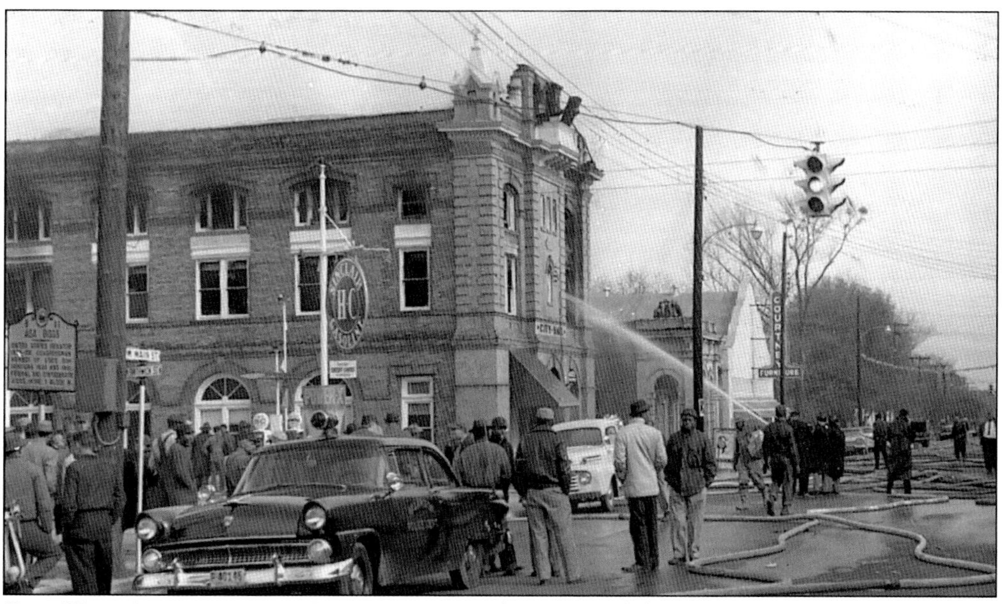

City Hall After the Fire, December 1958. (Courtesy of the Francis Manning Room.)

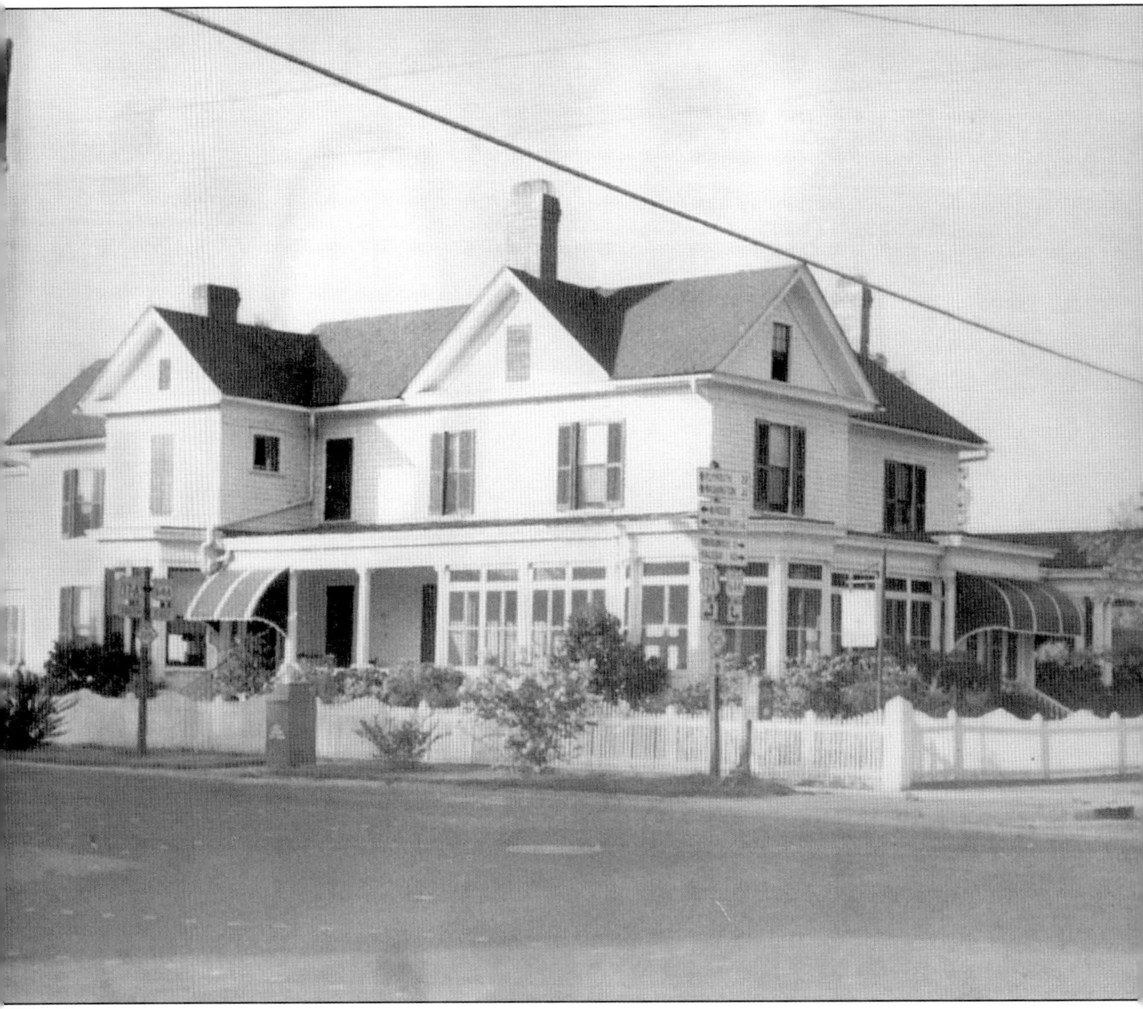

THE J.G. STATON HOME ON THE SOUTHWEST CORNER OF MAIN AND SOUTH HAUGHTON STREETS. Lumber merchant Dennis Simmons moved to Williamston from Jamesville in 1865 and built this home, which was later enlarged and modified over the years. Upon his death in 1902, Simmons's nephew Dennis Simmons Biggs inherited the home. Biggs died not long after, and his wife, Fannie Chase Biggs, later married James Grist Staton. The residence was torn down after Mrs. Staton's death in 1956. (Courtesy of J. Earl Bailey.)

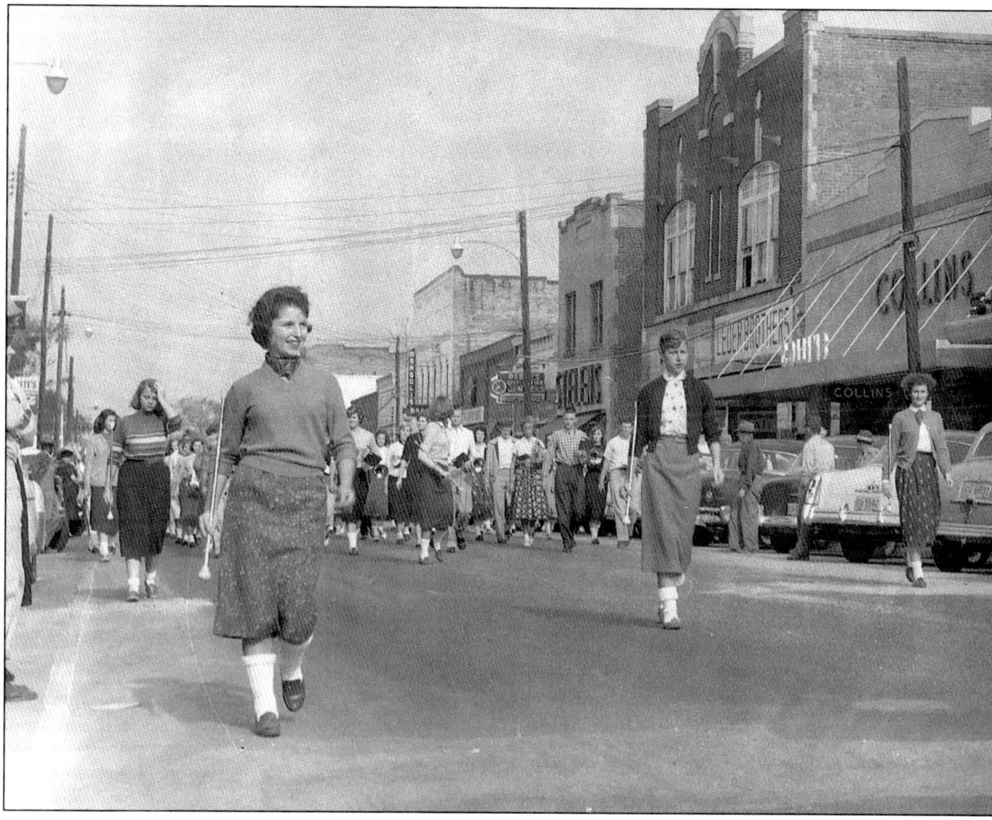

A MAIN STREET PARADE SCENE, C. MID-1950S. (Courtesy of Francis Manning Room.)

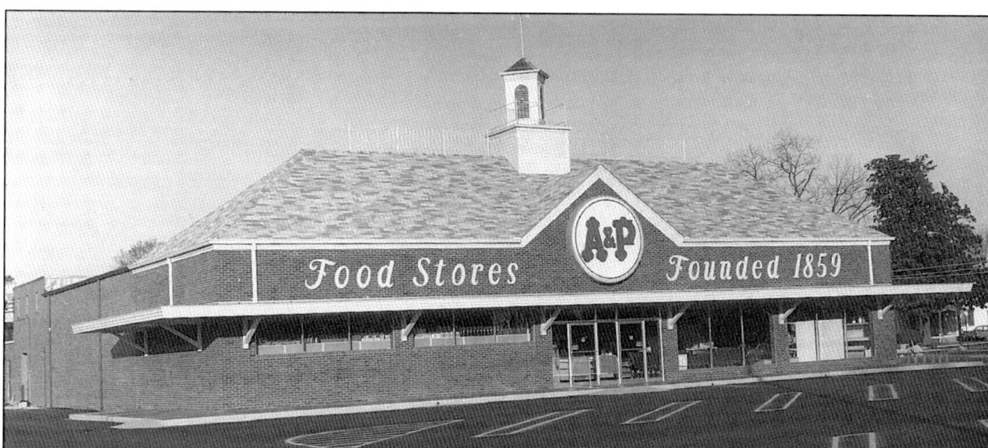

A 1962 VIEW OF AN A&P FOOD STORE. This grocery store was constructed on the property formerly occupied by the Staton home. (Courtesy of Fred W. Harrison Jr.)

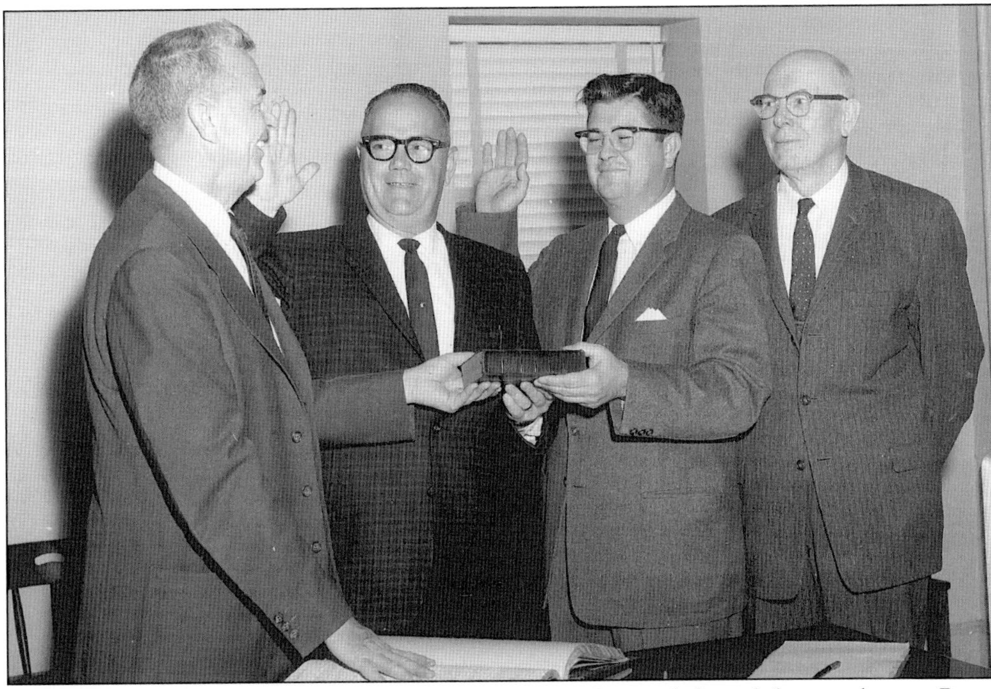

TAKING THE OATH OF OFFICE, DECEMBER 6, 1962. Pictured from left to right are Bruce Wynne, Henry S. Johnson, Joseph H. Thigpen, and J. Sam Getsinger. (Courtesy of the Francis Manning Room.)

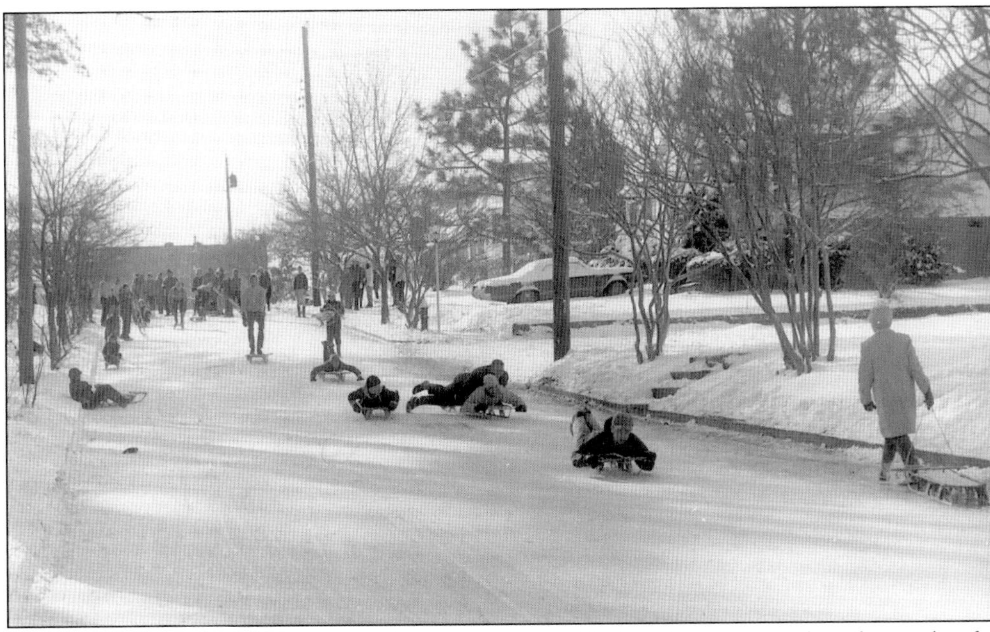

A HALIFAX STREET SNOW SCENE, JANUARY 17, 1965. Residents enjoy the aftermath of a snowfall that measured nearly 7 inches. (Courtesy of the Francis Manning Room.)

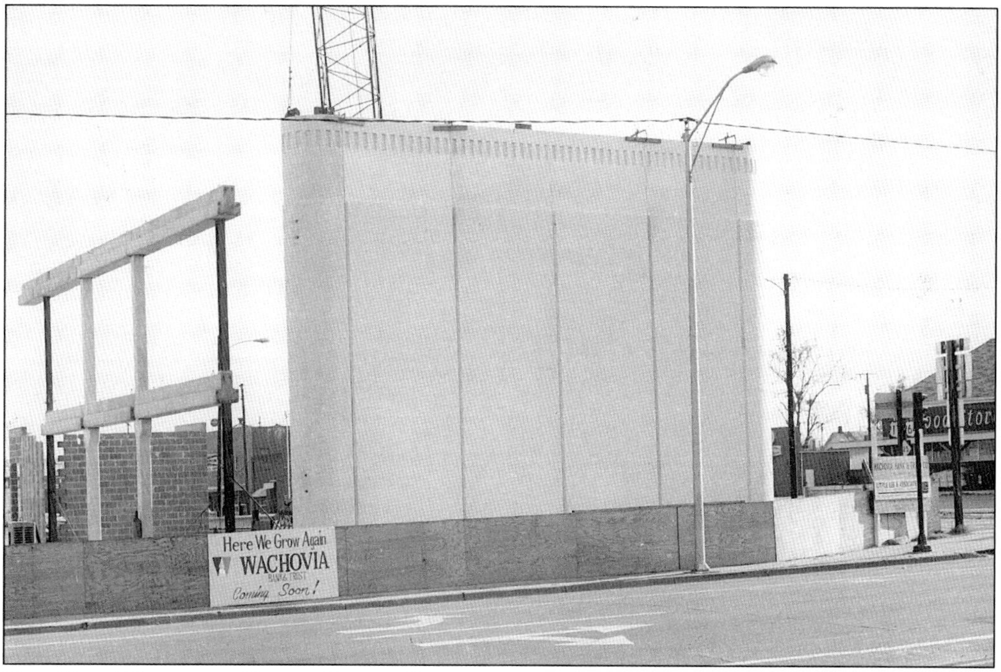

The New Wachovia Bank Under Construction on the Former Dunning Propert, c. 1970. (Courtesy of the Francis Manning Room.)

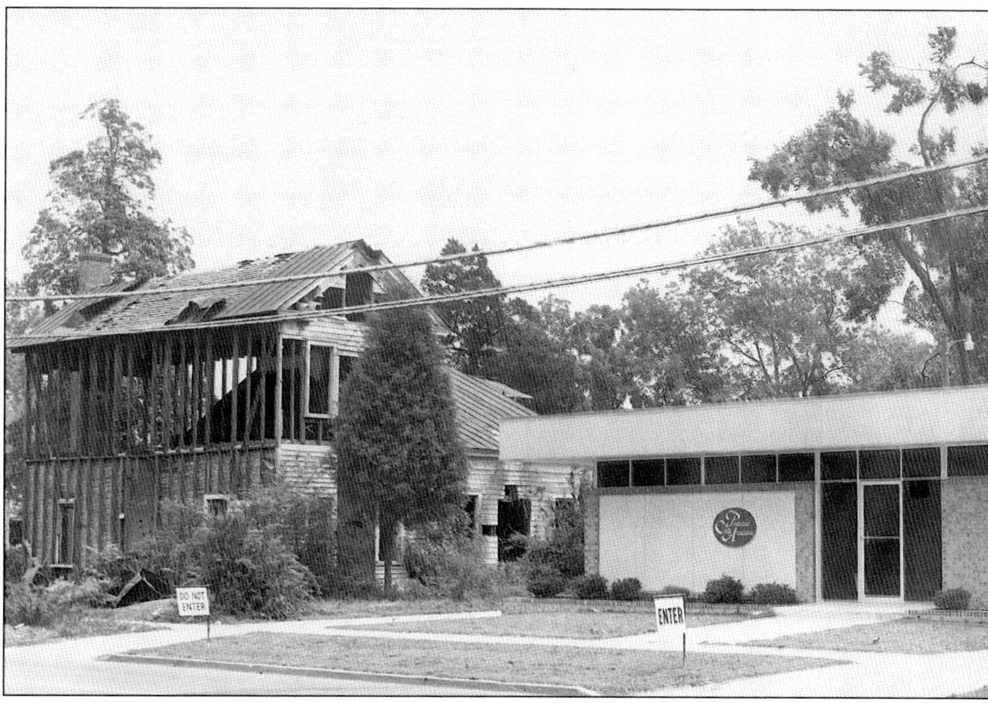

West Main Street, c. 1970. From the late 1950s to the early 1970s, many older homes along West Main Street were torn down to provide more room for commercial developments. Shown here is the old Moore home being demolished next to a recently built office. (Courtesy of the Francis Manning Room.)

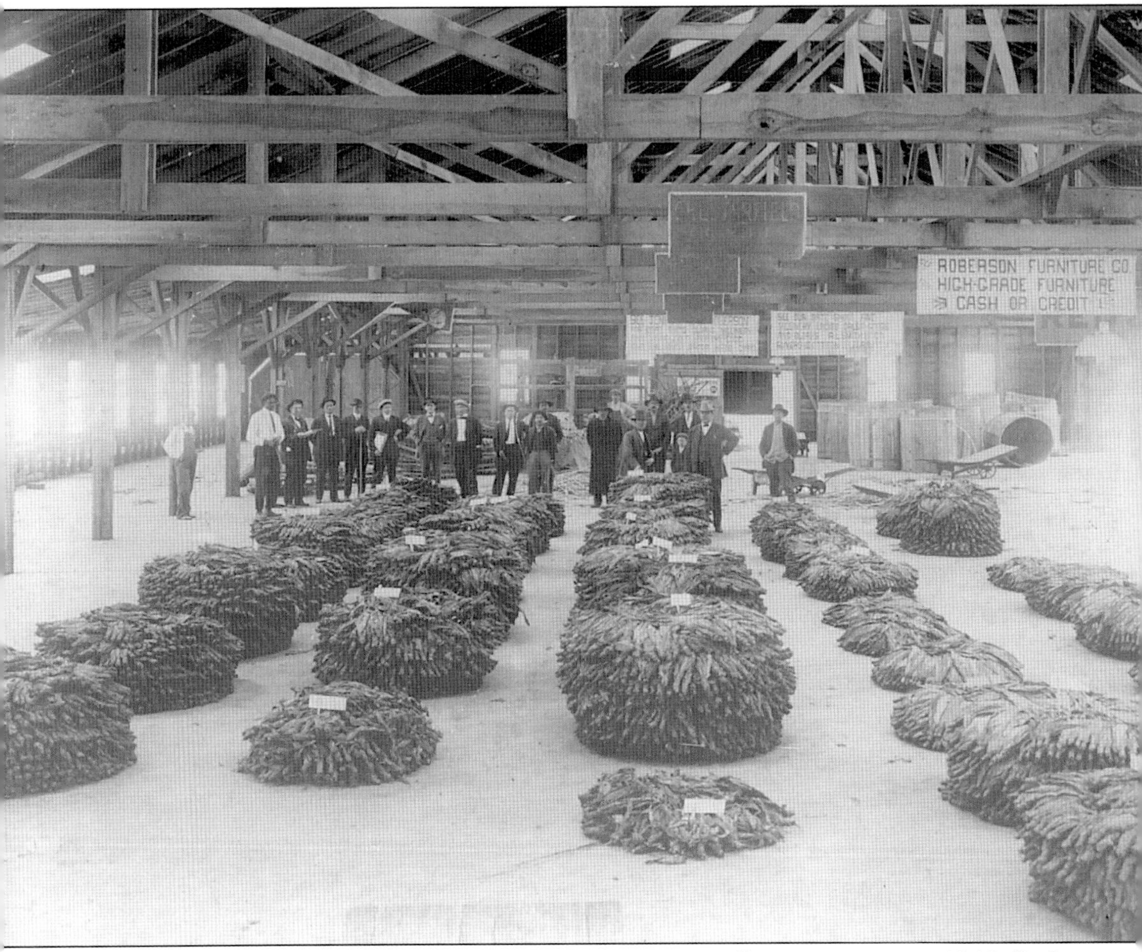

AN INSIDE VIEW OF THE ADKINS AND BAILEY WAREHOUSE IN ROBERSONVILLE, C. 1910. Built in 1902 as the Taylor Warehouse, the business later came under ownership of W.H. Adkins and R.A. Bailey. Their partnership was said to be the longest continuous one in the history of the tobacco industry in Martin County. (Courtesy of Doris L. Wilson.)

Three

ROBERSONVILLE

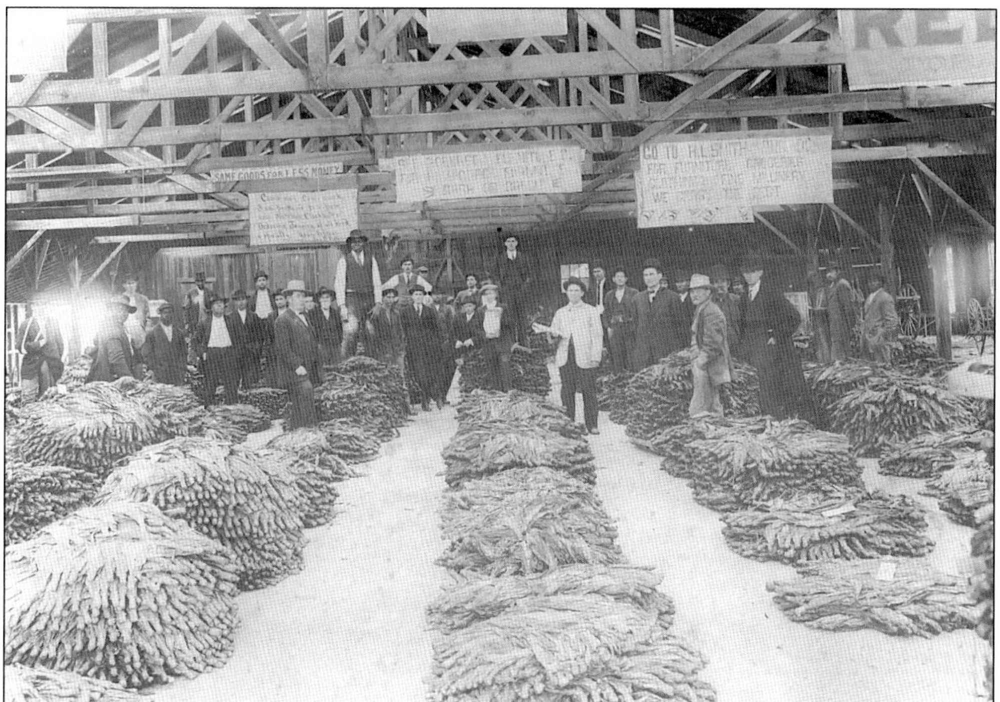

ANOTHER INSIDE VIEW OF THE ADKINS AND BAILEY WAREHOUSE, C. 1910. The first auction sale of tobacco in Martin County occurred in Robersonville on August 7, 1900. (Courtesy of Doris L. Wilson.)

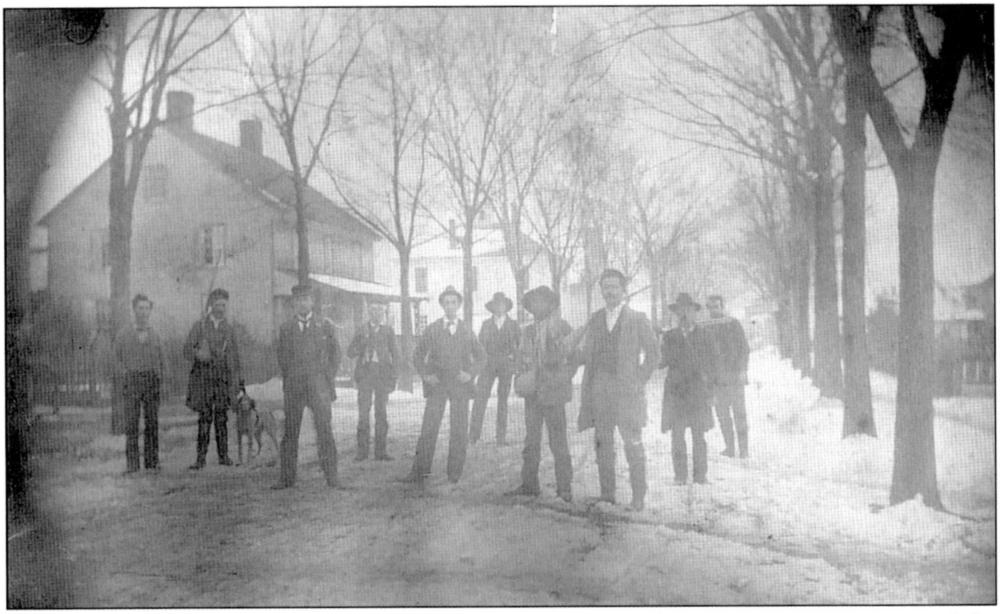

ROBERSONVILLE'S MEMORABLE SNOWSTORMS IN THE 1890S. This *c.* 1892 picture is one of the earliest-known images of downtown Robersonville. These men are standing just north of the present railroad crossing on Main Street. The old Grimes house in the background sits on what was the site of the former Cox Motor Company property. (Courtesy of Josephine R. Smith.)

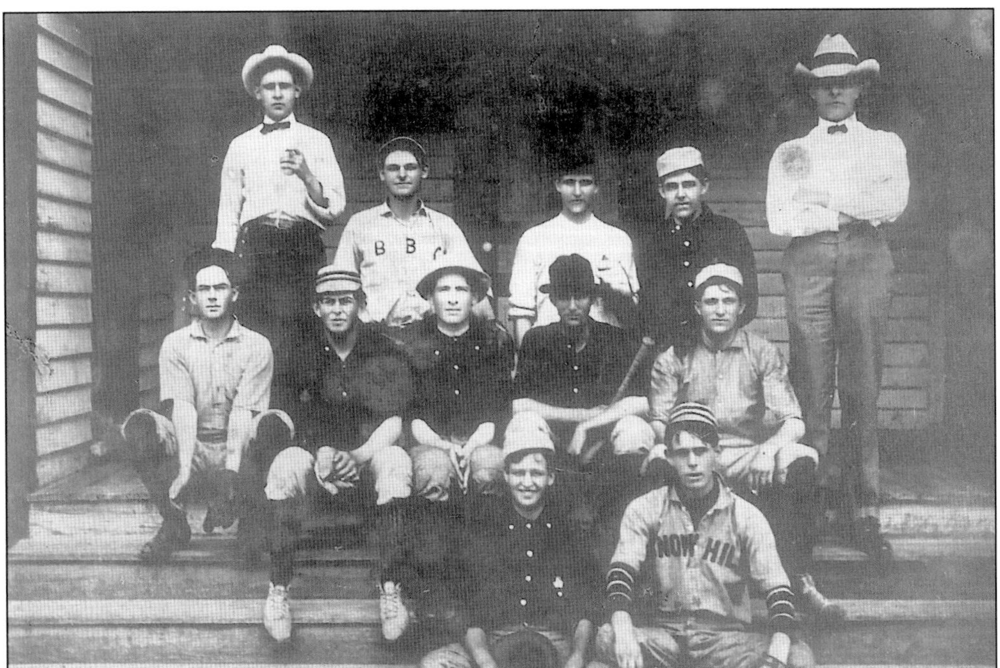

AN EARLY BASEBALL TEAM IN ROBERSONVILLE, C. 1905. Calvin Smith is standing on the right in this view. The names of the other men pictured are unknown. (Courtesy of the Francis Manning Room.)

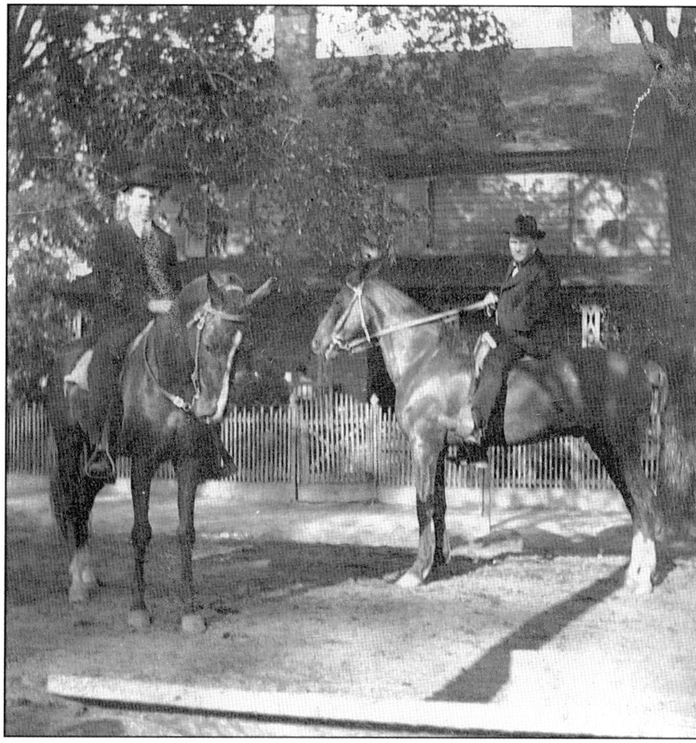

R.E. GRIMES AND AN UNIDENTIFIED MAN IN FRONT OF THE OLD GRIMES HOME ON MAIN STREET, C. 1900. (Courtesy of Josephine R. Smith.)

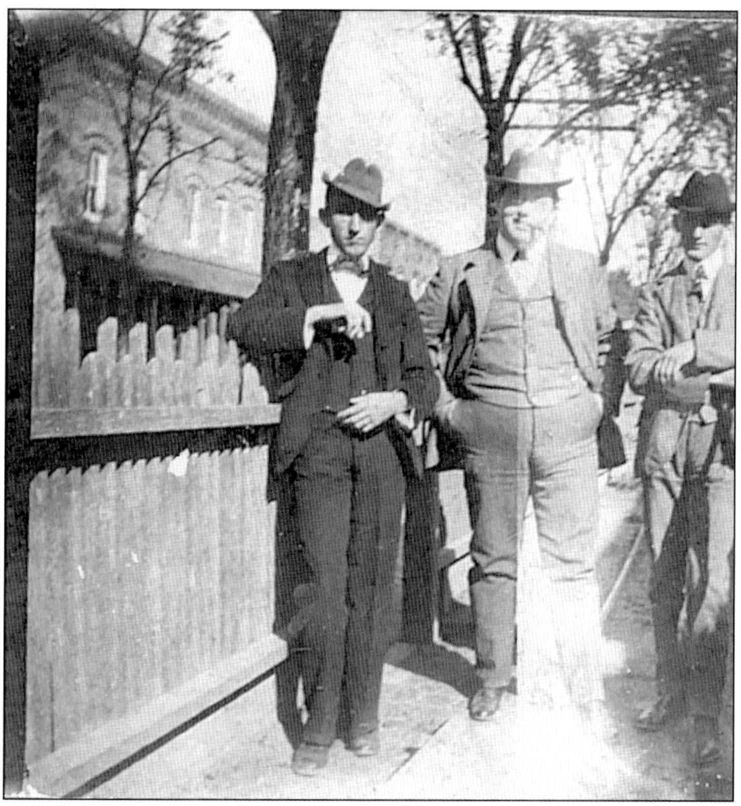

ALONG MAIN STREET, LOOKING NORTH, C. 1900. Pictured from left to right are Will Keel, John Ross, and Arthur Roberson. (Courtesy of Josephine R. Smith.)

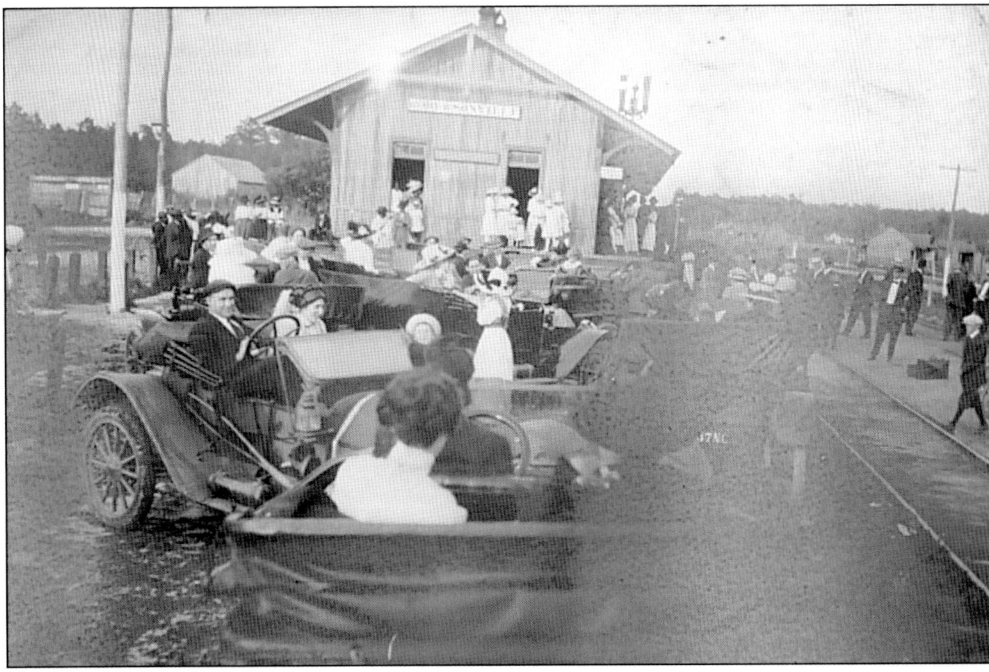

A CROWD AWAITS A TRAIN AT THE ROBERSONVILLE DEPOT, c. 1915. (Courtesy of Josephine R. Smith.)

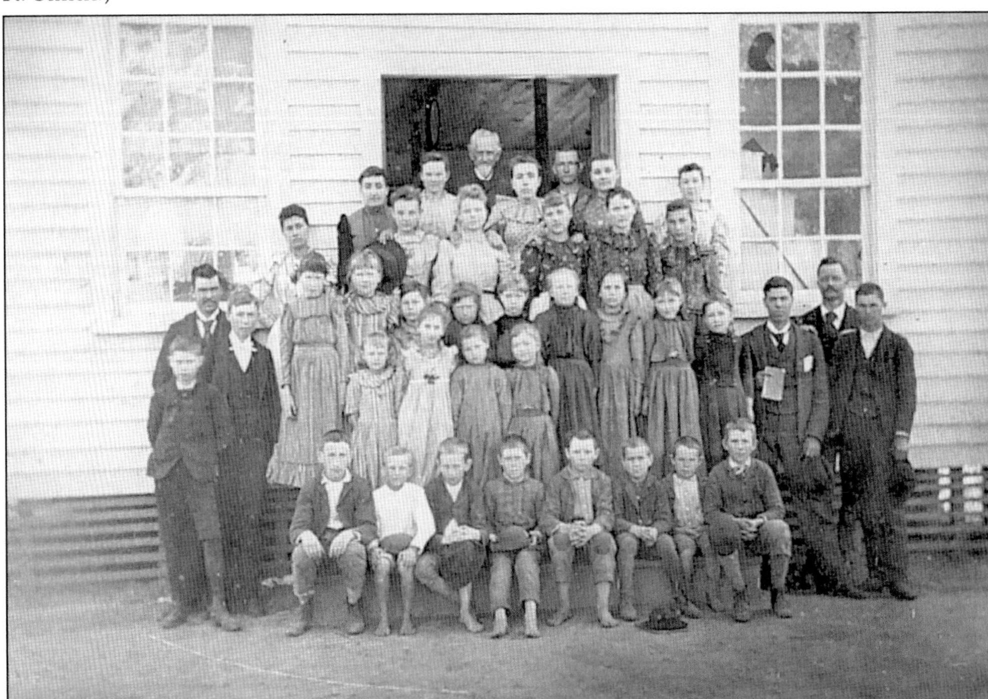

STUDENTS AND FACULTY AT ROBERSONVILLE GRADED SCHOOL, c. 1905. This wood-frame school was replaced in 1924 with the brick building later known as Robersonville Elementary School. (Courtesy of Josephine R. Smith.)

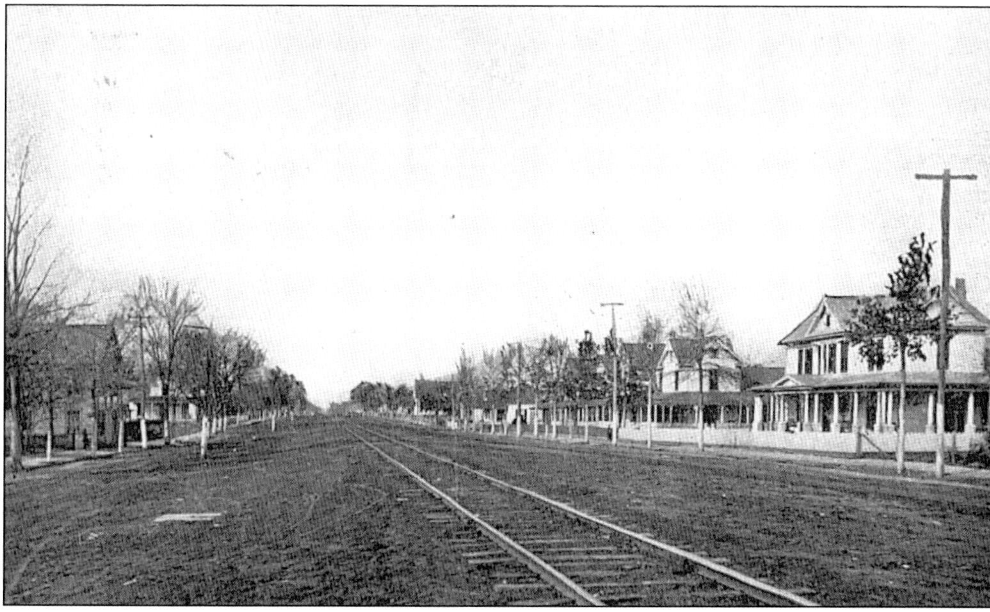

A Postcard View of Residences Along Railroad Street, Looking West, c. 1910. (Courtesy of the Sarah M. Pope Collection.)

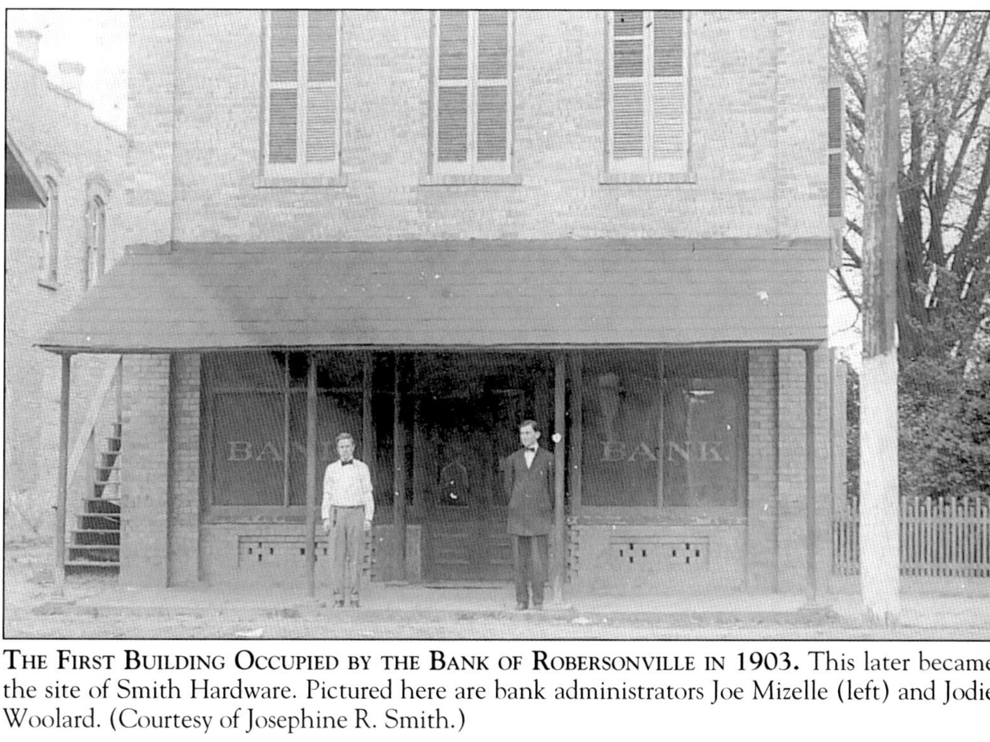

The First Building Occupied by the Bank of Robersonville in 1903. This later became the site of Smith Hardware. Pictured here are bank administrators Joe Mizelle (left) and Jodie Woolard. (Courtesy of Josephine R. Smith.)

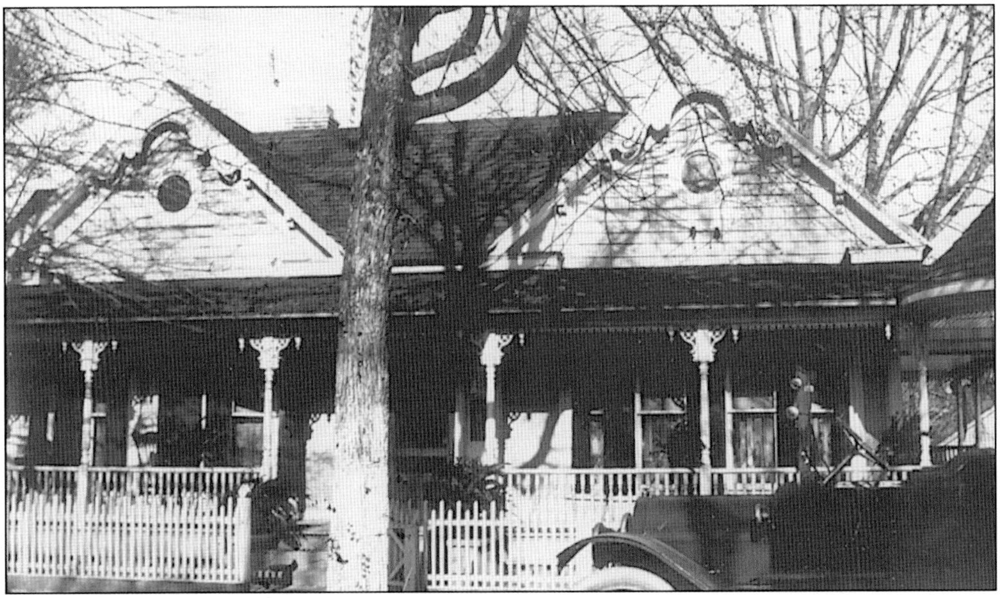

The R.A. Bailey Residence on South Broad Street, c. 1920. Bailey was a well-known tobacconist and part owner of the Adkins and Bailey Warehouse. (Courtesy of Doris L. Wilson.)

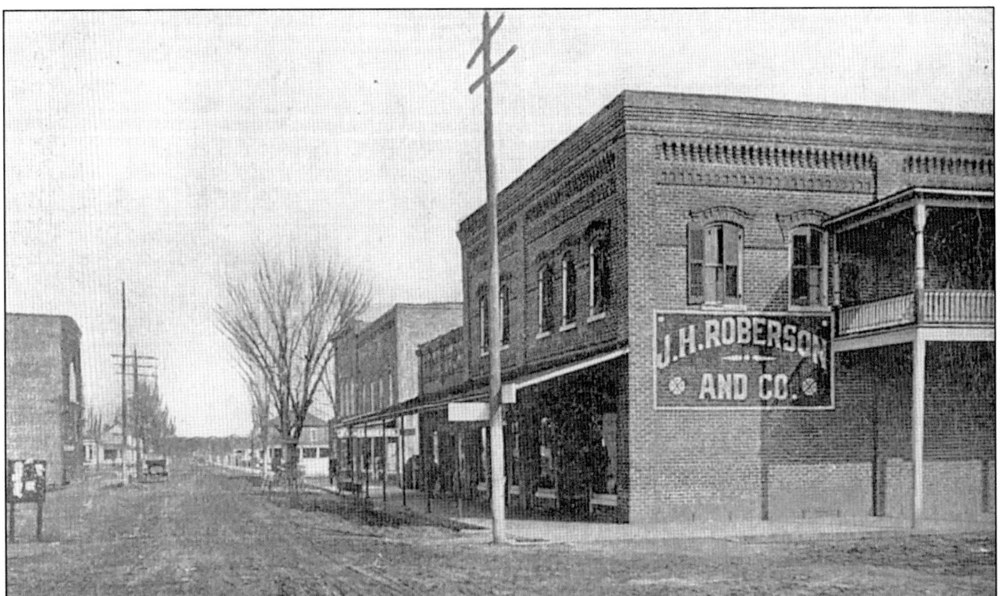

A Postcard View of the J.H. Roberson and Co. Store Along Main Street, Looking North, c. 1918. (Courtesy of the Sarah M. Pope Collection.)

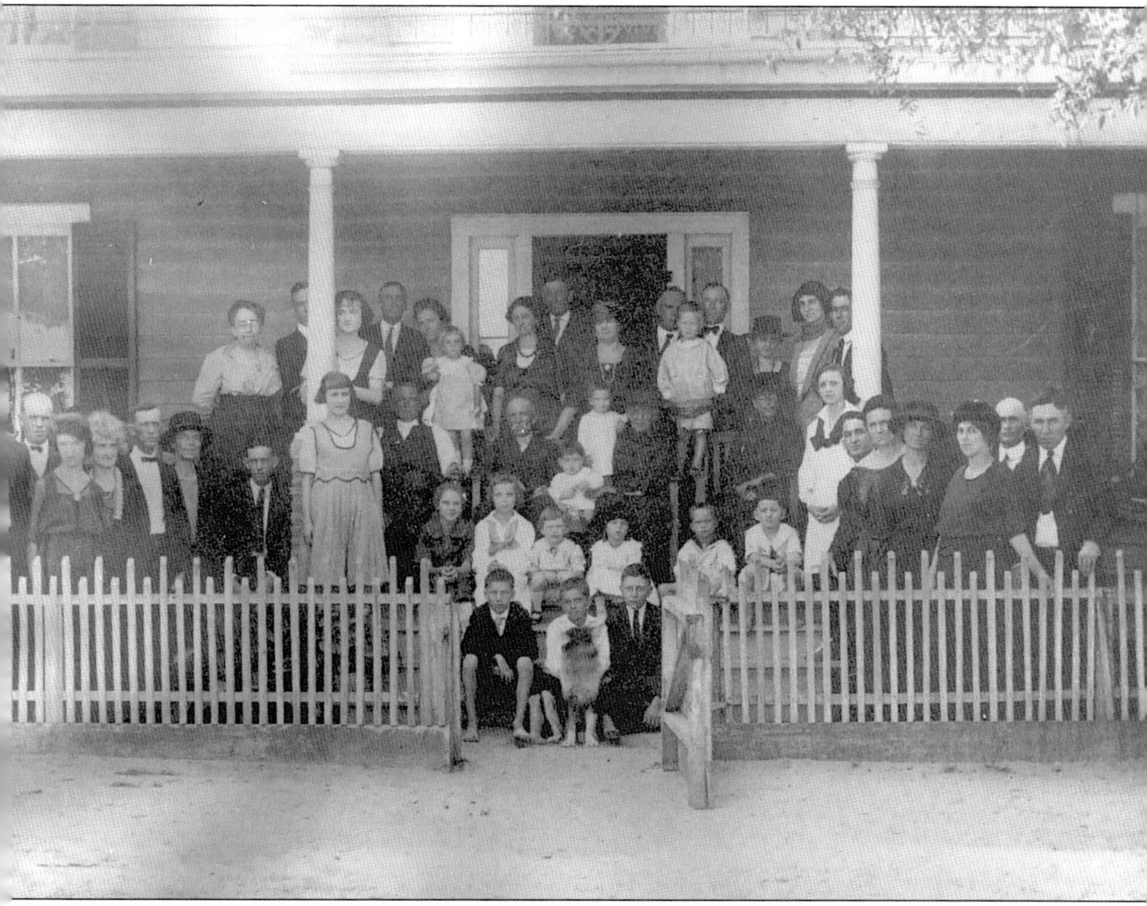

ROBERSON FAMILY REUNION, C. EARLY 1920S. Family members pictured in this view include Willie Harvey Crofton, Frank Crofton, Helen Crofton, Mrs. Frank Crofton, George Crofton, Ida Roberson Crofton, George Ben Crofton, Hulda Roberson, Lucy Matt Crofton, Cloe Roberson, Emeline Roberson, unidentified, Ander Morgan Munford, unidentified, Clayton Crofton, Harry Roberson, Heber Munford, Vivian Roberson Roberson, Helen Edmondson, C. Abrum Roberson, Bunyon Edmondson, Rodney Roberson, Ben H. Roberson, Fannie Coburn Roberson, John E. Roberson, Sarah Coburn Roberson, Mary Barden Crofton, C. Leon Wilson, Fannybel Roberson Wilson, Lena Parker Roberson, Harvey Roberson, Dixie D. Roberson, Ander Roberson, Berta Roberson, unidentified, Henry Roberson, Mrs. Henry Roberson (Daisy Johnson), Janie Yates Everett, Armita Roberson Everett, H. Lester Everett, Allie Pool Roberson, Margaret Roberson, A. Pitt Roberson, and Daisy J. Roberson's sister. (Courtesy of Doris L. Wilson.)

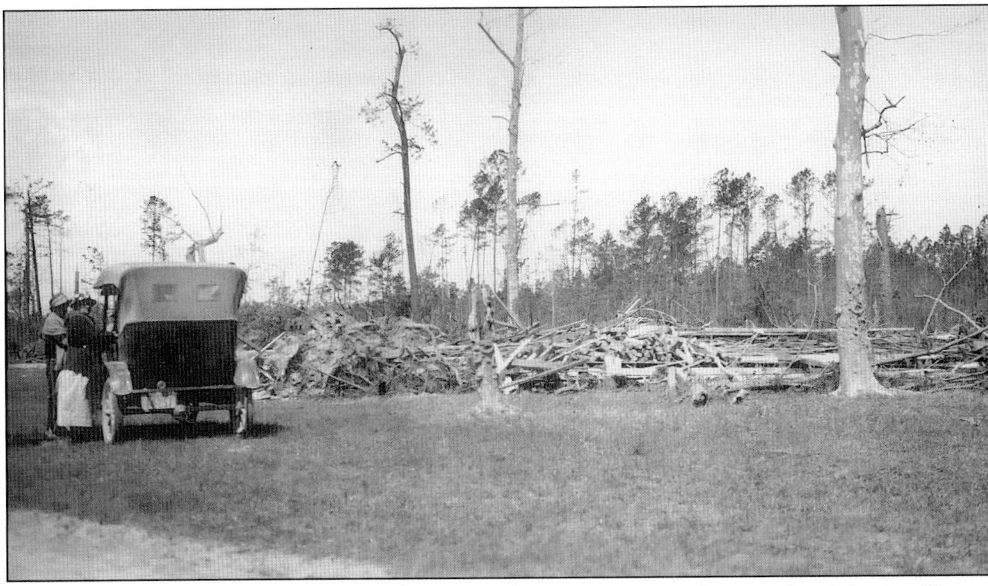

THE TORNADO OF 1924. One of the most devastating tornadoes to hit Martin County occurred on April 30, 1924. Damage was particularly heavy near Robersonville. Shown here are the remains of the Flat Swamp Primitive Baptist Church located on the Martin and Pitt County line near Robersonville after it was hit by the tornado. (Courtesy of the Francis Manning Room.)

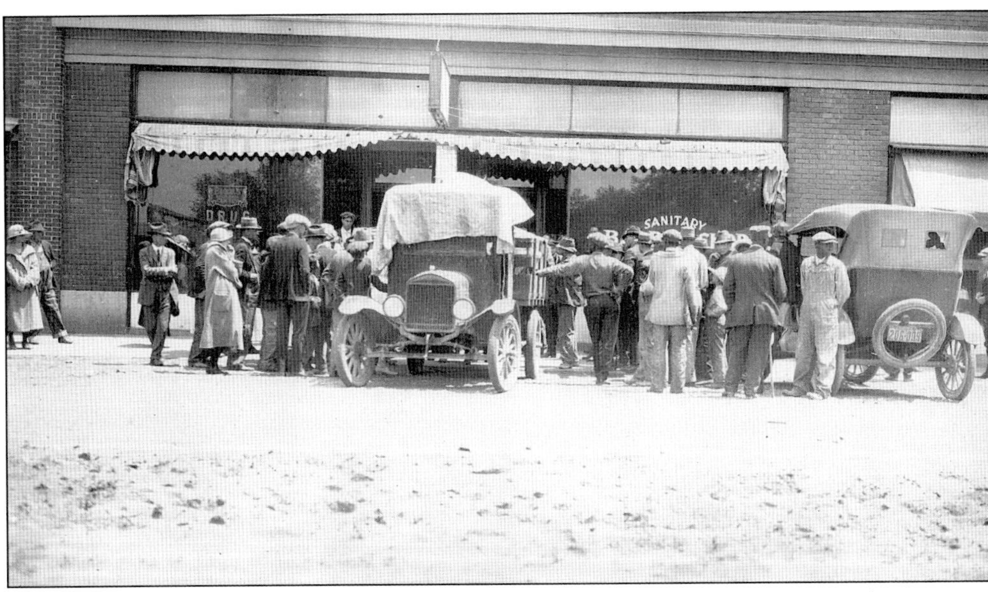

UNLOADING VICTIMS OF THE 1924 TORNADO IN ROBERSONVILLE, MAY 1924. A temporary hospital was set up downtown to care for the injured. (Courtesy of the Francis Manning Room.)

James Harvey Roberson and His Wife, Laverna Little Roberson. The Robersons are seen here at their home on the corner of North Main and Academy Streets, *c.* 1920s. (Courtesy of Patsy R. Miller.)

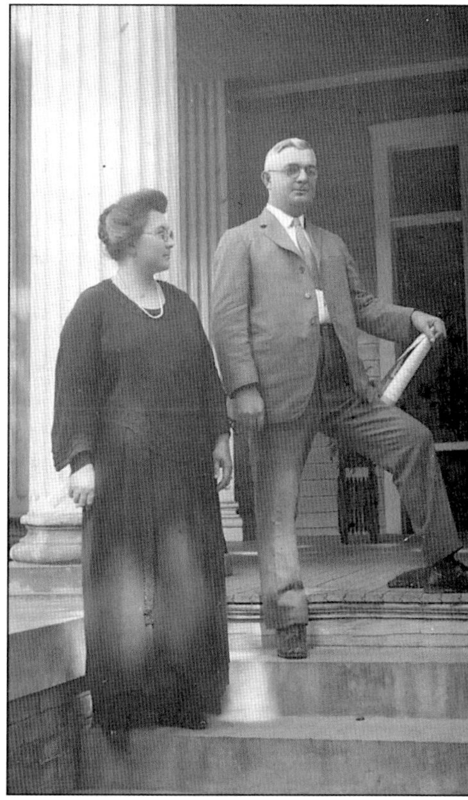

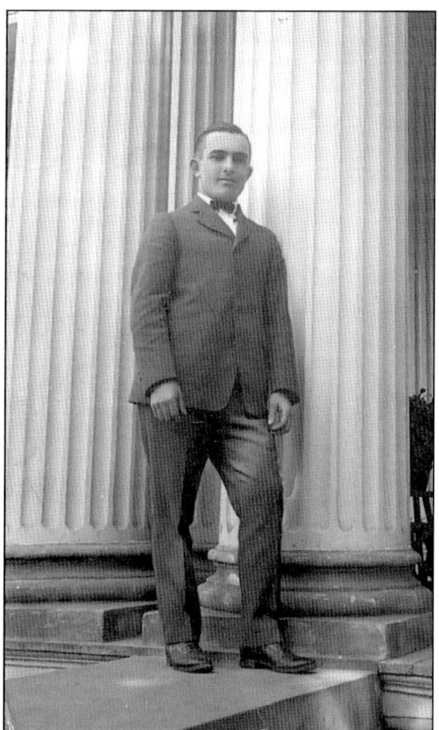

Vance L. Roberson, c. 1920s. Vance was the son of Mr. and Mrs. J.H. Roberson. (Courtesy of Patsy R. Miller.)

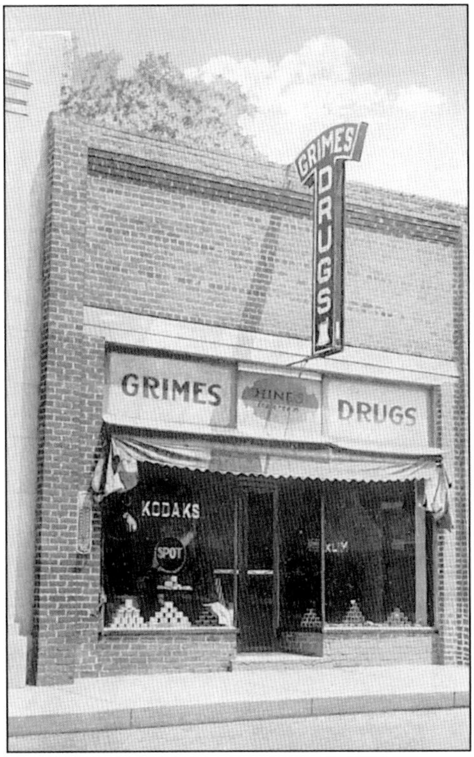

DAVID GRIMES'S DRUG STORE ON MAIN STREET, c. 1930. Grimes began this business in 1922 after working for C.L. Cannon's Drugstore. (Courtesy of the Sarah M. Pope Collection.)

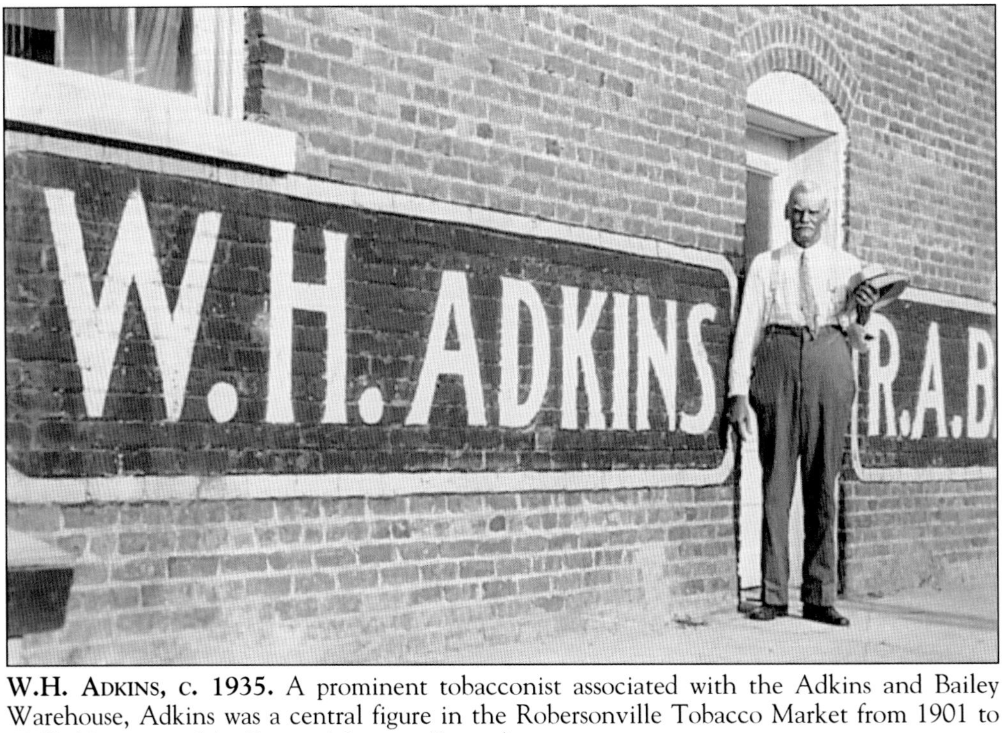

W.H. ADKINS, c. 1935. A prominent tobacconist associated with the Adkins and Bailey Warehouse, Adkins was a central figure in the Robersonville Tobacco Market from 1901 to 1947. (Courtesy of the Francis Manning Room.)

HATTIE GREEN ON THE GREEN FARM JUST OUTSIDE OF ROBERSONVILLE, C. 1930. (Courtesy of Patsy R. Miller.)

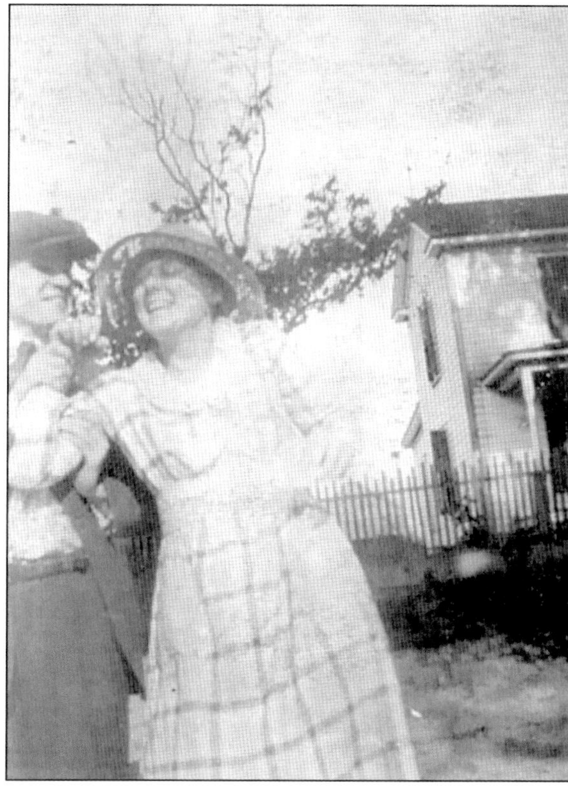

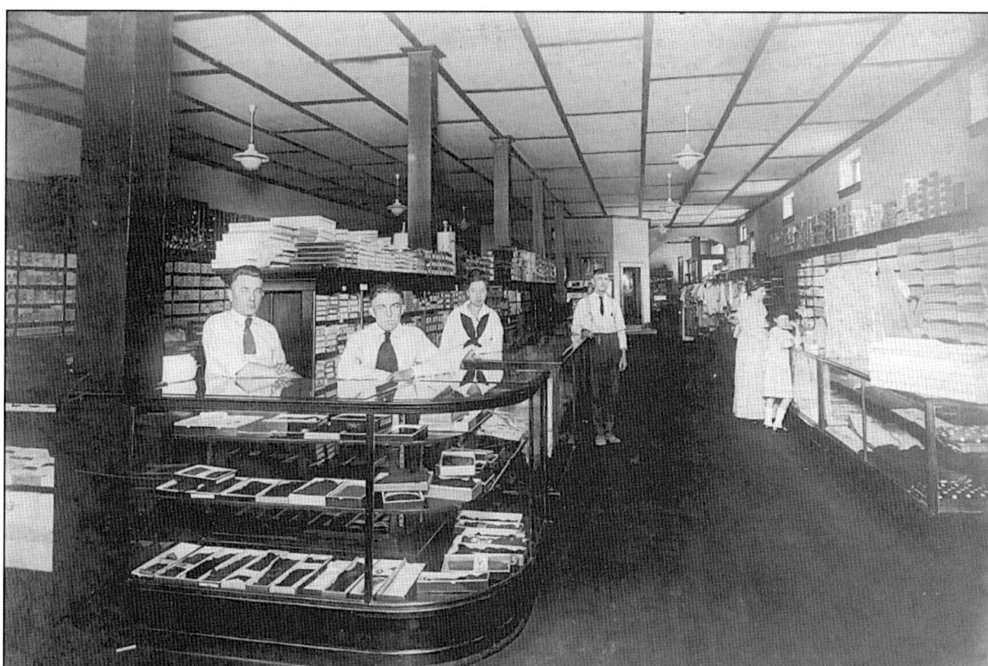

AN INTERIOR VIEW OF THE J.H. ROBERSON AND SON STORE, C. 1929. This business was located on the corner of Main and Railroad Streets. (Courtesy of Patsy R. Miller.)

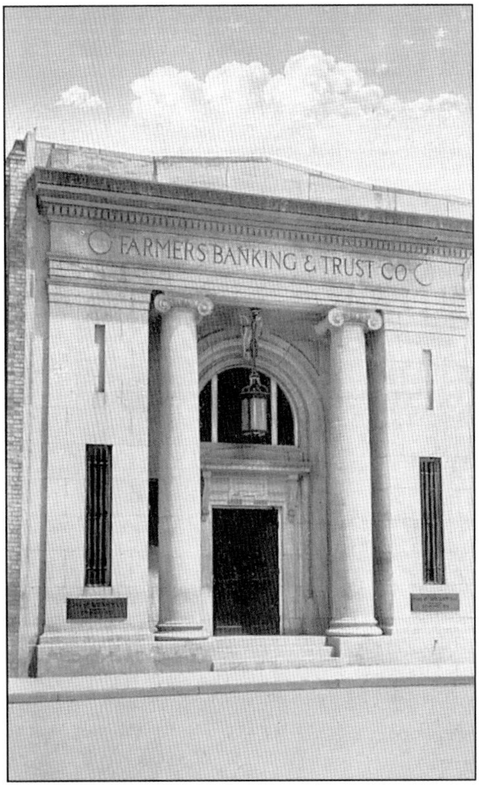

THE FARMERS BANKING AND TRUST CO. Opened for business in 1921, the Farmers Banking and Trust Co. occupied this building until it was taken over by the Bank of Robersonville in 1926. In 1938, it was renamed Guaranty Bank and later Wachovia Bank. The structure currently serves as the Robersonville Town Hall. (Courtesy of the Sarah M. Pope Collection.)

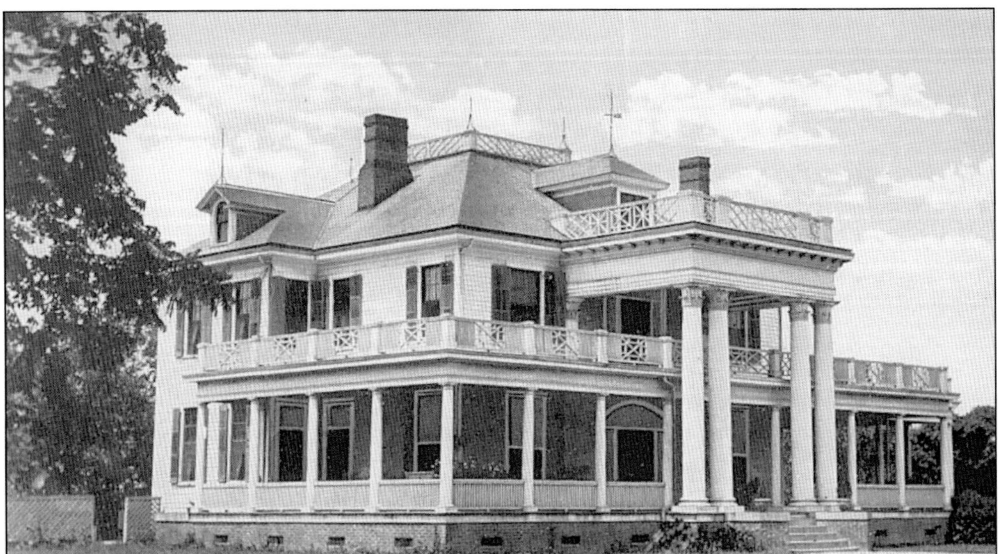

A 1930S POSTCARD VIEW OF THE W.J. LITTLE RESIDENCE. Located on the southwest corner of Main and Academy Streets, this impressive home was built for W.J. (Bill) Little and his family in 1914. The Little family moved to Robersonville from the Flat Swamp section of Pitt County. In later years, Little's son Mayo and Mayo's wife, Ethel Bailey Little, occupied the home in which they reared their two children, Doris and Mayo Jr. (Courtesy of the Sarah M. Pope Collection.)

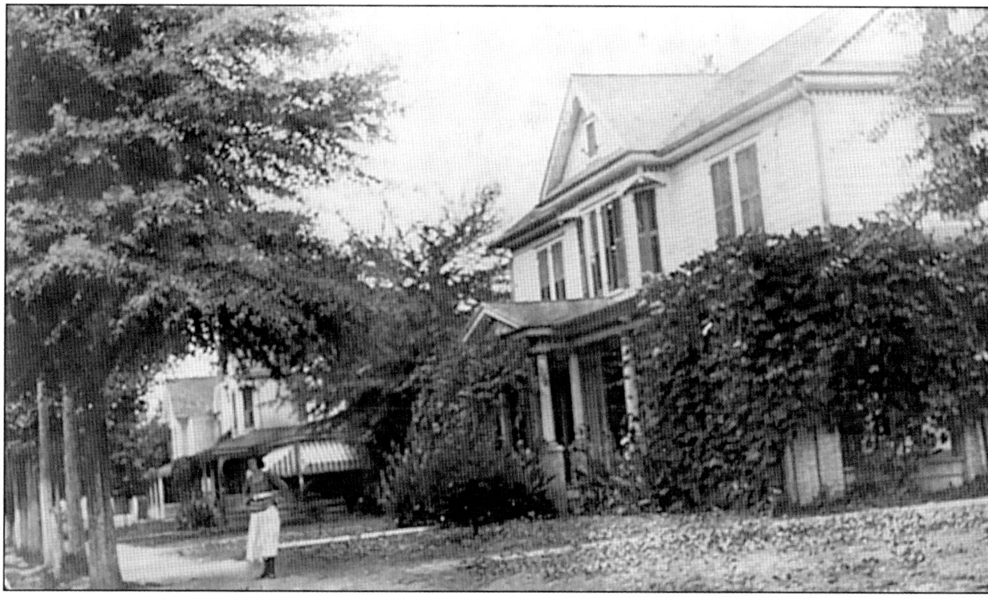

The Arch Roberson Home on Railroad Street, c. 1930s. This residence was located on the site where the Cooperative Savings and Loan currently stands. (Courtesy of Virginia B. Rodgers.)

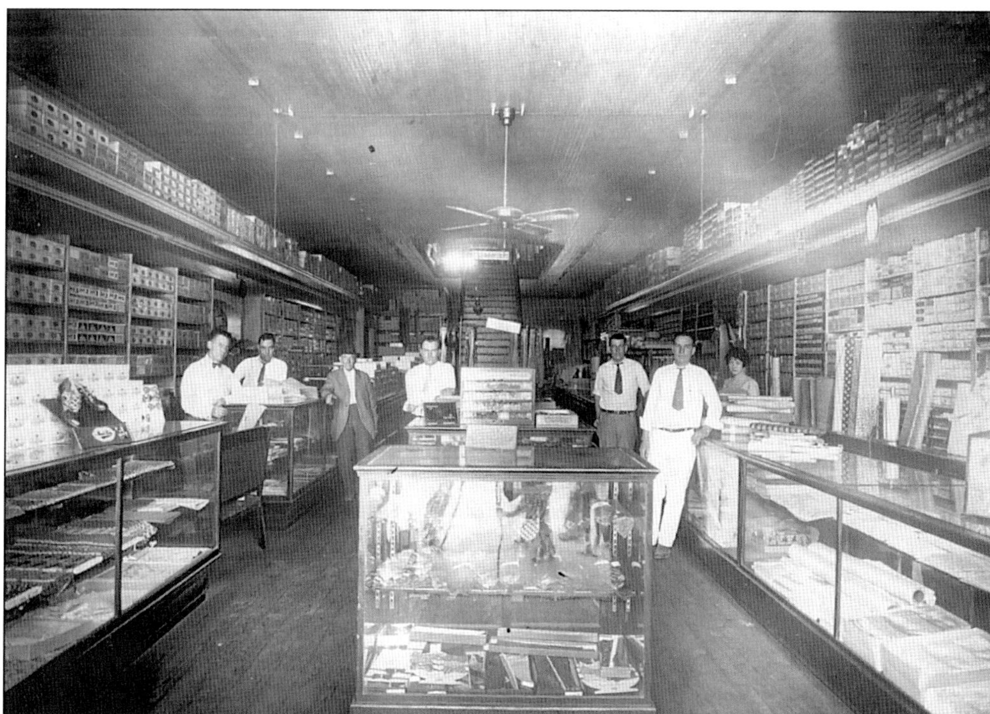

The R.L. Smith and Co. Store's Interior, c. Late 1920s. Pictured here, from left to right, are Bob Smith, Irving Smith, unidentified, unidentified, Jim Gray, Willie Johnson, and unidentified. (Courtesy of Josephine R. Smith.)

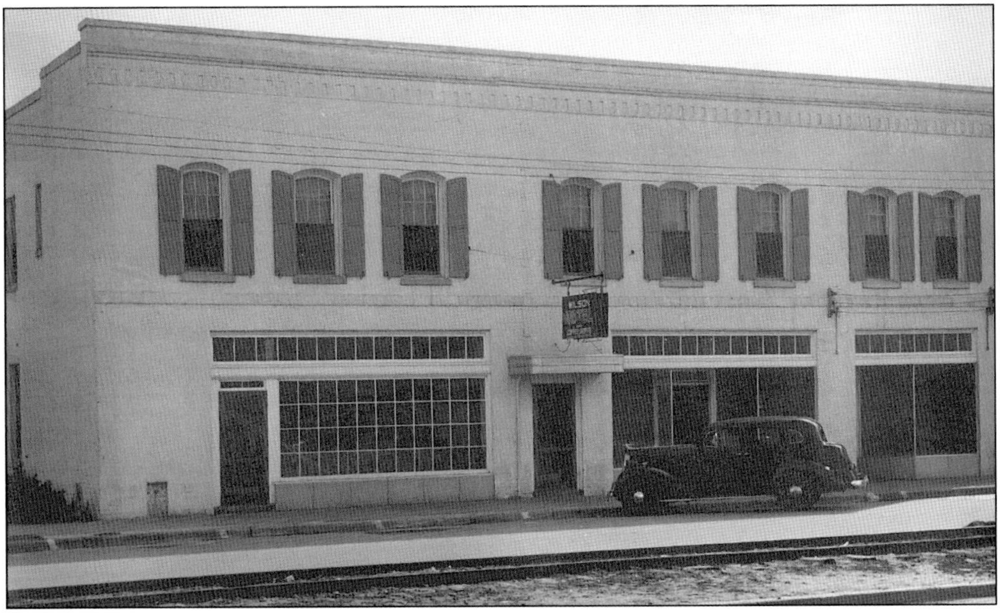

Wilson Hotel. Robersonville businessman C.L. Wilson began this full-service hotel on Railroad Street in 1939. It ceased operations in 1961. (Courtesy of Doris L. Wilson.)

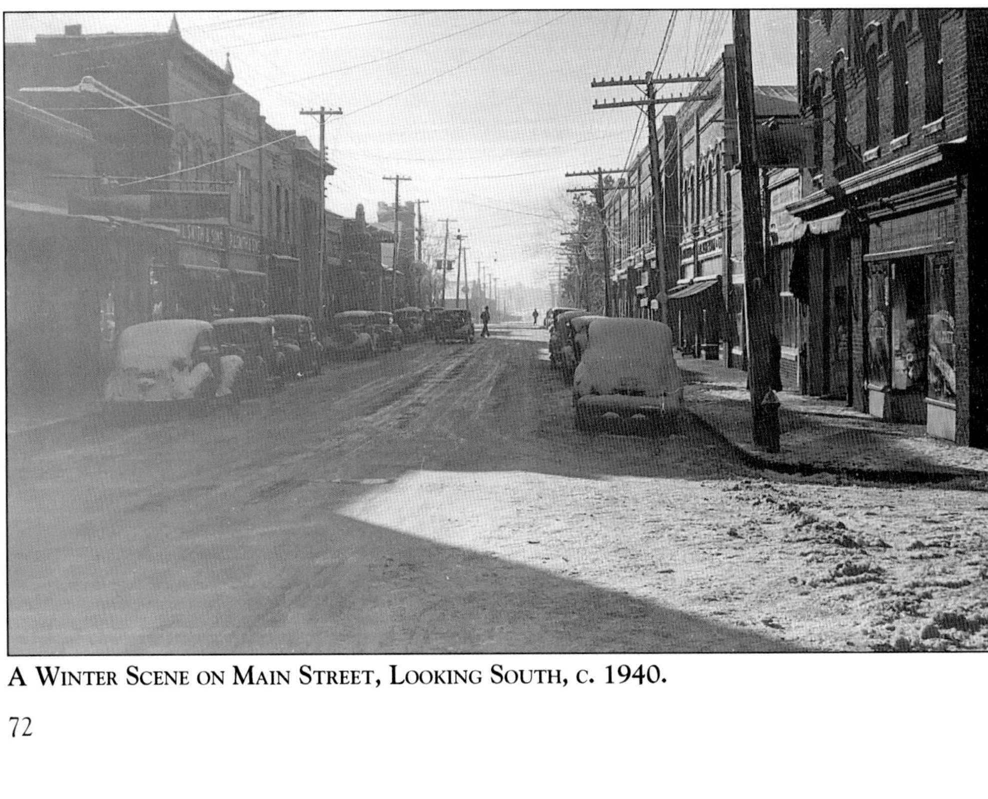

A Winter Scene on Main Street, Looking South, c. 1940.

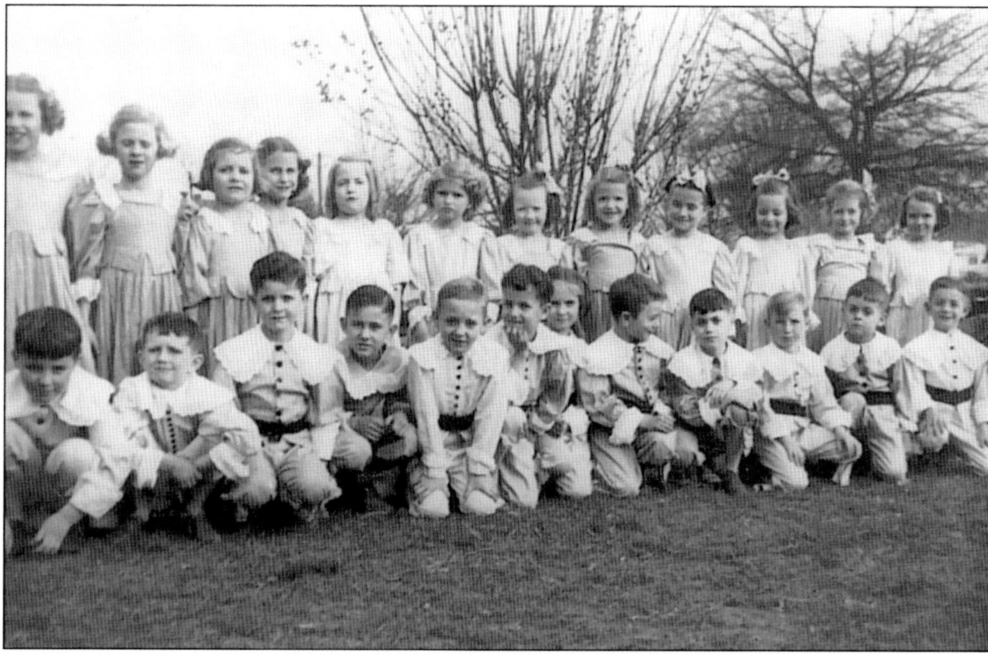

May Pole Activity, c. 1940. Pictured from left to right are as follows: (front row) Irving Smith, Joe Johnson, Donnie Everett, Billy Green, unidentified, Ralph Mobley, Gertie Oakley, Everett Parker, Dick Mathews, Gussie Bunting, William Taylor, and Kenneth Andrews; (back row) Jean Cargile, Mary Anne Anderson, Patsy Roberson, Betty Jean Coburn, Frances Smith, Peggy Cherry, unidentified, Ruth Coltrain, Marianne Roebuck, Claudia James, Annel Ayers, and Shirley Roberson. (Courtesy of Patsy R. Miller.)

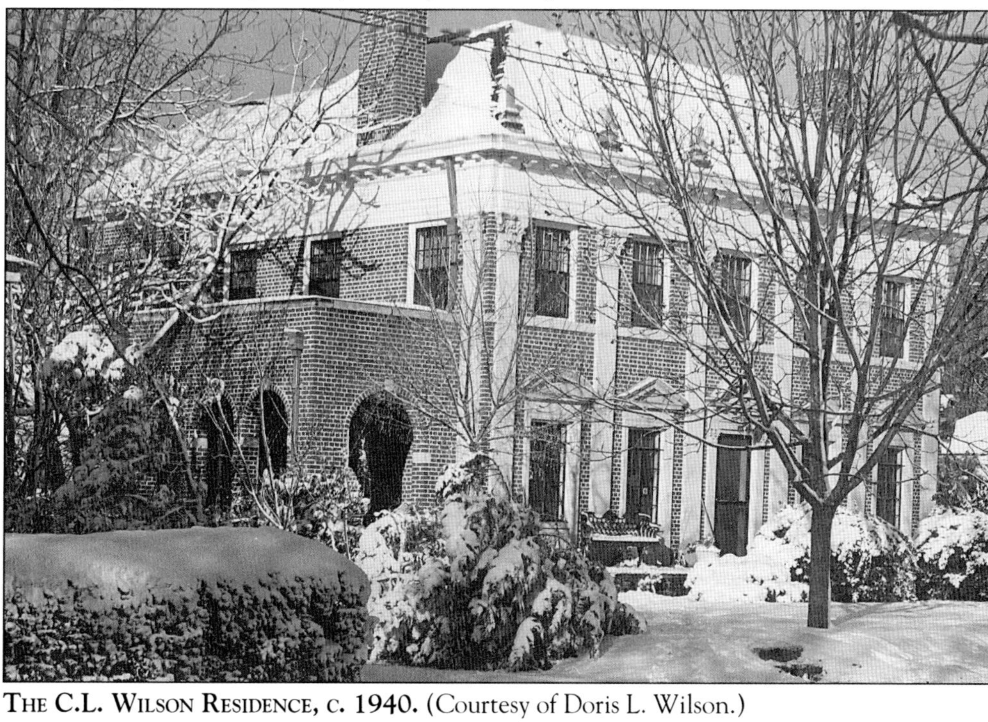

The C.L. Wilson Residence, c. 1940. (Courtesy of Doris L. Wilson.)

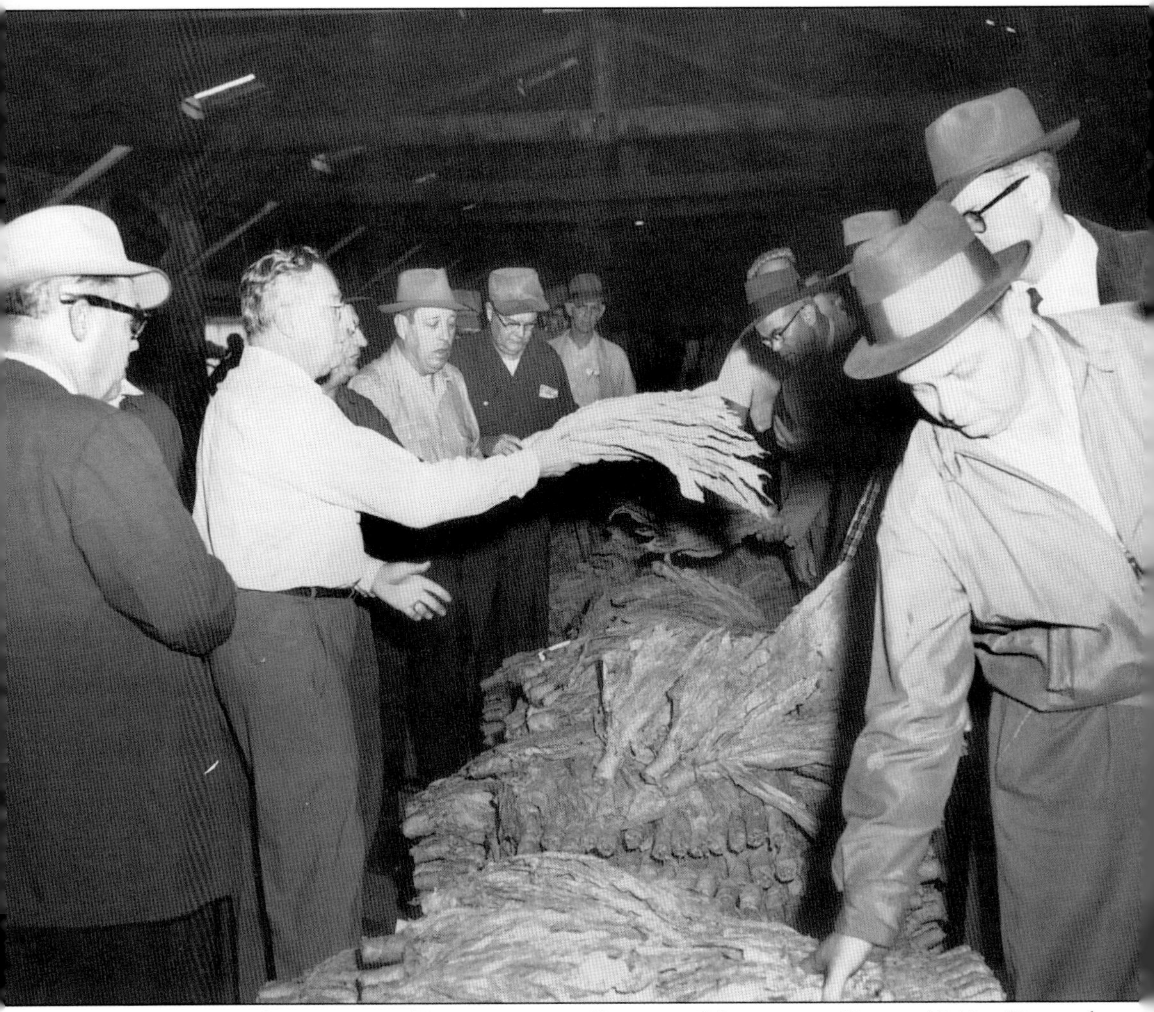

An Auction Sale at the Robersonville Tobacco Market, c. Early 1940s. Pictured from left to right are Charlie Gray, Mayo Little, Jake Taylor, Jim Gray, unidentified, Robert Adkins, Oscar Burch, unidentified, unidentified, and A.B. Ayers. (Courtesy of Doris L. Wilson.)

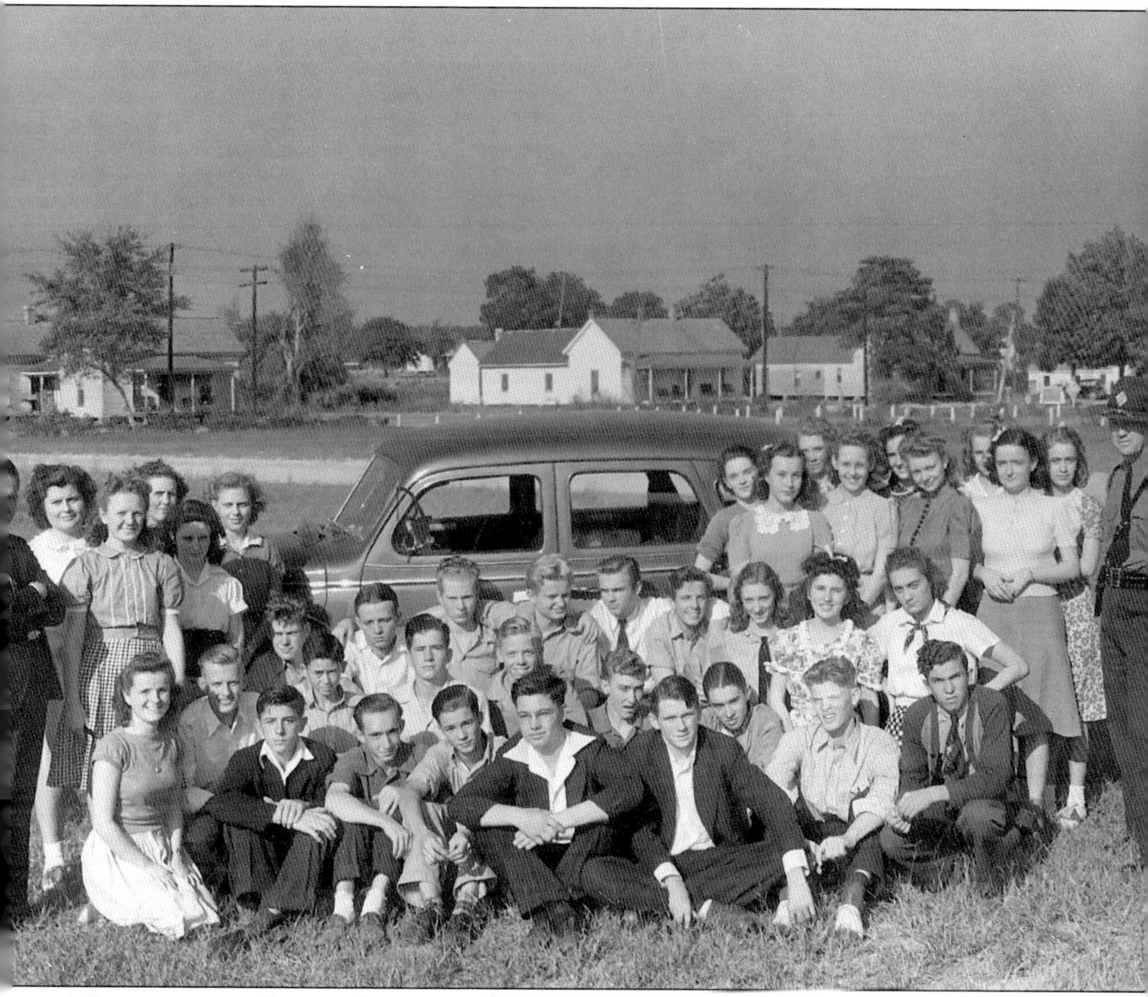

A ROBERSONVILLE DRIVERS EDUCATION CLASS, C. EARLY 1940S. Pictured from left to right are as follows: (front row) unidentified, unidentified, unidentified, John Roberson, Donald Jenkins, and Herman Rawls; (second row) Muriel Wynn, Grover Everett, unidentified, Herbert Taylor, Nelson Leggett, Wallace Roberson, Harvey Lee Winberry, and Edward Ashley Roberon; (third row) Leighton Cockran, unidentified, Wayland Wilson, Joe Ward, Roy Wilson, Robert Whichard, unidentified, unidentified, and unidentified; (standing) L.W. Anderson (principal), unidentified, unidentified, unidentified, unidentified, unidentified, Miriam Johnson, Maxine Smith, Ethel Smith, Gladys Roebuck, unidentified, unidentified, Loretta Osborne, unidentified, Lula Purvis Gray, and a highway patrolman. (Courtesy of Josephine R. Smith.)

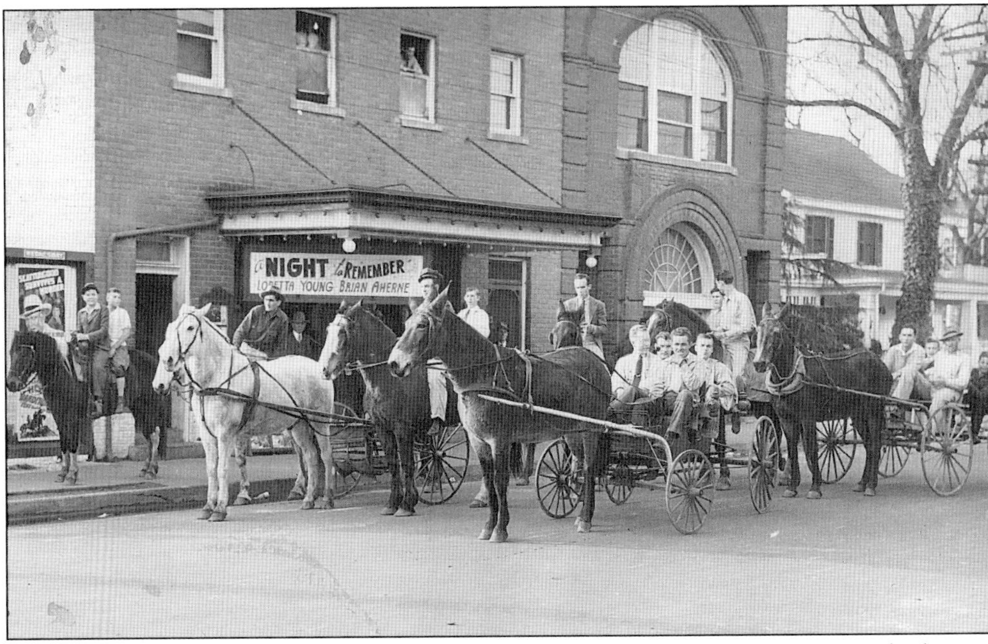

THE TRIO THEATRE ON NORTH MAIN STREET, C. 1940S. The home of Dr. Jesse Ward is located to the right. Both structures sat in the area now occupied by Southern Bank. (Courtesy of Josephine R. Smith.)

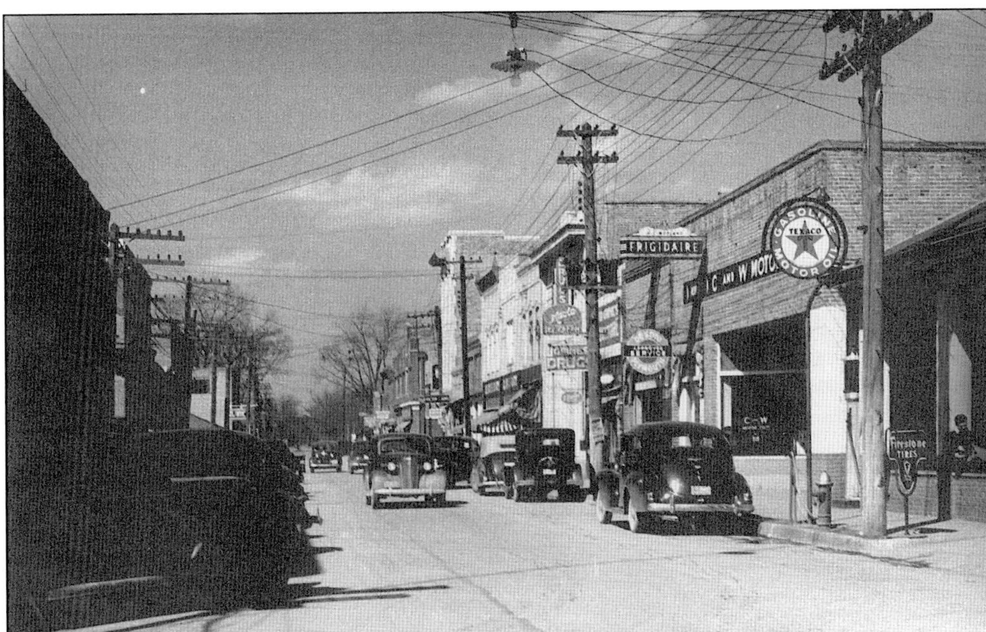

THE EAST SIDE OF MAIN STREET, LOOKING NORTH, C. EARLY 1940S. (Courtesy of Josephine R. Smith.)

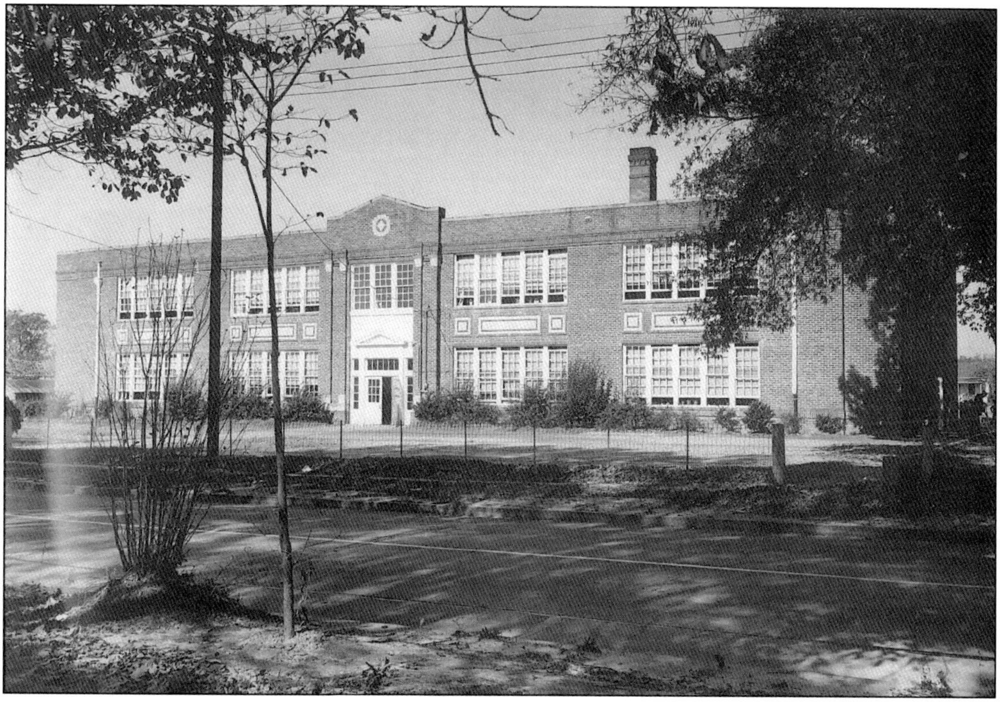

ROBERSONVILLE ELEMENTARY SCHOOL. First occupied in January 1924, this building replaced the 1902 wood-frame graded school building. Built at a cost of $62,406, the school was one of the first in the area to enjoy electric lights, indoor plumbing, and janitorial service. Telephone service was added in 1926. The building saw continuous use until it was demolished c. 1974. (Courtesy of the Francis Manning Room.)

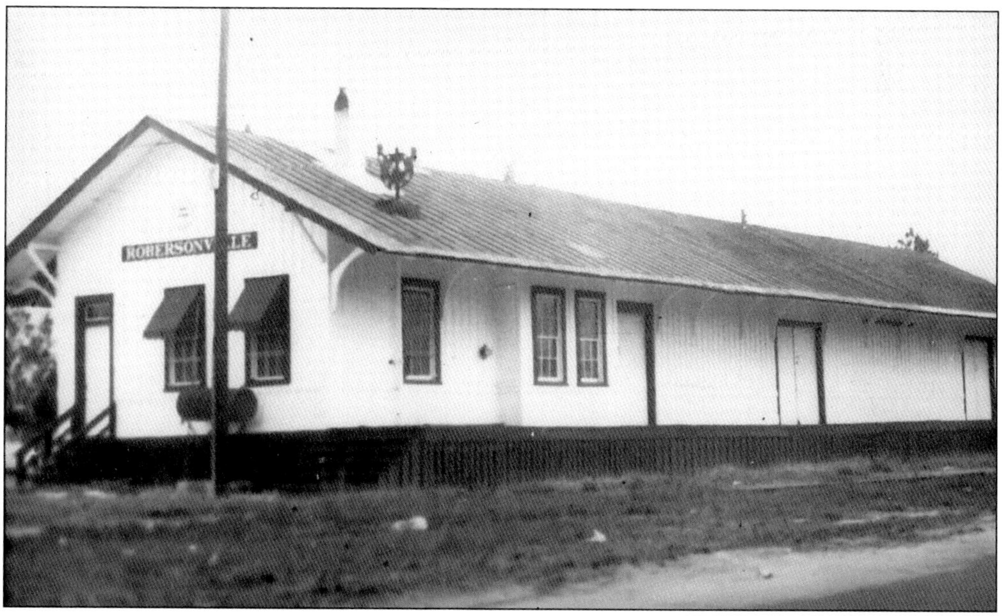

A POSTCARD VIEW OF THE ROBERSONVILLE DEPOT, c. 1950. On August 24, 1882, Robersonville residents celebrated the arrival of the first train in town. (Courtesy of the Sarah M. Pope Collection.)

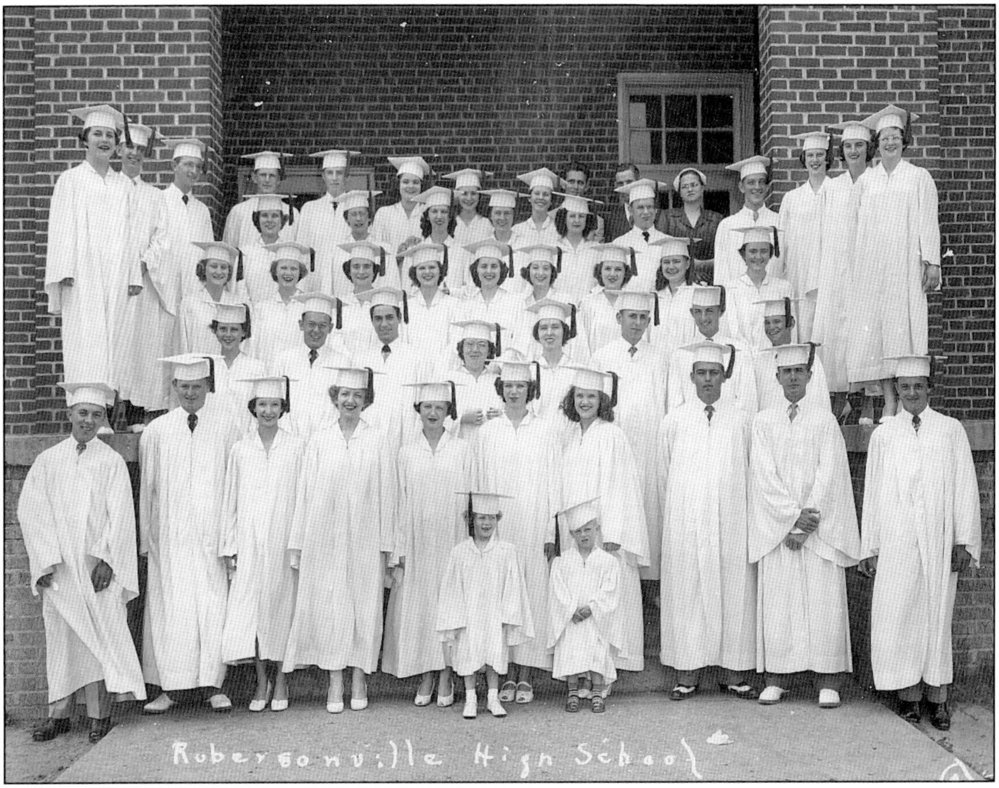

The 1952 Graduating Class of Robersonville High School. (Courtesy of Patsy R. Miller.)

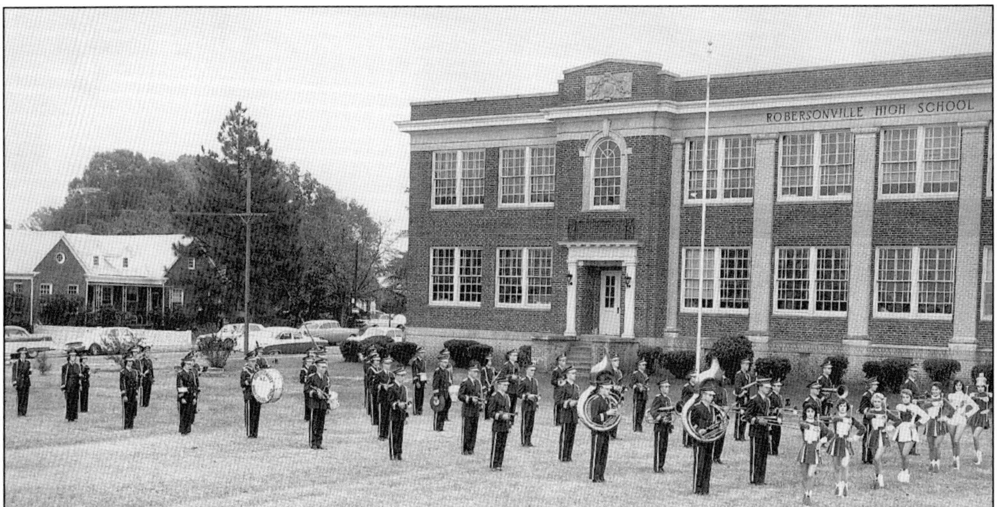

The 1955–1956 Robersonville High School Marching Band. The town's first high school band had its beginnings in the mid-1930s under the direction of J.E. Aiken. (Courtesy of the Francis Manning Room.)

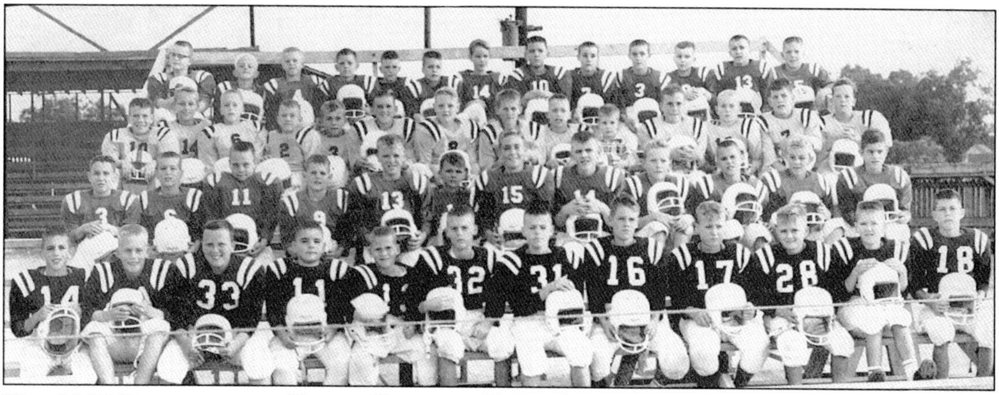

THE 1962 ROBERSONVILLE YOUTH FOOTBALL TEAM. (Courtesy of Josephine R. Smith.)

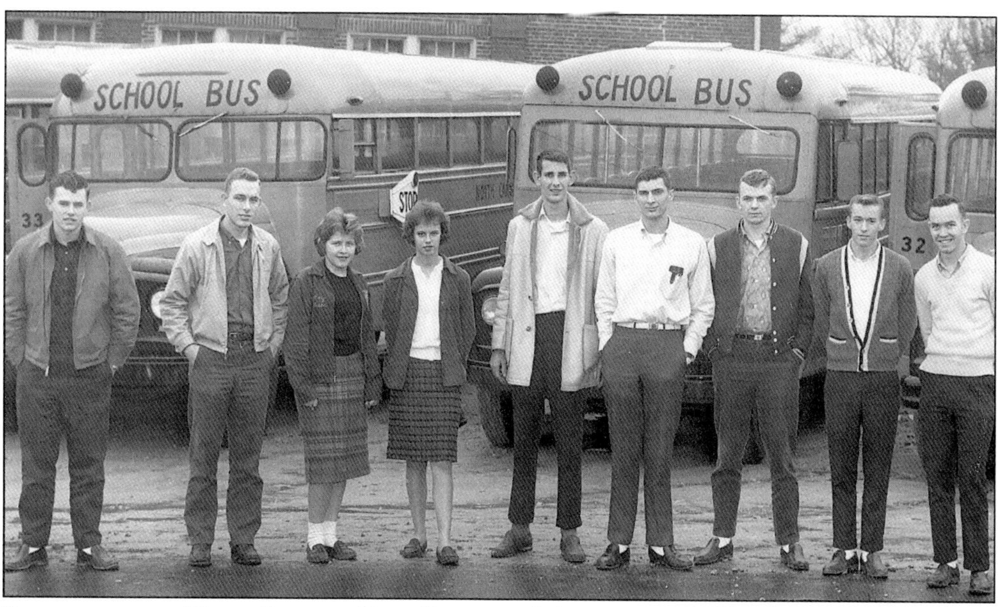

ROBERSONVILLE HIGH SCHOOL BUS DRIVERS, MARCH 1963. (Courtesy of the Francis Manning Room.)

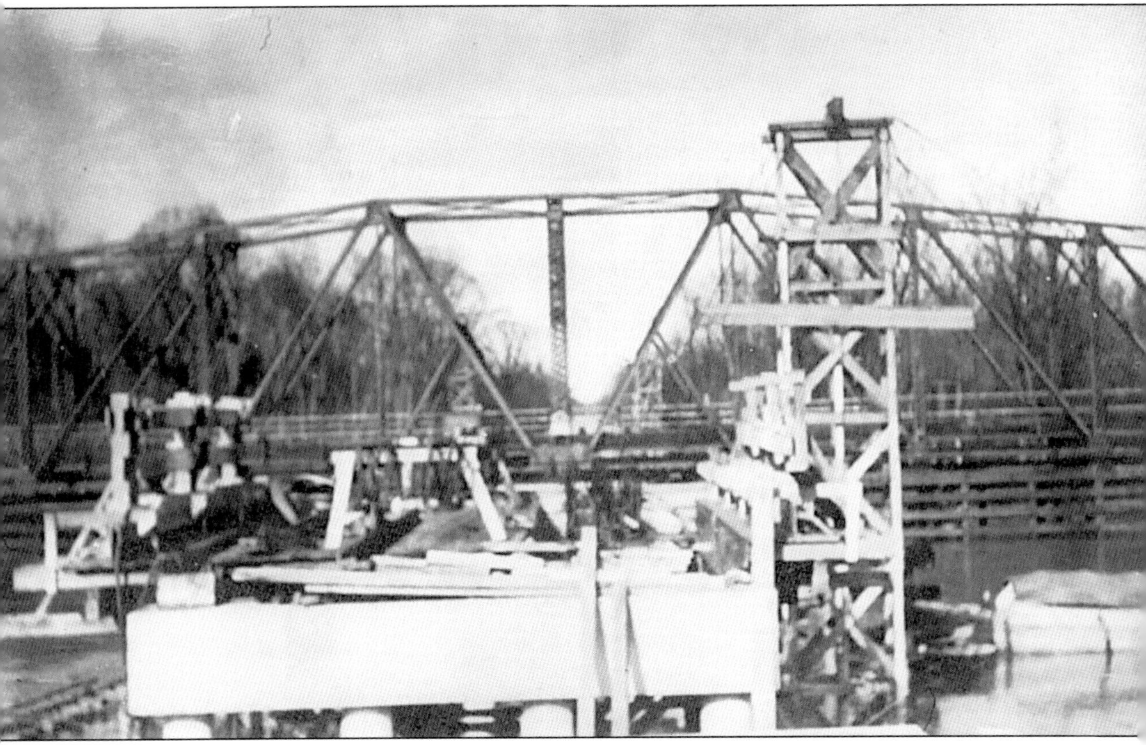

A View of the Construction of the First Roanoke River Bridge Linking Bertie and Martin Counties, c. 1921–1922. Formally opened on September 7, 1922, the bridge project, which had its beginnings as far back as May of 1918, was considered to be the most impressive of its kind in the state up to that time. Over 1,000 cars traveled over the main structure and several causeway bridges during opening day ceremonies. The total cost of the project was $590,000. (Courtesy of Ann H. McKeel.)

Four

The 1940 Flood

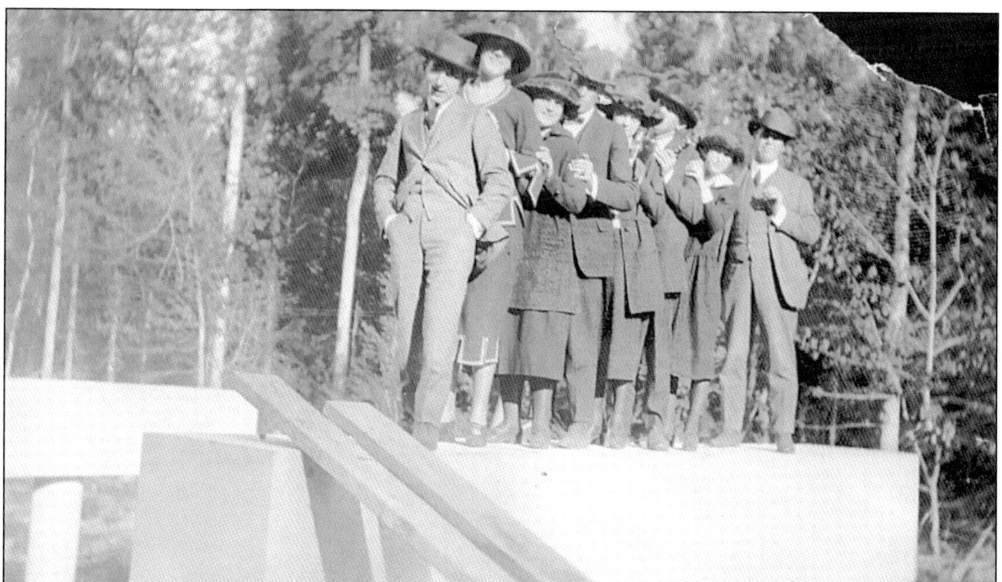

Inspecting Bridge Construction, c. 1921. Pictured from left to right are Frank Margolis, Bessie Page Horton, unidentified, unidentified, Leona Page Roberson, Hugh Horton, Martha Mizell Ward, and the bridge superintendent. The photo was taken by Irving Margolis. (Courtesy of the Francis Manning Room.)

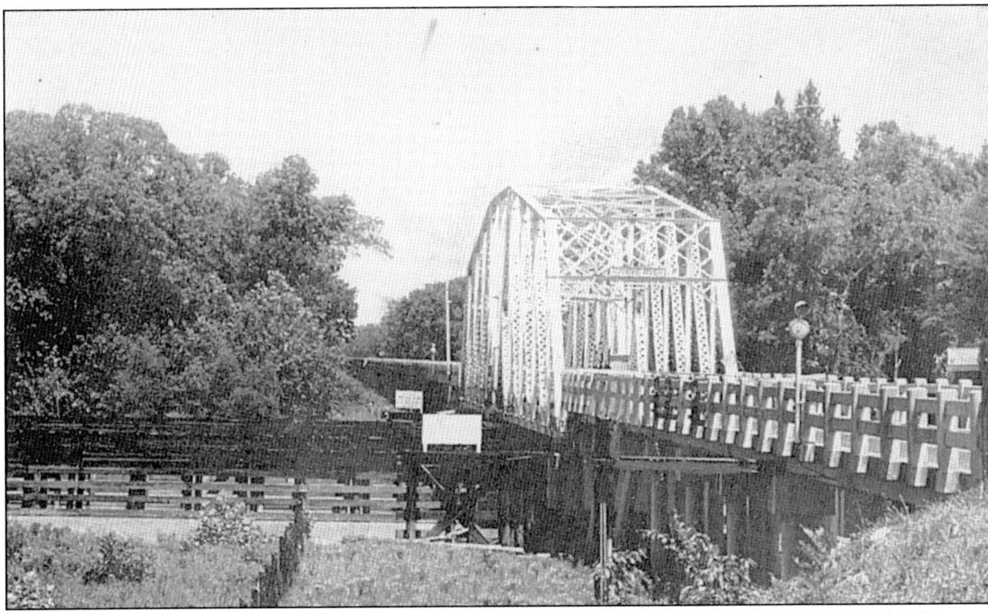

A Late 1930s Postcard View of the Roanoke River Bridge. (Courtesy of the Francis Manning Room.)

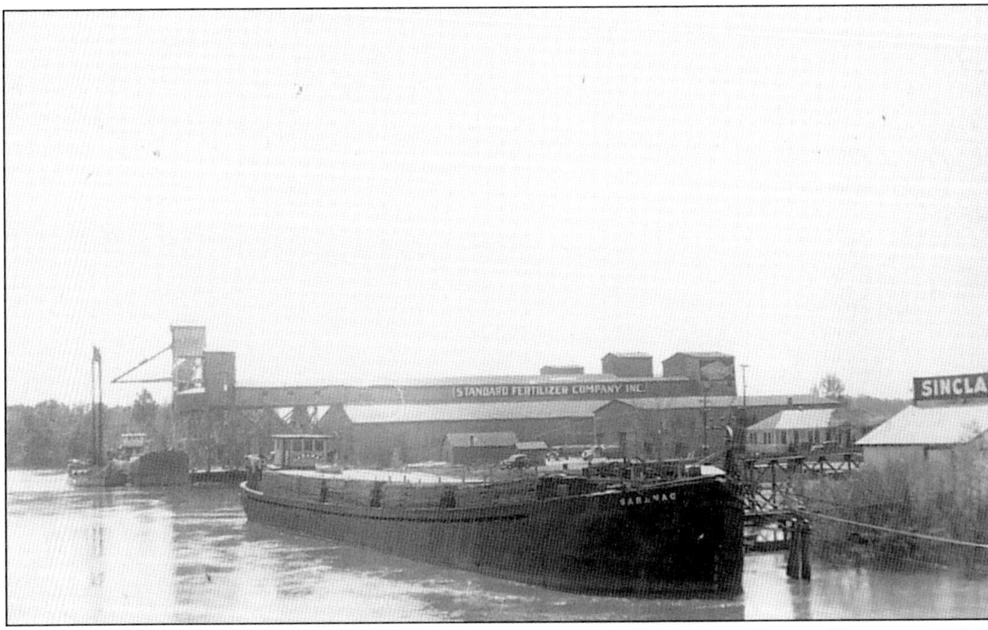

The Standard Fertilizer Company Dock near the Roanoke River Bridge, 1937. (Courtesy of the Francis Manning Room.)

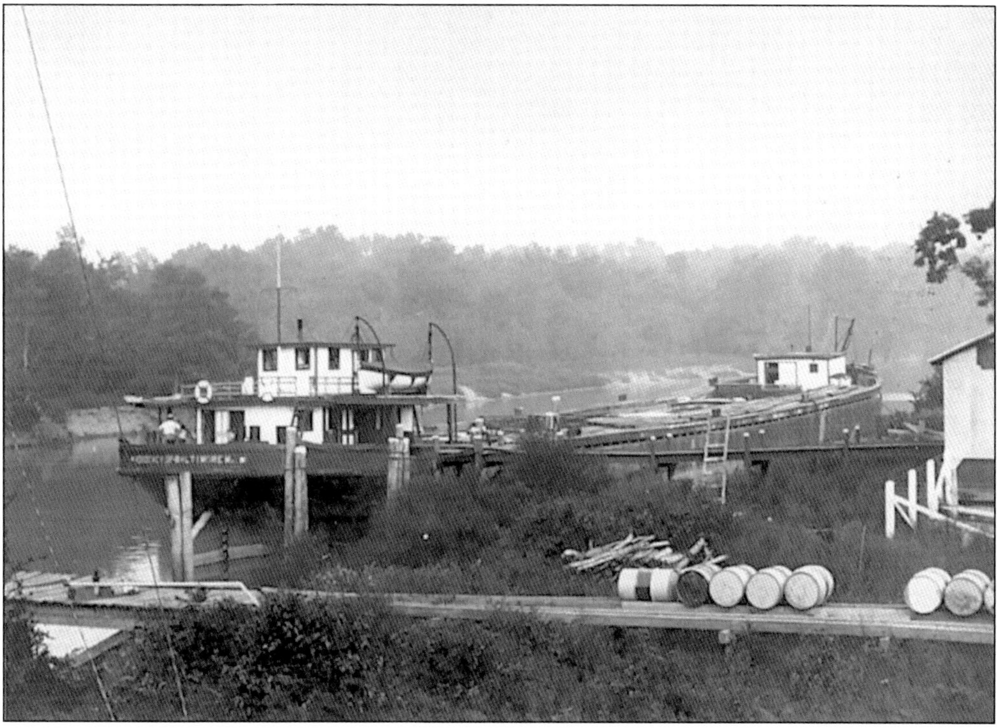

A LOG-LUMBER BARGE AT THE STANDARD FERTILIZER COMPANY WHARF, C. 1938. (Courtesy of the Francis Manning Room.)

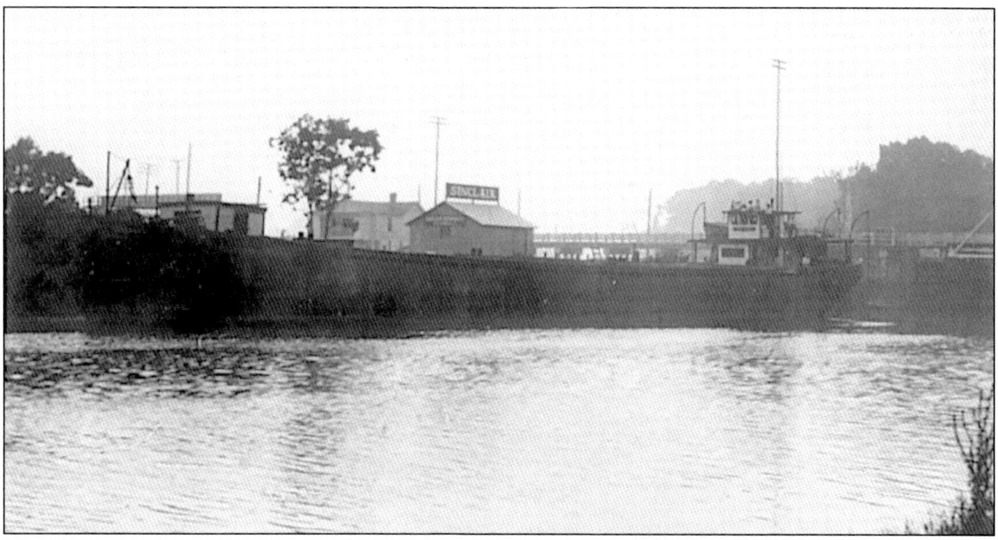

THE WHARF AS SEEN FROM THE BERTIE COUNTY SIDE OF THE RIVER, C. 1938. (Courtesy of the Francis Manning Room.)

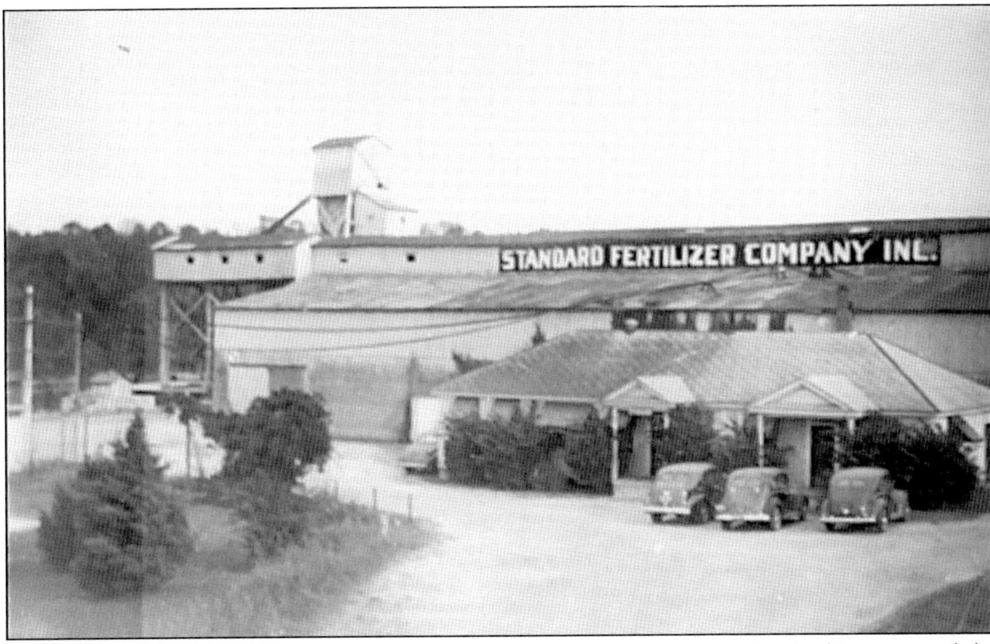

THE STANDARD FERTILIZER COMPANY MAIN PLANT AND OFFICES, C. 1937. (Courtesy of the Francis Manning Room.)

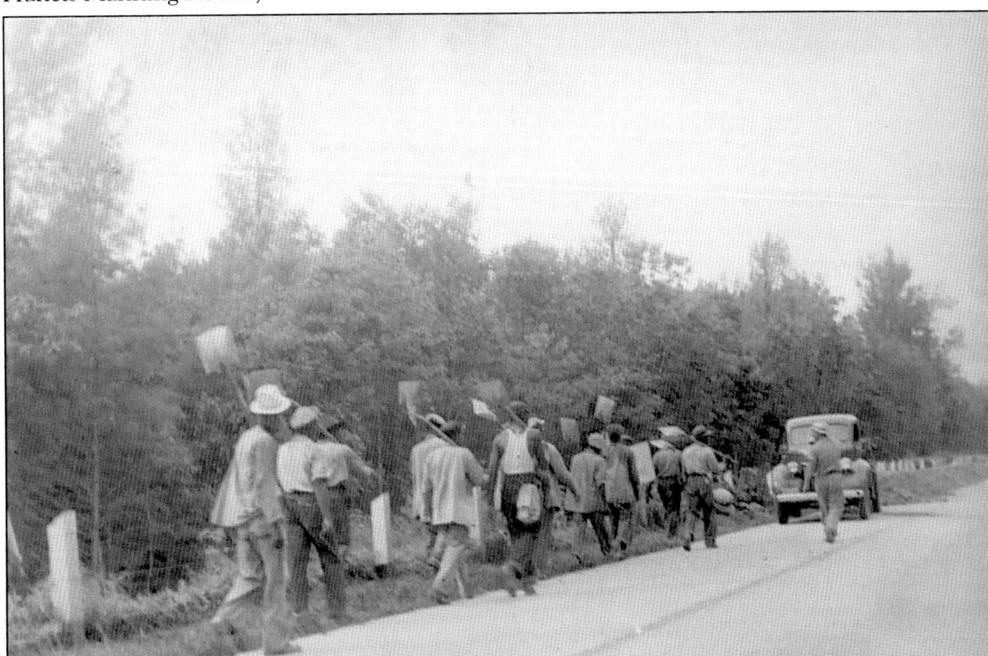

A CONVICT CREW TRYING TO SAVE THE RIVER FILL PRIOR TO THE AUGUST 1940 FLOOD. The great flood of 1940 was perhaps the most destructive of all recorded floods on the Roanoke. Except for the main bridge, the flood destroyed almost all of the causeway and the smaller bridges leading into Bertie County. A record high-water mark was set on August 22 when the river rose 10 feet above flood stage. Shown here is a convict crew trying to save what is still referred to as the river fill prior to the flood. (Courtesy of the Francis Manning Room.)

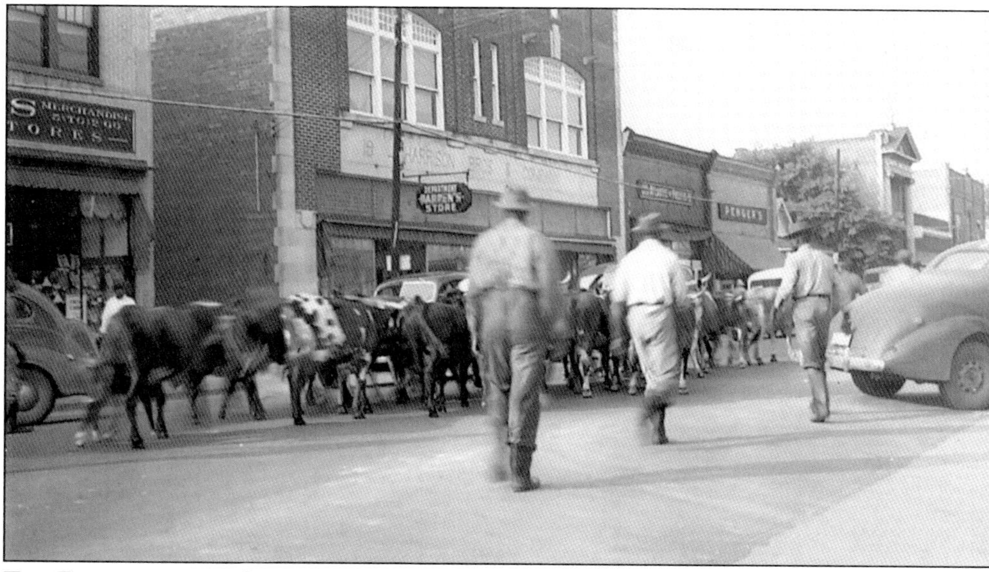

THE EVACUATION OF CATTLE ALONG MAIN STREET IN WILLIAMSTON, PRIOR TO THE FLOOD. (Courtesy of the Francis Manning Room.)

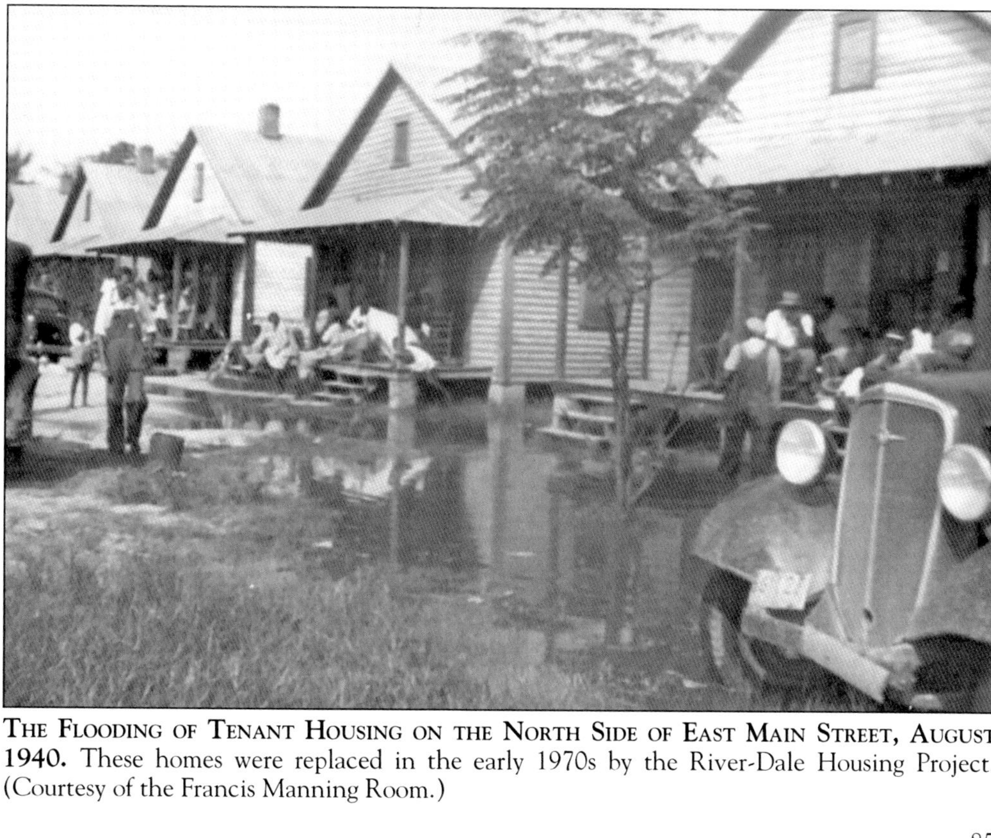

THE FLOODING OF TENANT HOUSING ON THE NORTH SIDE OF EAST MAIN STREET, AUGUST 1940. These homes were replaced in the early 1970s by the River-Dale Housing Project. (Courtesy of the Francis Manning Room.)

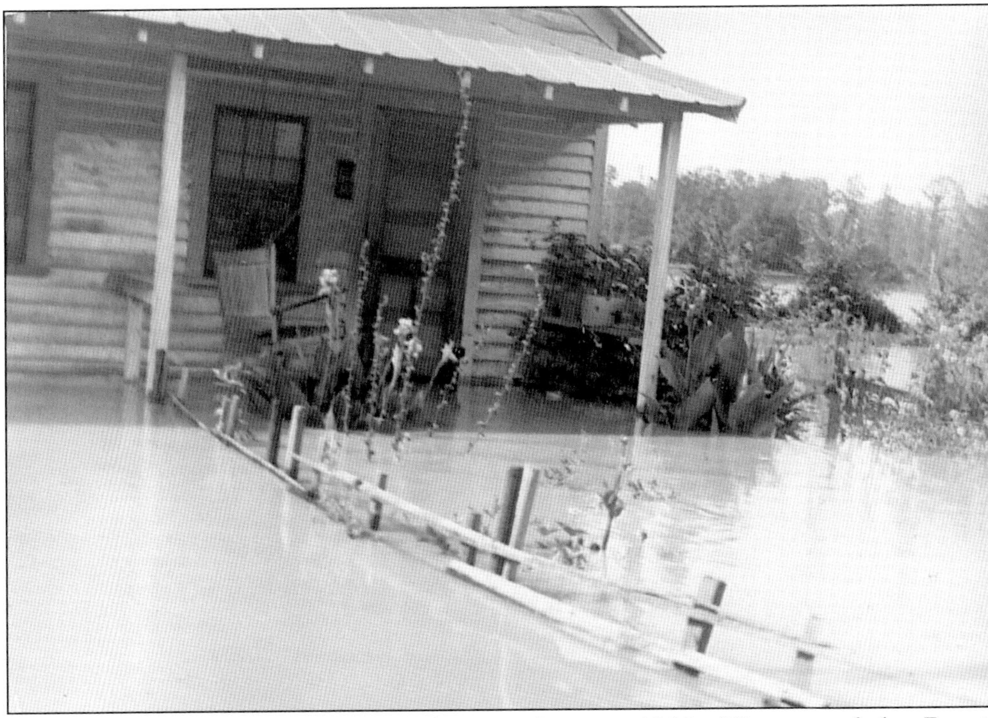

A FLOODED HOME ON EAST MAIN STREET, AUGUST 1940. (Courtesy of the Francis Manning Room.)

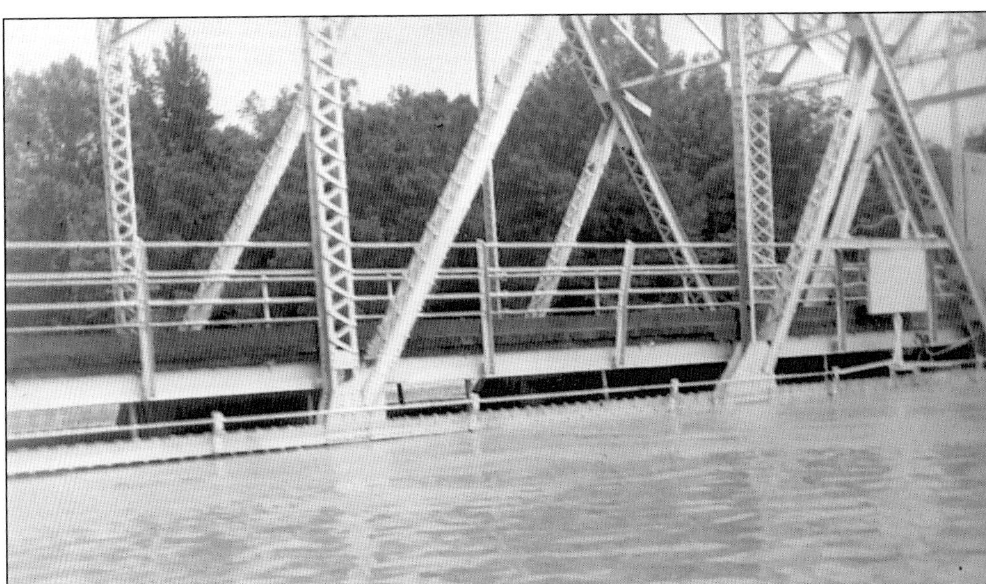

THE DRAW SPAN OF THE ROANOKE RIVER BRIDGE DURING THE HEIGHT OF THE FLOOD, AUGUST 1940. (Courtesy of the Francis Manning Room.)

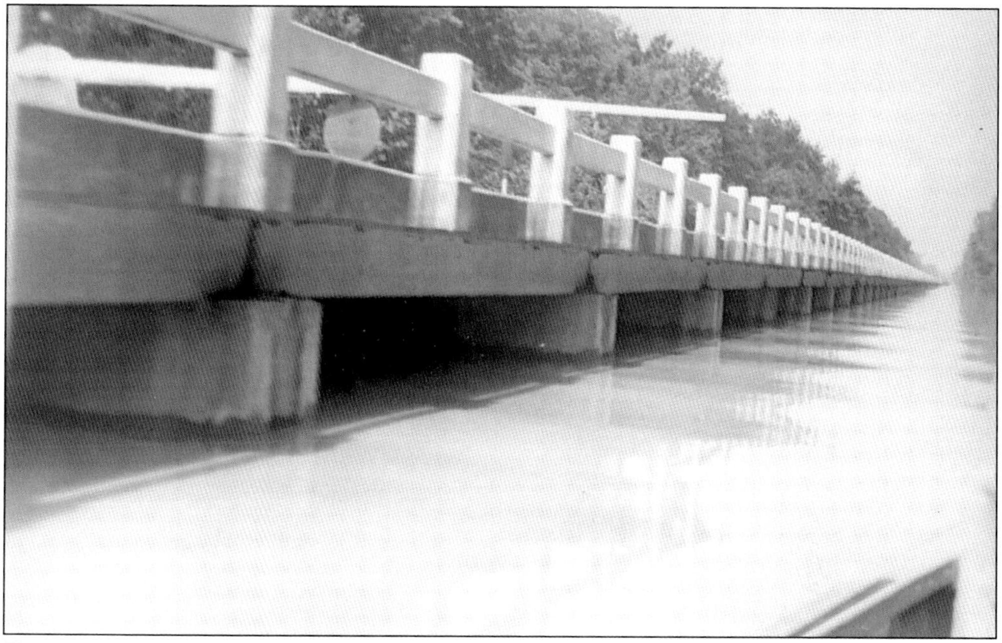

The Bertie County Side of the River Fill Leading to the Main Bridge. More than a year of work and an excess of $300,000 were required to replace and repair damages to the bridge and fill after the flood. (Courtesy of the Francis Manning Room.)

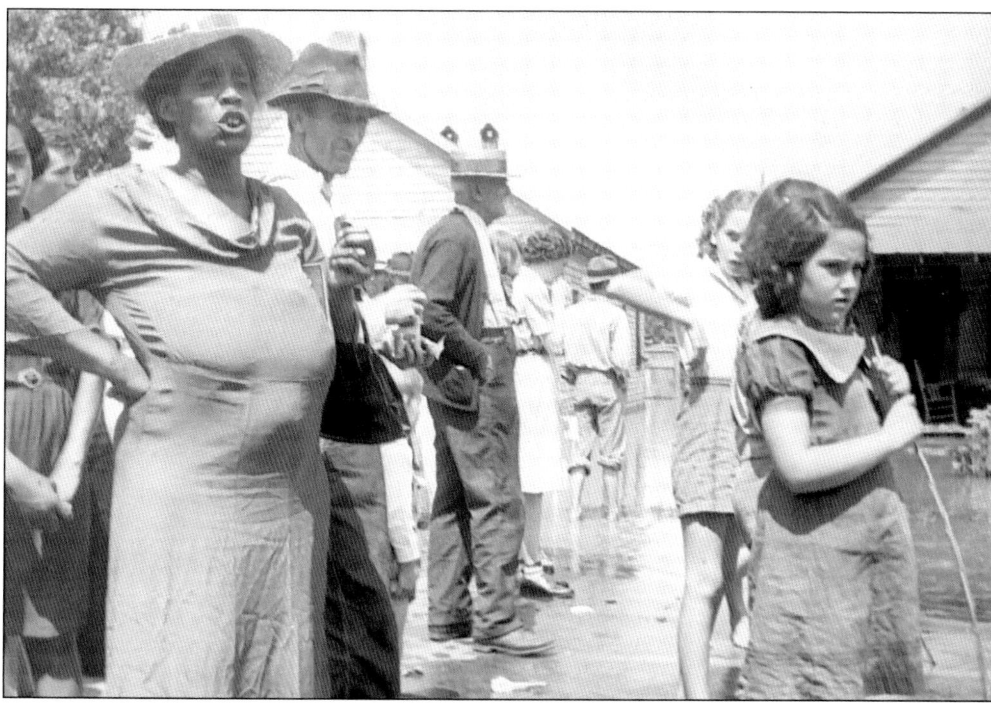

Spectators Gather on Lower East Main Street to View the Flood Damage, August 1940. (Courtesy of the Francis Manning Room.)

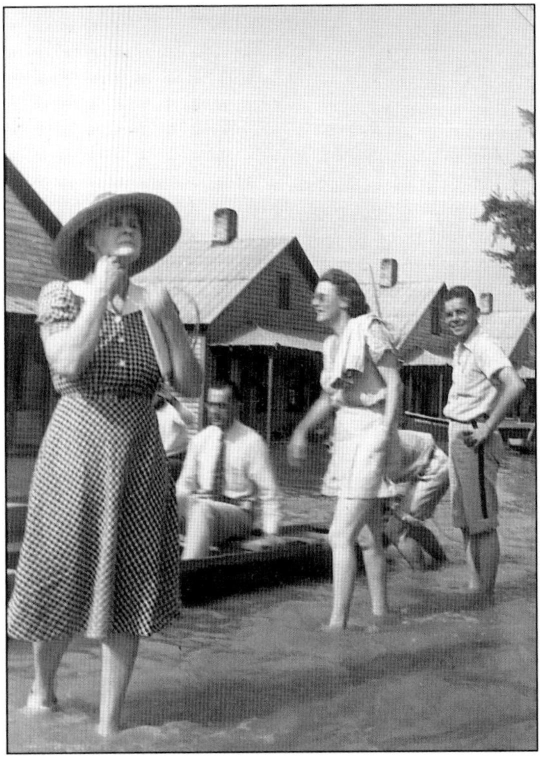

Touring the Flood Scene, August 1940. Shown standing from left to right are Mrs. Myrt Harris, Mrs. Paul Jones, and Jimmy Watts. Wigg Watts is the man in the boat. (Courtesy of the Francis Manning Room.)

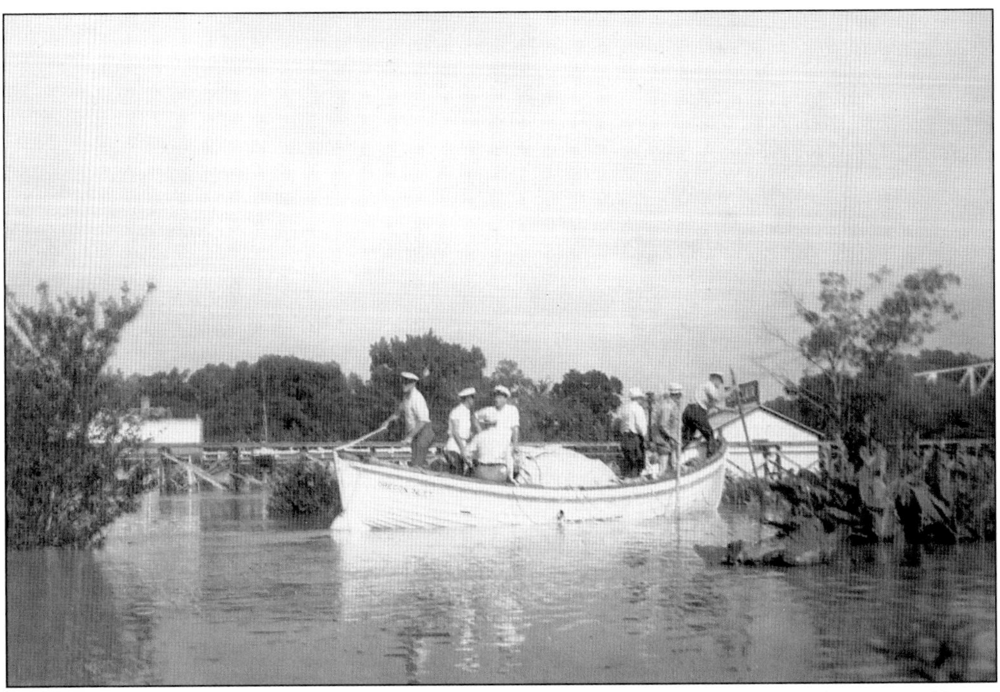

A Coast Guard Crew Moving Through the Standard Fertilizer Company Yard, August 1940. (Courtesy of the Francis Manning Room.)

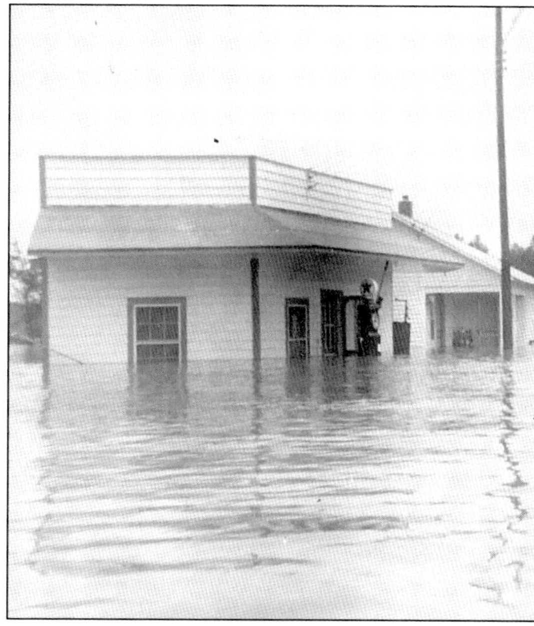

Flood Waters Consume a Gas Station on East Main Street. (Courtesy of the Francis Manning Room.)

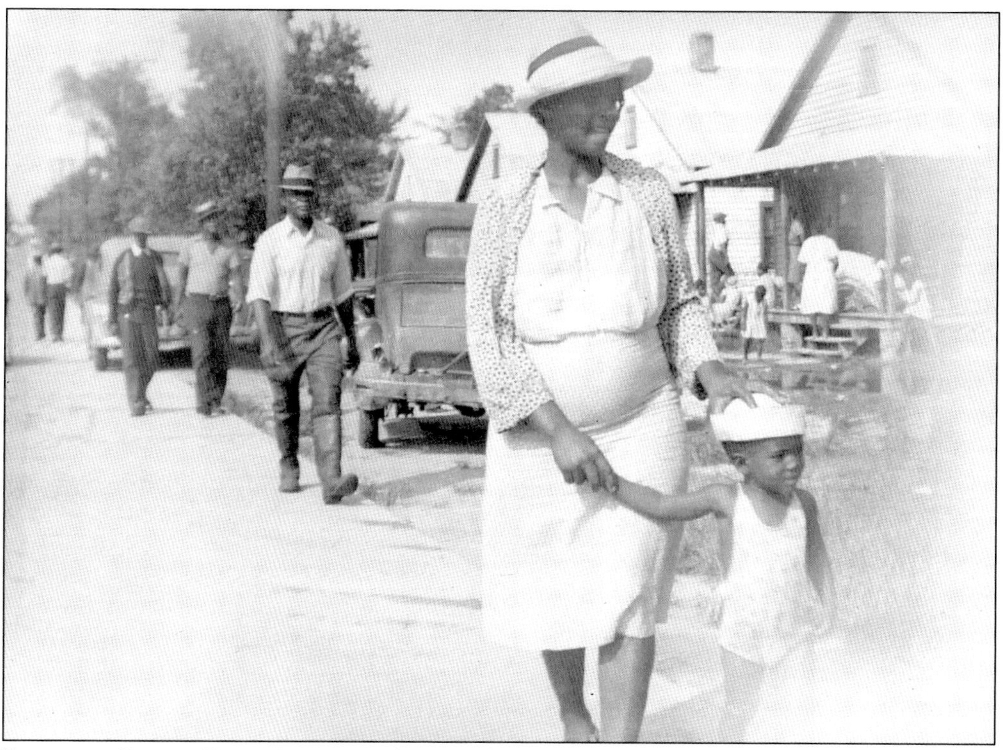

Residents Survey Flood Damage. The 1940 flood is still considered one of the most memorable events in Martin County. Business losses were extremely heavy, especially in Williamston where operations such as the Goldman Packaging Company, Wicomico Lumber Company, Saunders and Cox Lumber Mill, and others were closed down for a considerable amount of time. (Courtesy of the Francis Manning Room.)

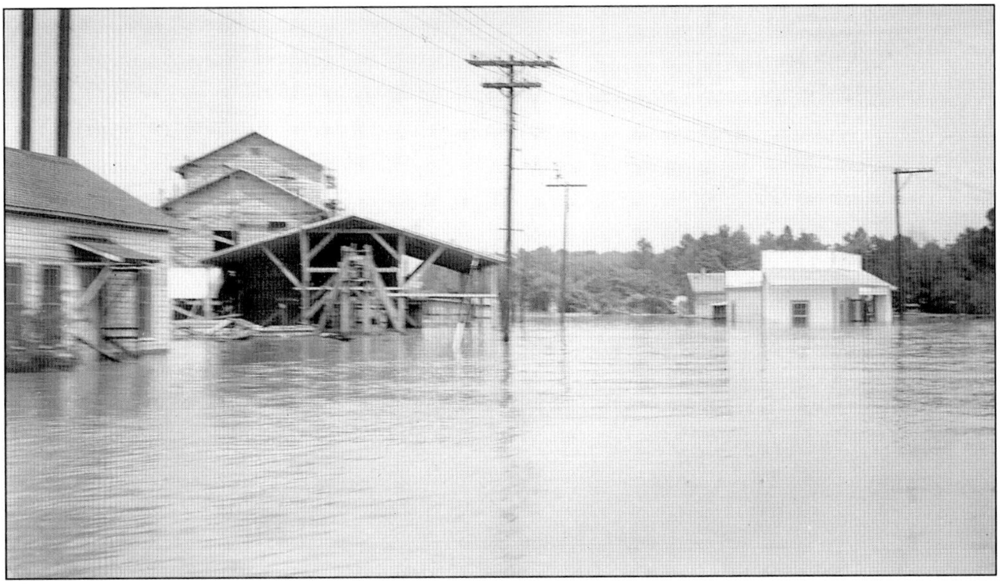

THE SAUNDERS AND COX LUMBER MILL SURROUNDED BY FLOOD WATERS, AUGUST 1940. (Courtesy of the Francis Manning Room.)

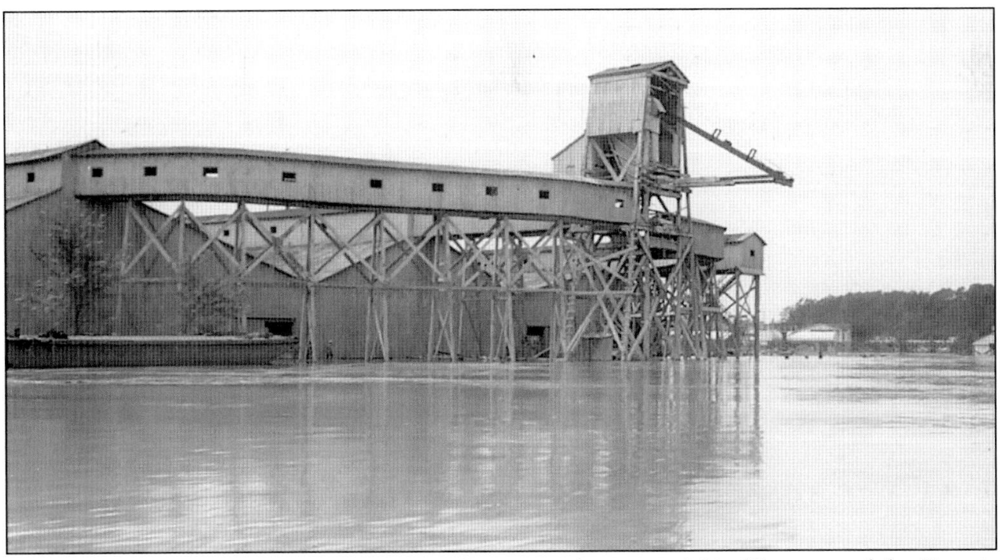

A PORTION OF THE STANDARD FERTILIZER COMPLEX, AUGUST 1940. (Courtesy of the Francis Manning Room.)

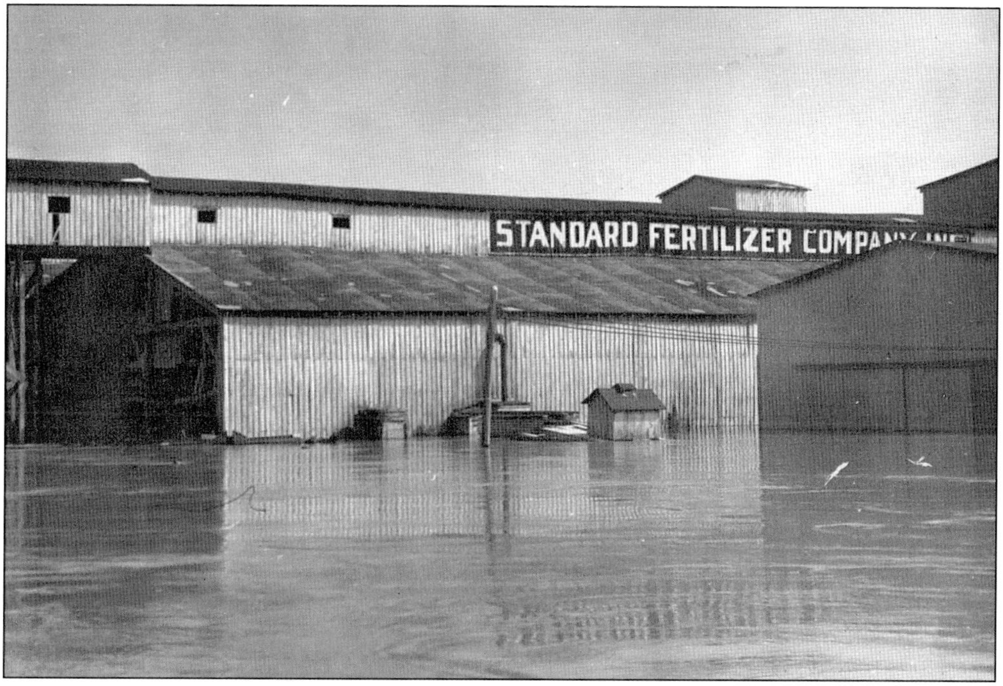

THE STANDARD FERTILIZER COMPANY UNDER WATER, AUGUST 1940. (Courtesy of the Francis Manning Room.)

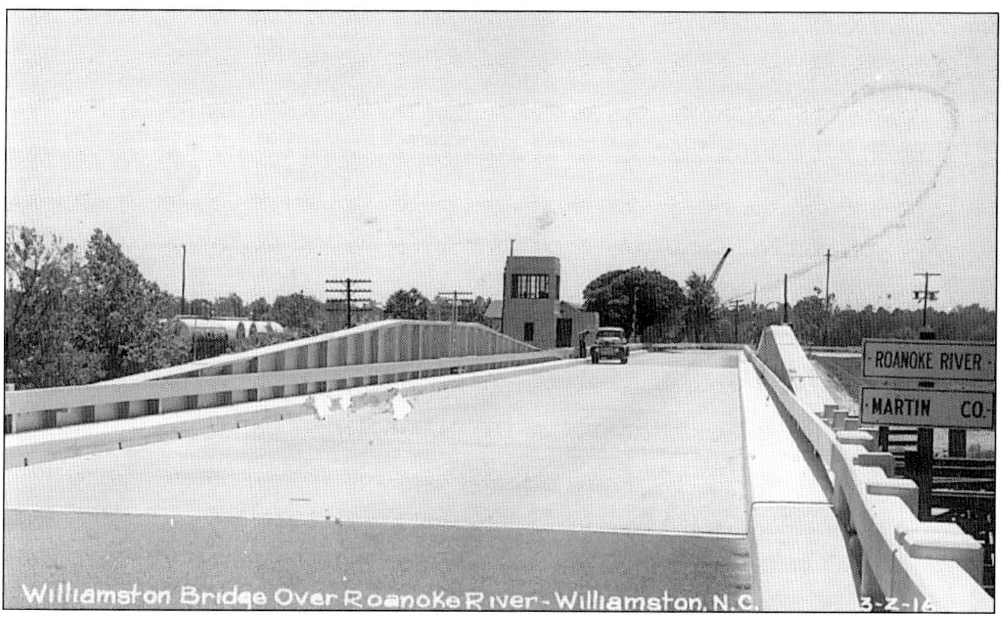

A POSTCARD VIEW OF A REFURBISHED ROANOKE RIVER BRIDGE, C. 1950. (Courtesy of the Francis Manning Room.)

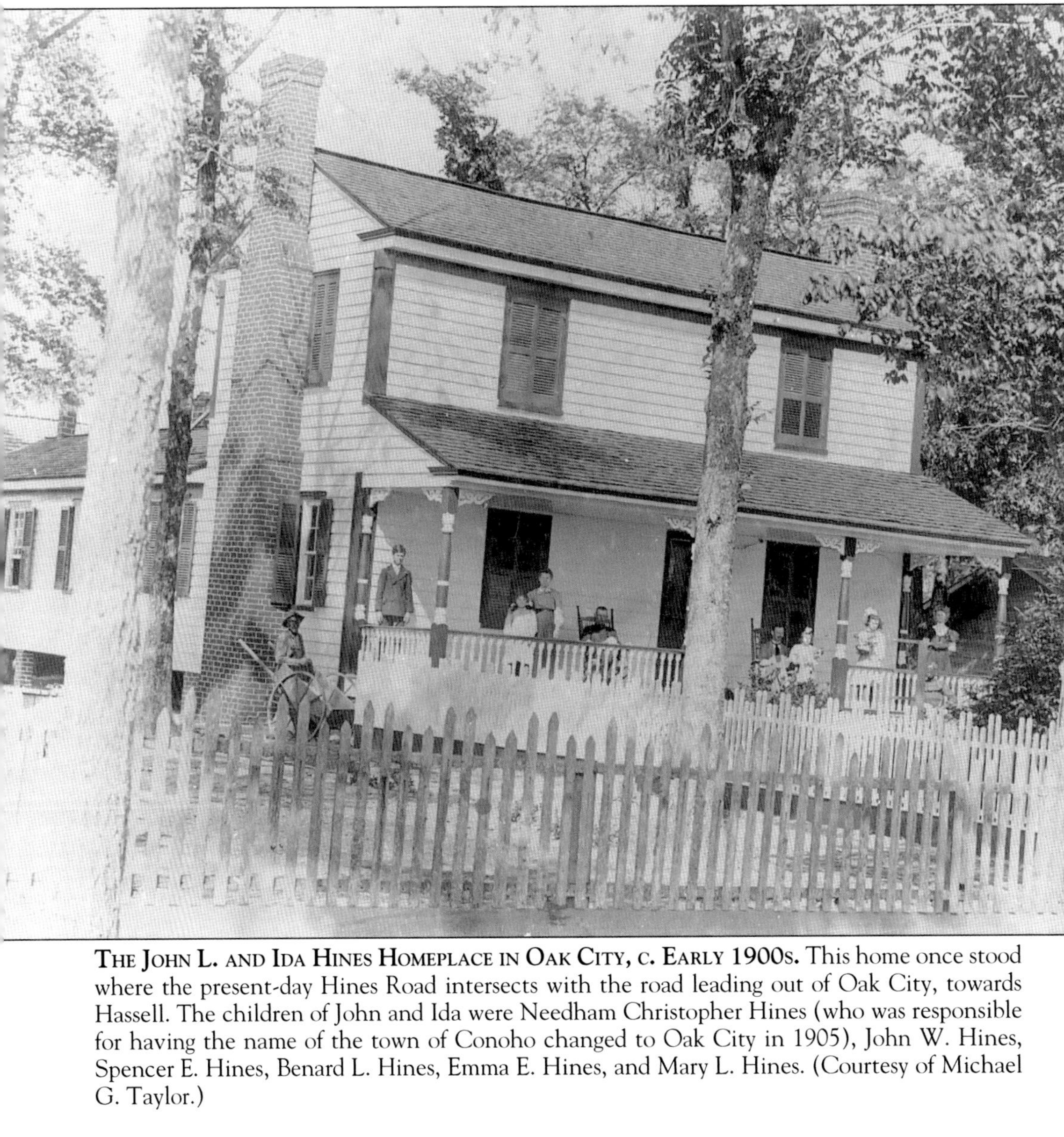

The John L. and Ida Hines Homeplace in Oak City, c. Early 1900s. This home once stood where the present-day Hines Road intersects with the road leading out of Oak City, towards Hassell. The children of John and Ida were Needham Christopher Hines (who was responsible for having the name of the town of Conoho changed to Oak City in 1905), John W. Hines, Spencer E. Hines, Benard L. Hines, Emma E. Hines, and Mary L. Hines. (Courtesy of Michael G. Taylor.)

Five

Rural Communities

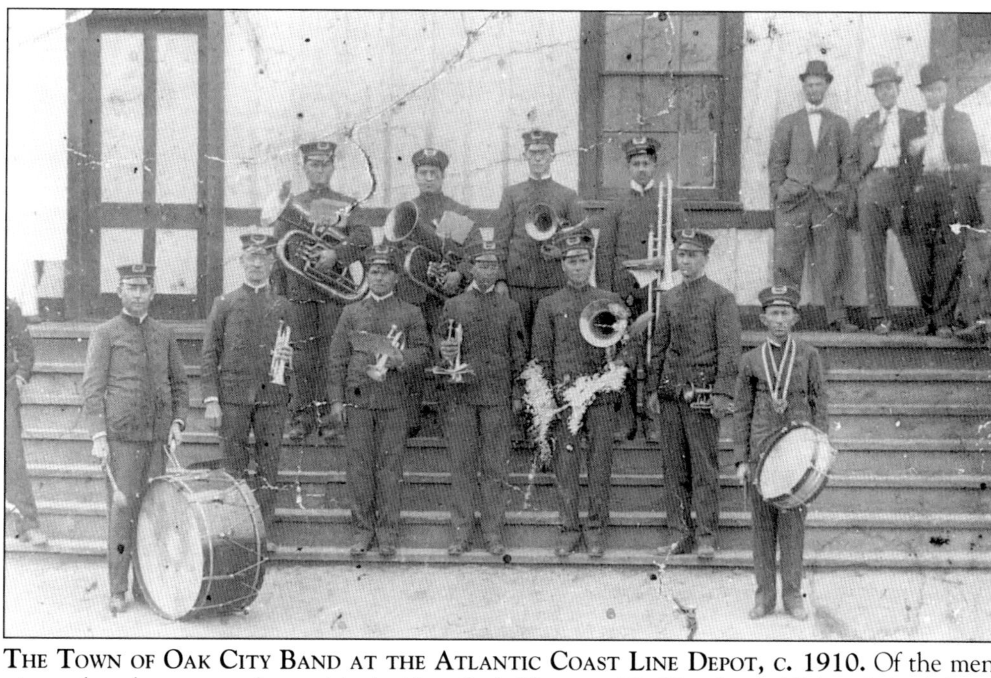

The Town of Oak City Band at the Atlantic Coast Line Depot, c. 1910. Of the men pictured, only two can be positively identified. They are T. Cleveland Allsbrook (at left on drum) and Jimmy Council (at right on drum). (Courtesy of Michael G. Taylor.)

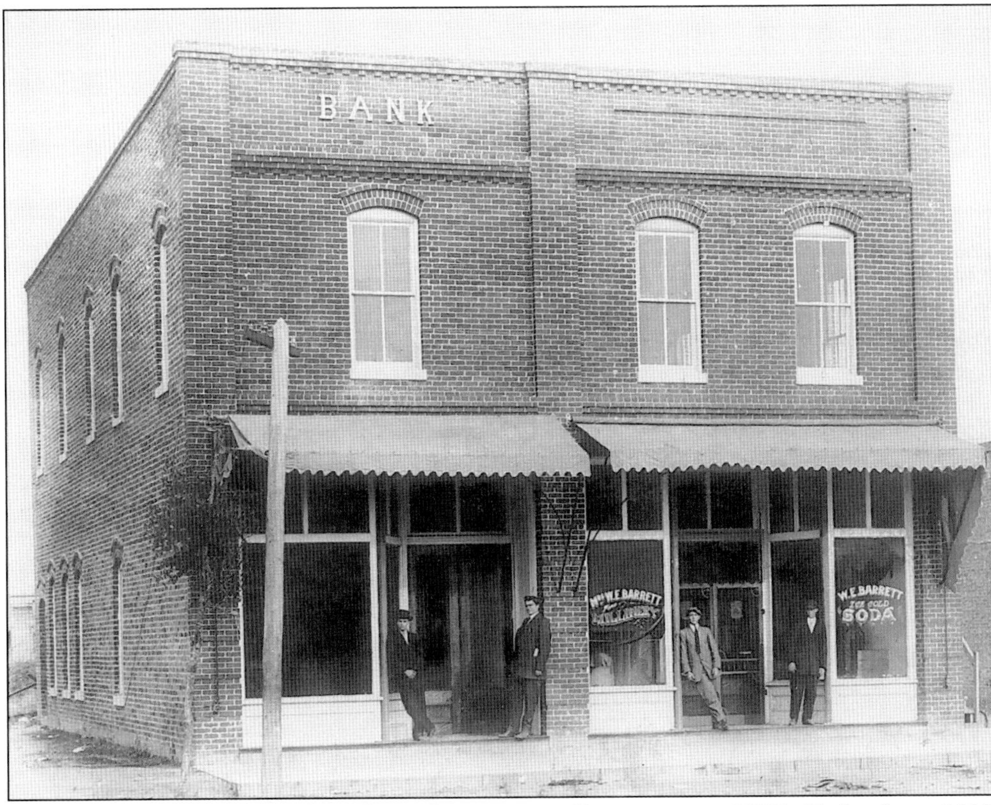

A Postcard Picture of Oak City Commercial Building, c. 1920. Built about 1910, this building served a variety of purposes; it was the headquarters for the Bank of Oak City, W.E. Barrett's Drug Store, a soda shop, a millinery shop, and an office for Dr. E.E. Pittman. Benjamin M. Worsley, pictured second from left, served as a cashier for the bank before it closed in the 1930s. (Courtesy of Michael G. Taylor.)

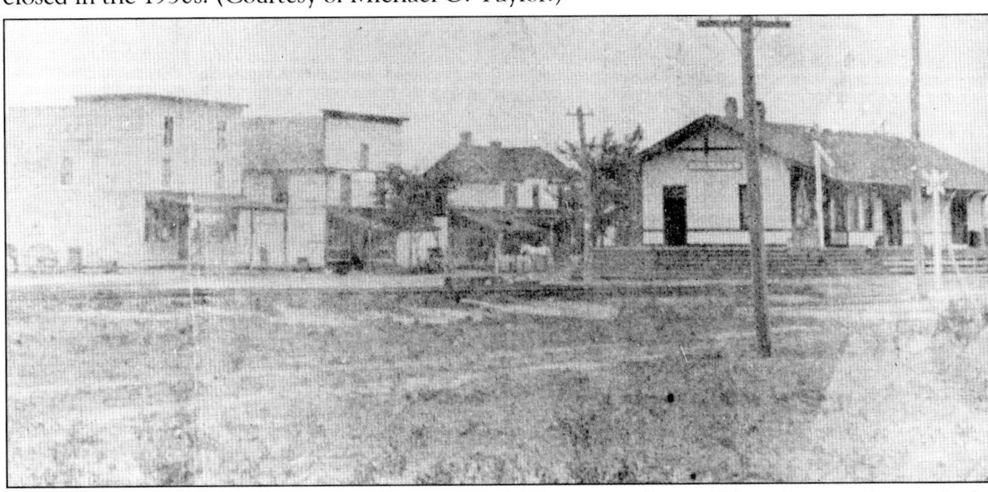

The Oak City Commercial District, c. 1905. The stores facing West Avenue (towards the depot) are, from left to right, T.W. Davenport and Co., Casper Brothers, and J.H. Ayers and Co. The house pictured in the center was built by John L. Hines and later owned by the Davenport, Rawls, and Harrell families. (Courtesy of Michael G. Taylor.)

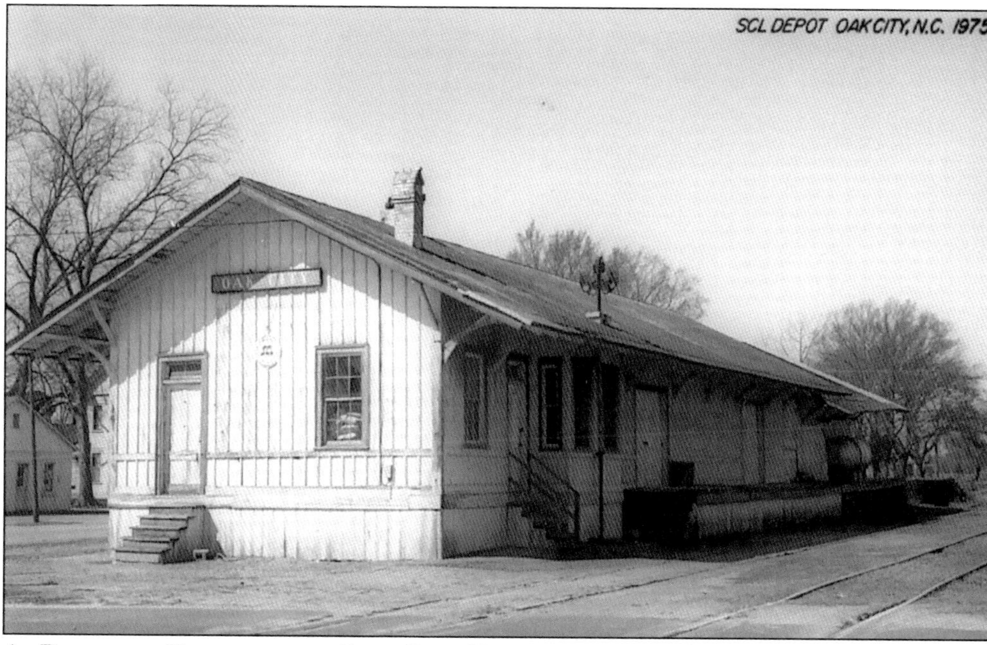

A POSTCARD VIEW OF THE OAK CITY DEPOT, C. 1975. (Courtesy of the Sarah M. Pope Collection.)

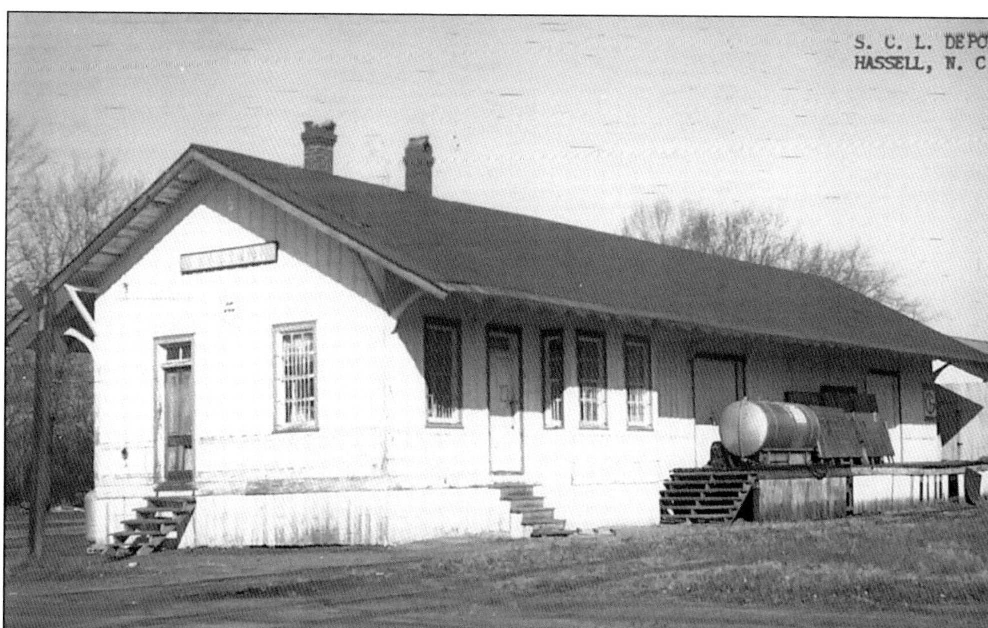

A POSTCARD VIEW OF THE HASSELL DEPOT, C. 1950. (Courtesy of the Sarah M. Pope Collection.)

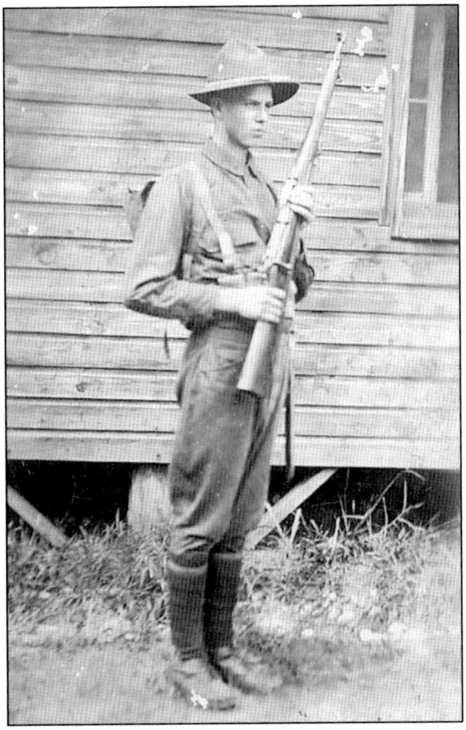

R.J. Hardison. A resident of Williams Township, Hardison is pictured at Camp Jackson during World War I. (Courtesy of Sallie H. Long.)

A 1937 Advertisement for Armour's Tobacco Fertilizer. This ad featured Robersonville residents Sarah Keel Powell and Cecil B. Powell with an endorsement by J. Augustus Powell. The fertilizer was used on the Powell farm near the community of Gold Point. (Courtesy of Michael G. Taylor.)

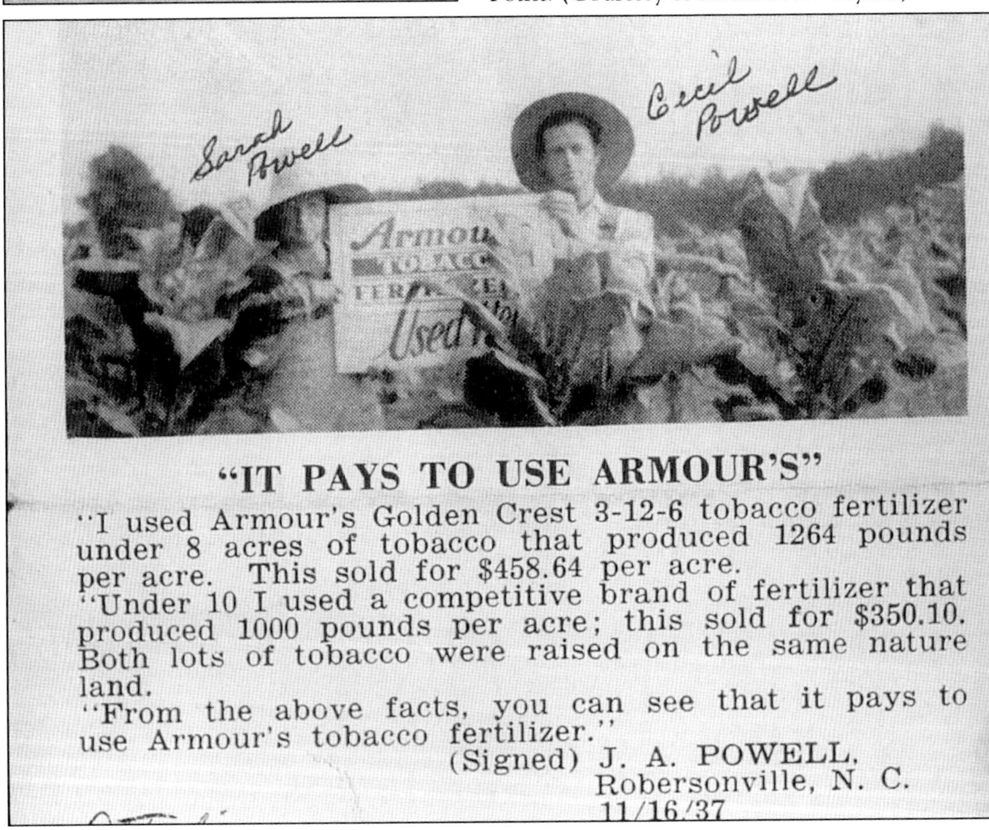

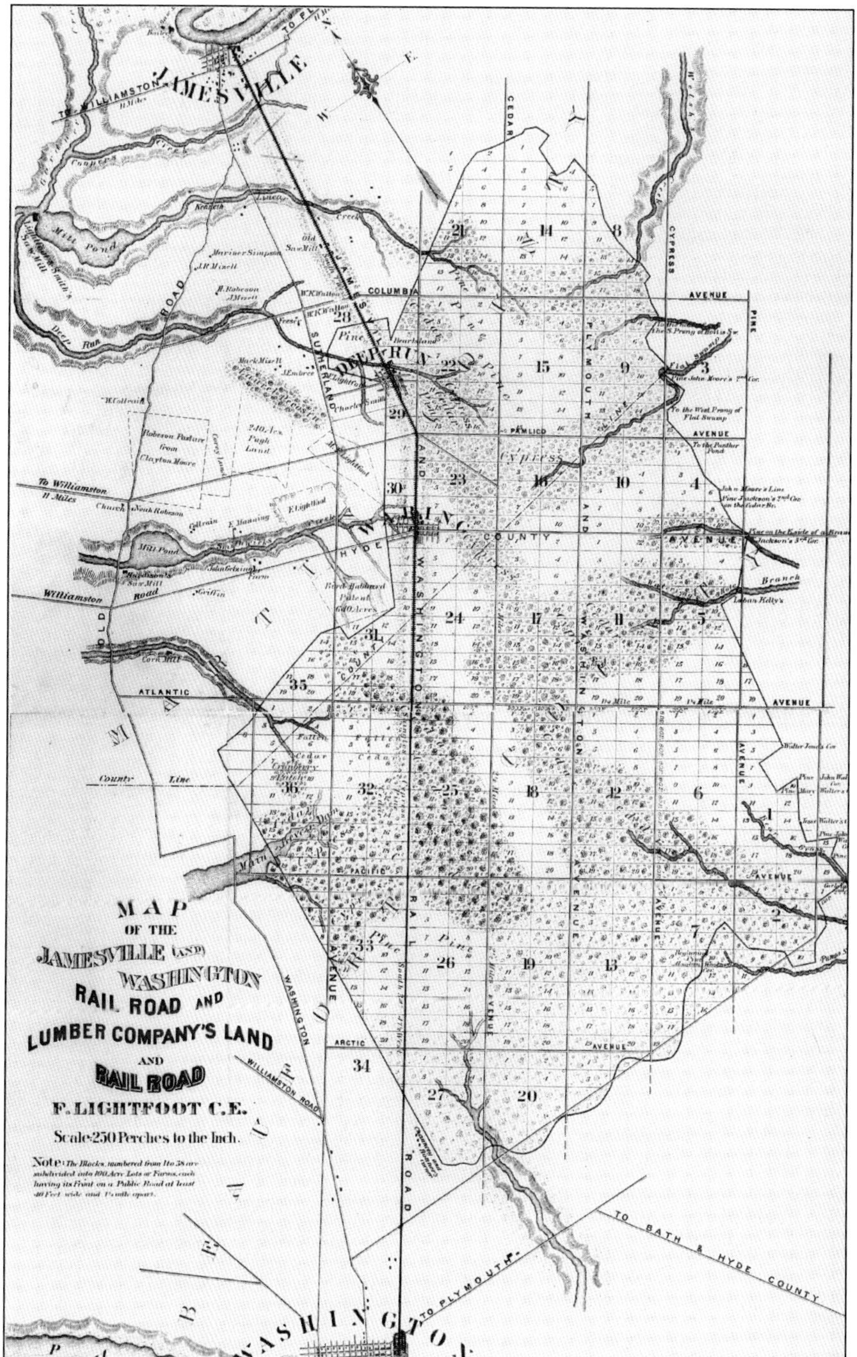

A Jamesville and Washington Railroad and Lumber Company Map. This company had its beginnings about 1868, when a group of Pennsylvania investors became interested in the area's vast timber resources. The firm eventually built a 21-mile railroad, the first in the county, between Jamesville and Washington in Beaufort County, and operated it until the mid-1890s. (Courtesy of the Getsinger Family Papers, East Carolina Manuscript Collection, East Carolina University.)

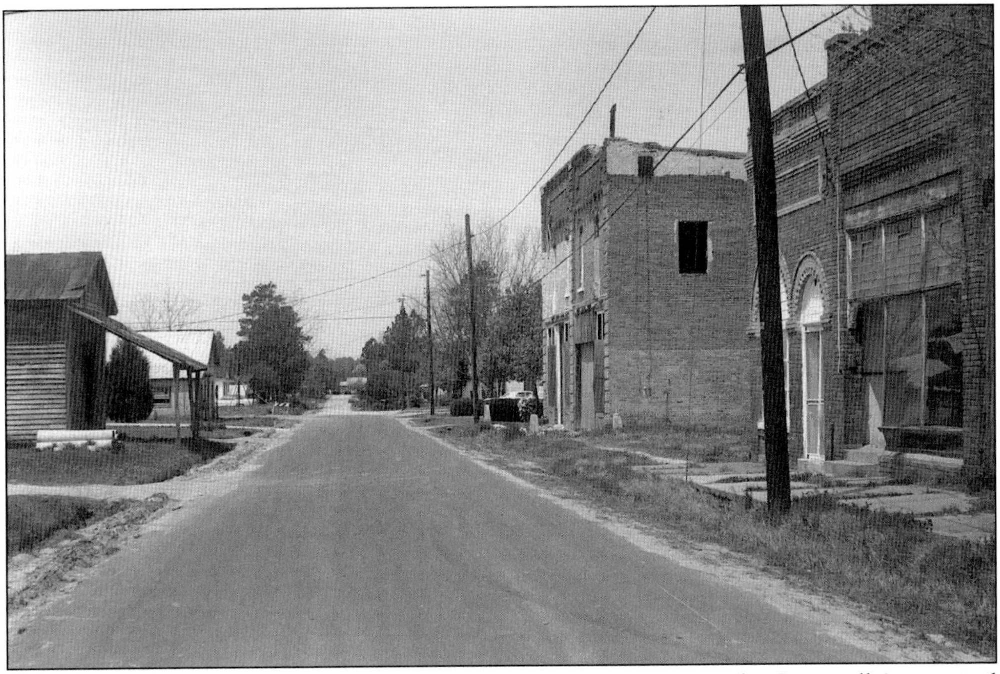

WATER STREET IN JAMESVILLE, C. 1970. This street, at one time, served as Jamesville's principal business district. (Courtesy of Fred W. Harrison Jr.)

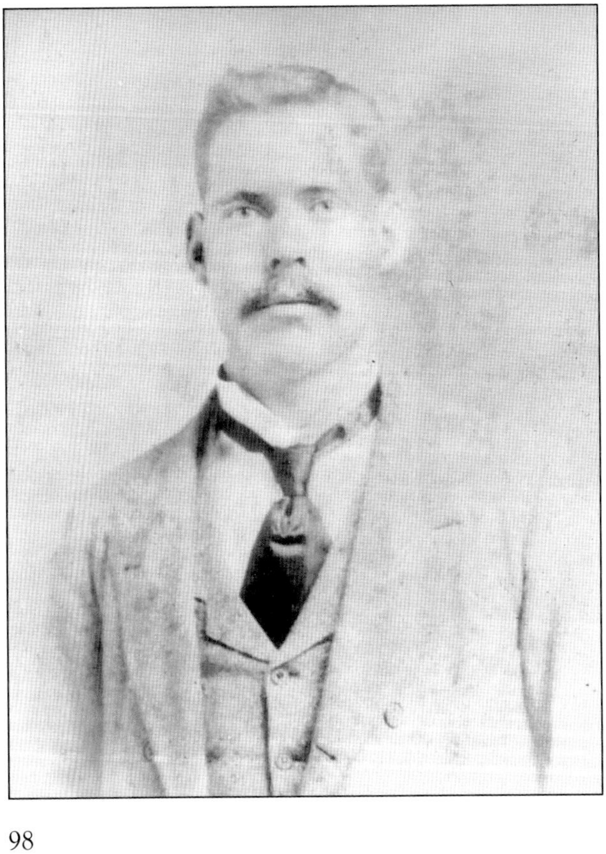

W. JACKSON HOLLIDAY, JAMESVILLE MERCHANT AND AREA FARMER, C. 1895. (Courtesy of Mary G. Dixon.)

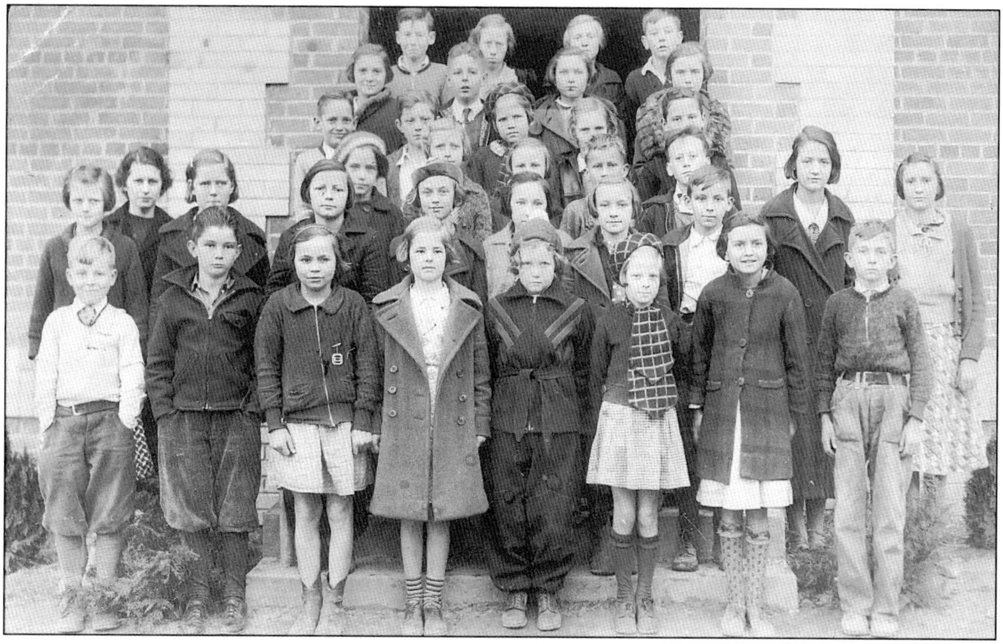

A Jamesville Elementary School Class. Fourth graders at the old Jamesville Elementary School posed for this class portrait around 1934. (Courtesy of Mary G. Dixon.)

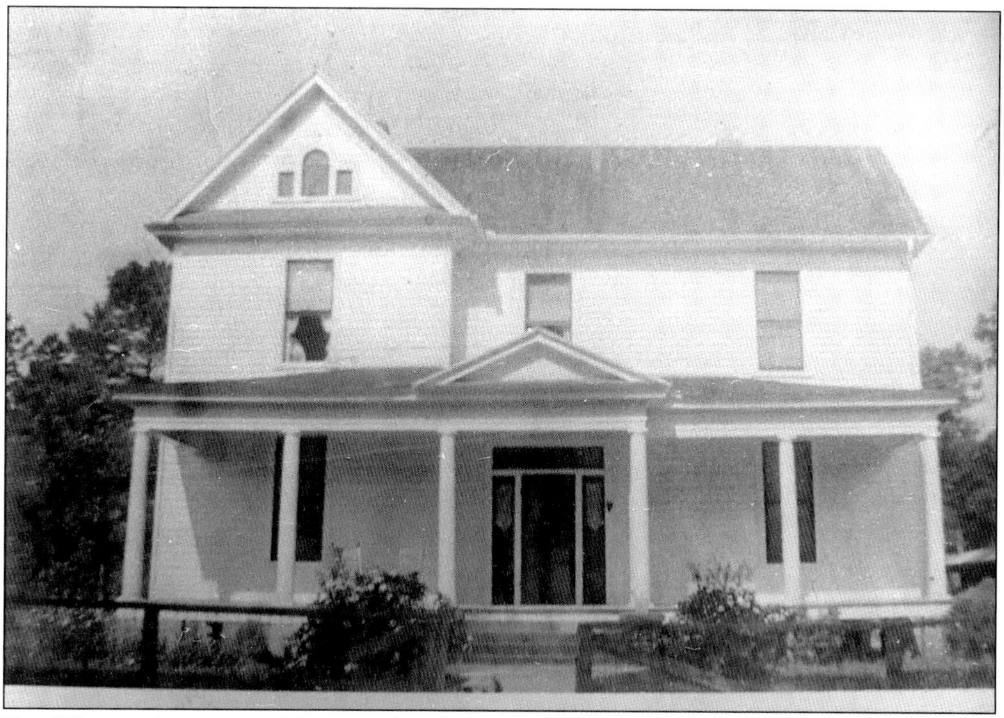

The Walter Alexander Manning Sr. Homeplace. Located in Griffins Township, this ample farmhouse was built in 1918 for W.A. Manning and his wife, Malinda. (Courtesy of Mary M. Jones Peele.)

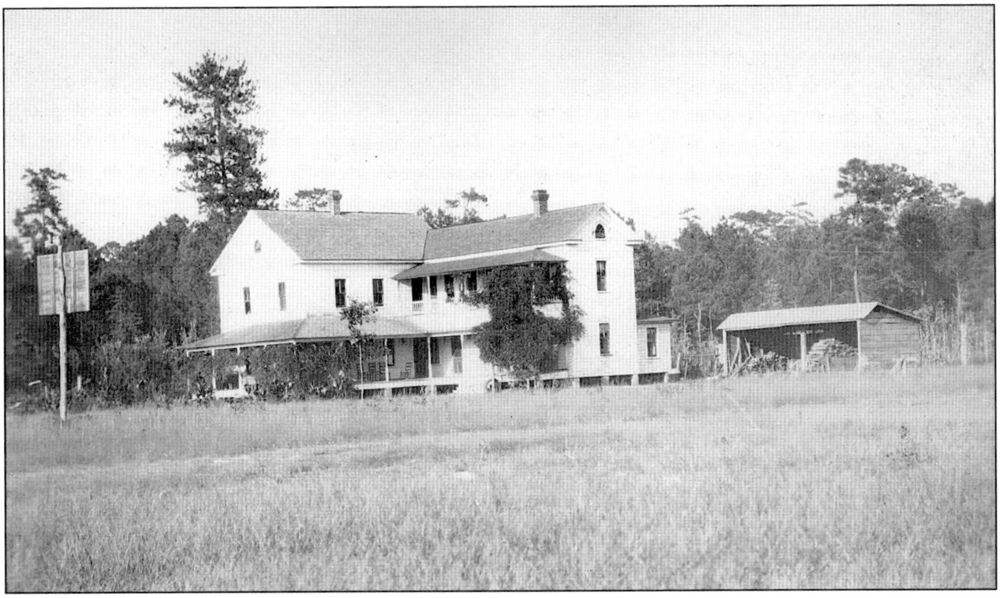

THE FARM LIFE SCHOOL TEACHERAGE, 1938. During the Depression Era, economic circumstances dictated one income per family. In general, local school boards required teachers to resign their positions upon marriage. Teacherages were a common feature at the time as a way of providing housing for unmarried teachers, many of whom were women. This teacherage was connected with Farm Life School in Griffins Township. (Courtesy of the Francis Manning Room.)

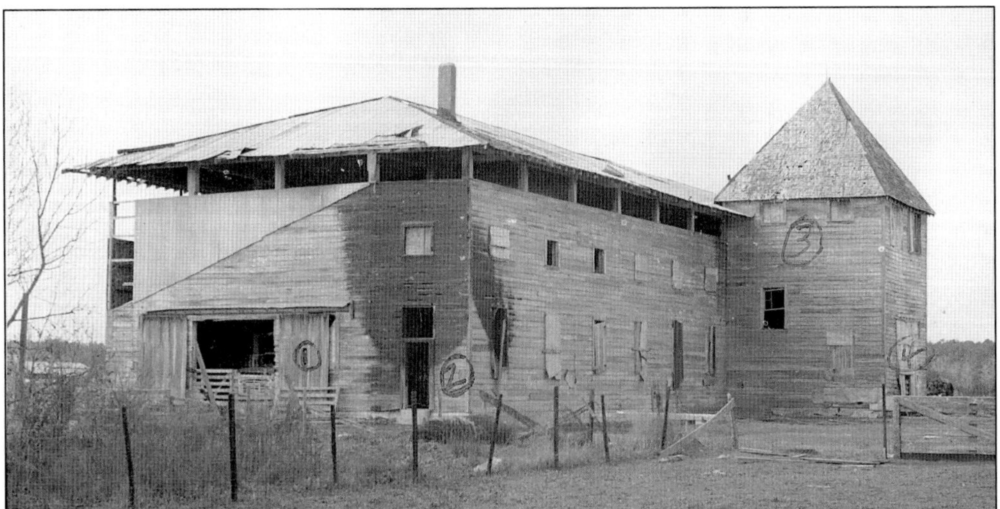

THE OLD GRANDSTAND AT THE MARTIN COUNTY FAIRGROUND, 1974. Shown here is one the last remnants of the old Martin County Fairgrounds complex as it appeared in 1974. In 1920, the Martin County Fair Association purchased 40 acres of land near Williamston in what was later to become the residential neighborhood referred to as West End. This grandstand, along with several exhibit halls, stables, a pavilion, a machinery shop, and other structures, was first opened in October 1920. The complex was operated continuously until sometime in the early 1940s. (Courtesy of the Francis Manning Room.)

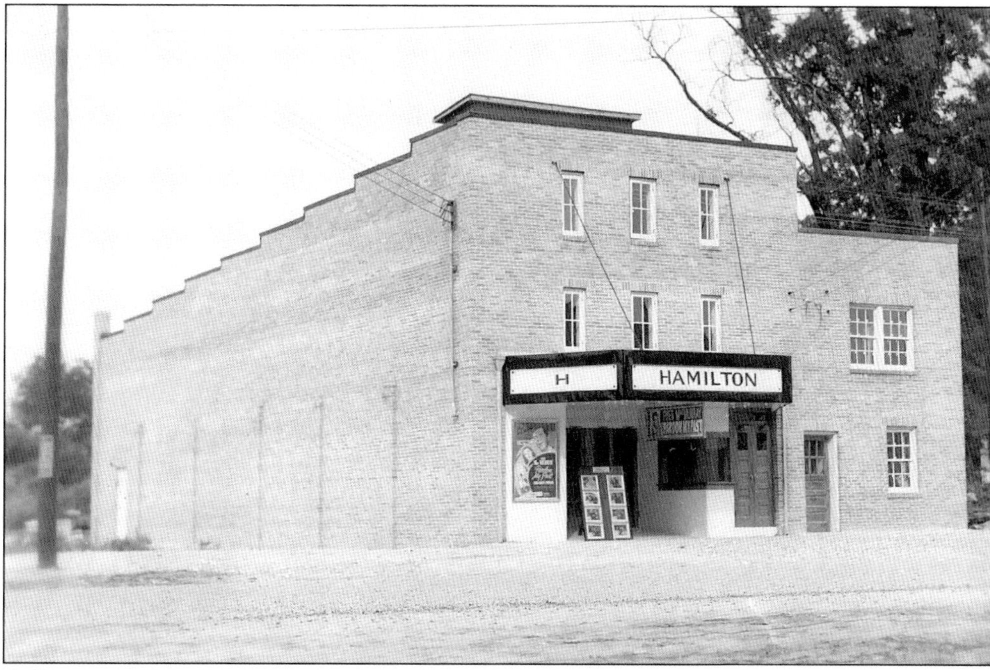

A Postcard View of the Hamilton Theatre in Hamilton, c. 1940s. (Courtesy of the Francis Manning Room.)

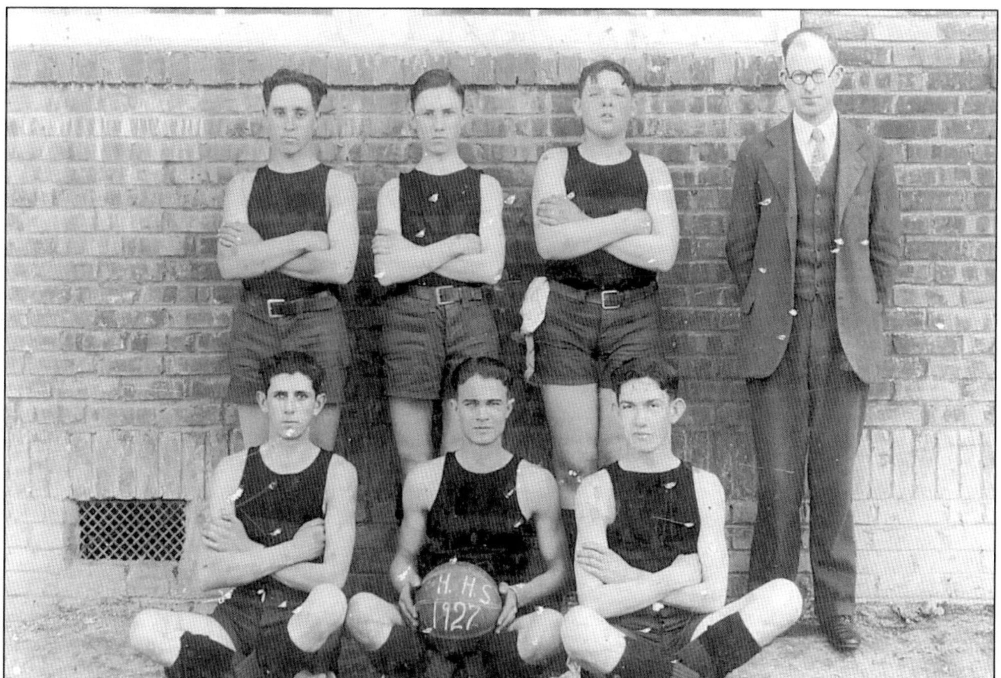

The Hamilton High School Basketball Team, c. 1927. Pictured on the back row, standing at left, is Edgar Hopewell. (Courtesy of Alton Hopewell.)

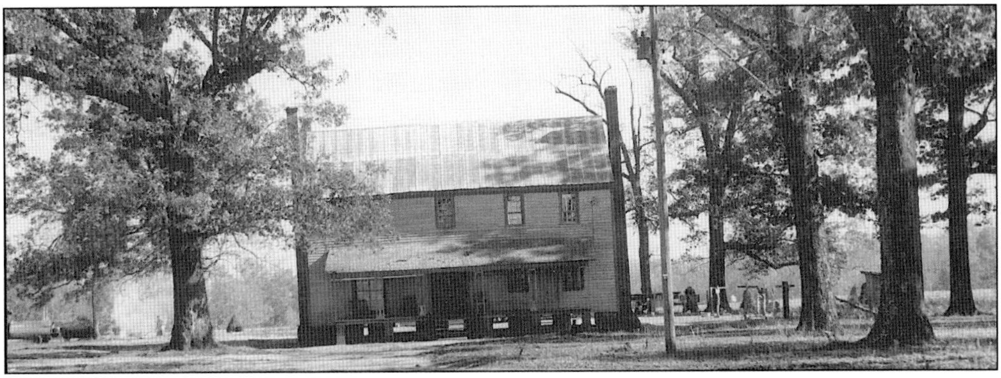

The Biggs House near Skewarkee Church. Dating back to the early 1800s, this large house was the seat of the equally large Biggs family of Williamston and Martin County. Joseph Biggs, a Virginia native, moved to Martin County sometime in the 1740s and eventually received a land grant for property extending from the present U.S. Highway 17 and 64 intersection on down Highway 17 to the Reedy Swamp Bridge and back over towards Bear Grass Township. An earlier home than the one pictured here was built c. 1755. Referred to in later years as Cedar Lane farm, the home seen here, which was the second home, is reputed to have had very detailed woodwork as well as a ballroom that occupied a portion of the second floor. The house was demolished in the 1950s. (Courtesy of the Francis Manning Room.)

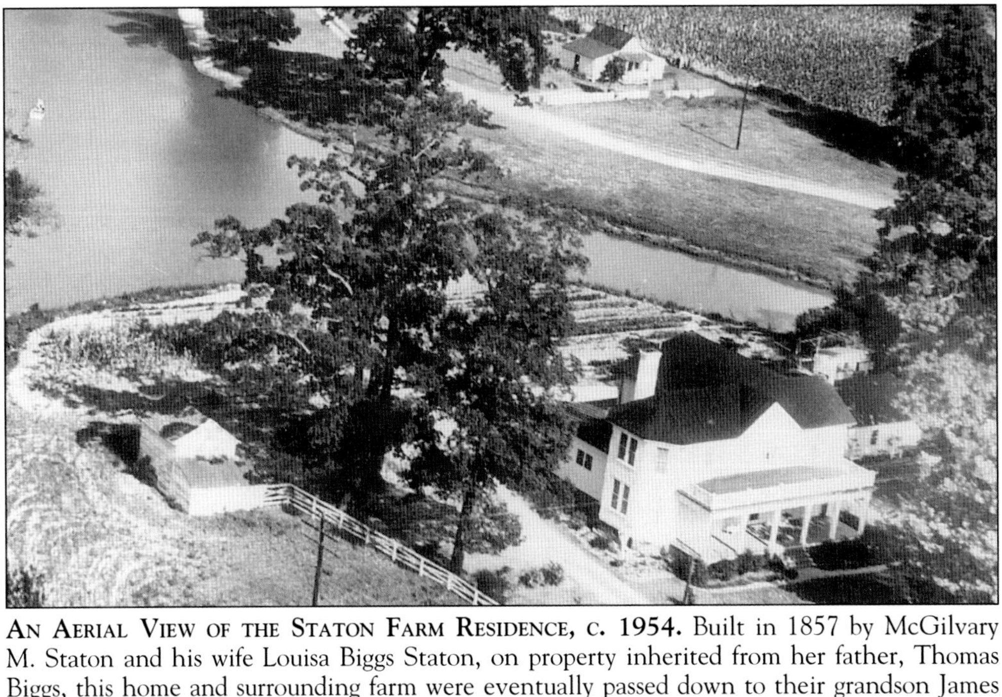

An Aerial View of the Staton Farm Residence, c. 1954. Built in 1857 by McGilvary M. Staton and his wife Louisa Biggs Staton, on property inherited from her father, Thomas Biggs, this home and surrounding farm were eventually passed down to their grandson James G. Staton. Under the younger Staton's management, the farm was known as Kelvin Grove and became one of the most progressive in the county. Staton was instrumental in bringing in the people and processes that led to the first series of successful peanut and tobacco crops in the county. Staton began liquidating his farm holdings in the early 1940s, and the house and much of the property was purchased by the Harris family. In 1959, the house was taken over and later enlarged by the Williamston Moose Lodge. Its current occupant and owner is Jenkins Antiques. (Courtesy of Becky Jenkins.)

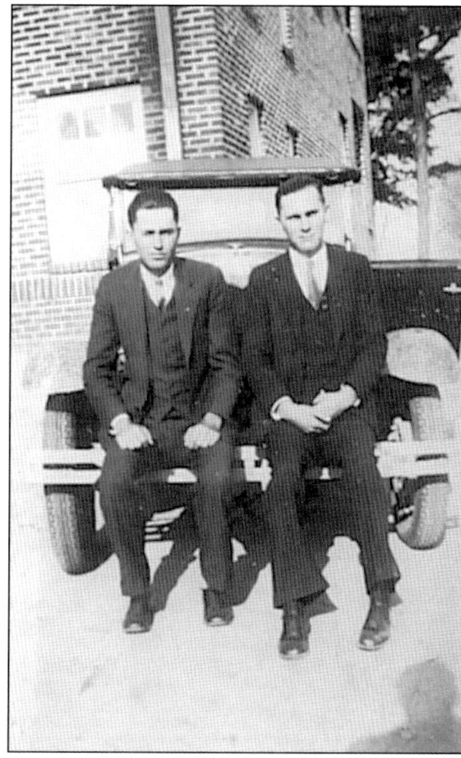

WILLARD B. HARRISON AND ROLAND T. ROGERS, C. 1931. The two young Bear Grass residents pictured here pose for the camera in Everetts while traveling down Highway 64. (Courtesy of Fred W. Harrison Jr.)

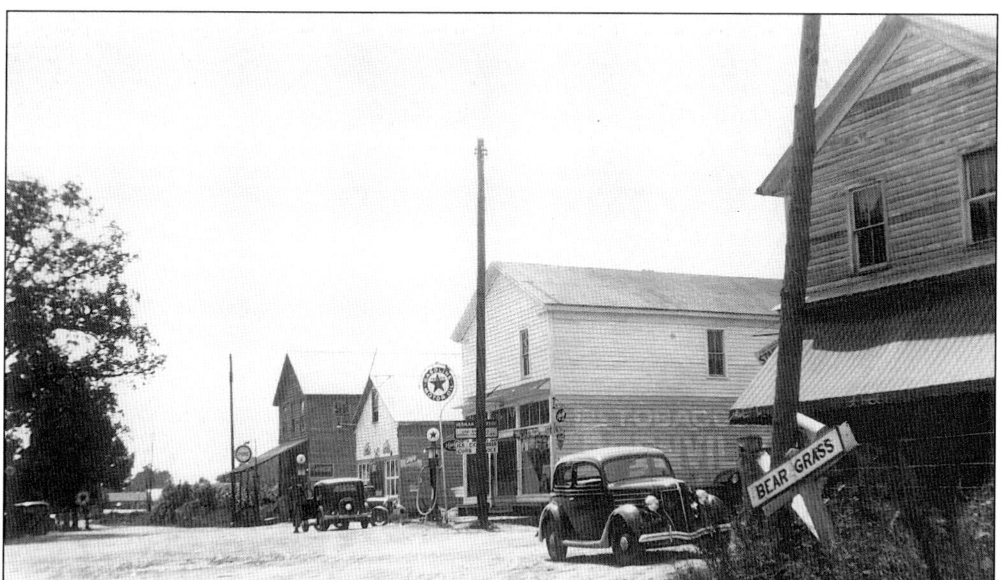

THE TOWN OF BEAR GRASS, 1937. The town was incorporated in 1909, on land belonging to W. Reddick Roberson. Roberson became the town's first mayor. (Courtesy of Fred W. Harrison Jr.)

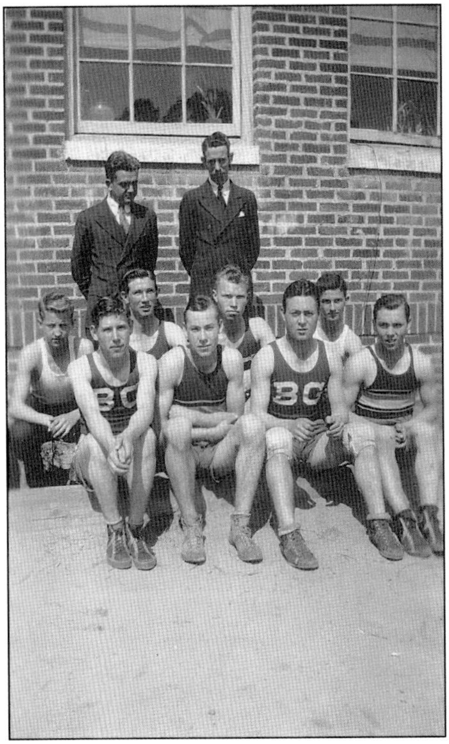

THE BEAR GRASS HIGH SCHOOL BASKETBALL TEAM, c. 1935. Pictured here, from left to right, are as follows: (front row) Hildreth Rogerson, Elbert Rawls, Leon Hall Rawls, and J.C. Rawls; (middle row) Leon Rogers, Benard Harrison, Joseph Keel, and Dan Peel; (standing) Principal Hickman and Coach Martin. (Courtesy of the Francis Manning Room.)

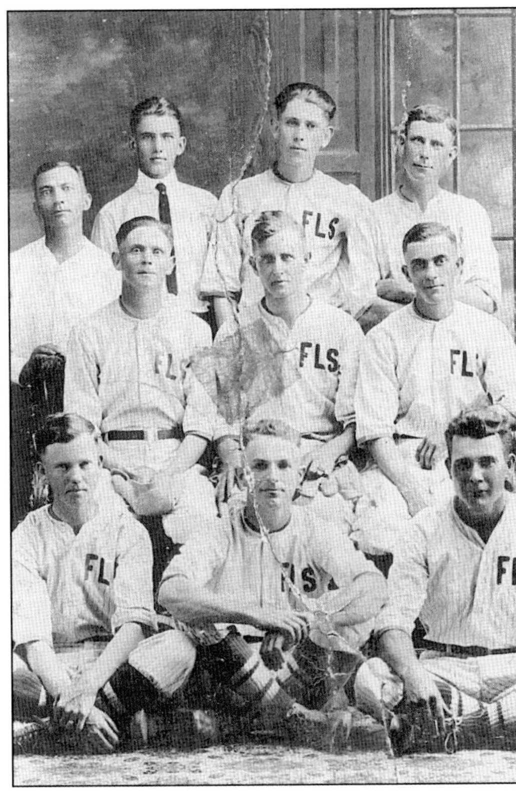

THE FARM LIFE SCHOOL BASEBALL TEAM, c. 1920. Pictured, from left to right, are as follows: (front row) Carl Griffin, Alfred Ellis, and Monroe Holliday; (middle row) Albert Gurkin, Prof Smithe (coach), and Perlie Lilley; (back row) Jessie Lilley, Daniel Peel, Johnnie Gurkin, and Jimmy Gurkin. (Courtesy of Chloe G. Tuttle.)

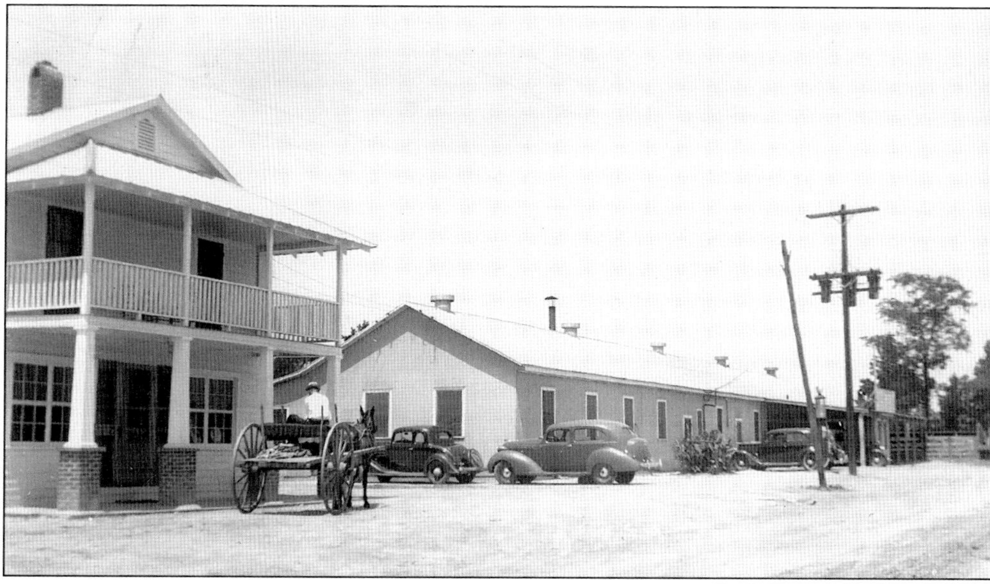

Roberson Slaughter House, 1937. Located on McCaskey Road near the railroad crossing just west of Williamston, this slaughterhouse was later purchased by Russell Griffin and George Peel, who renamed it he Williamston Packing Company. (Courtesy of Francis Manning Room.)

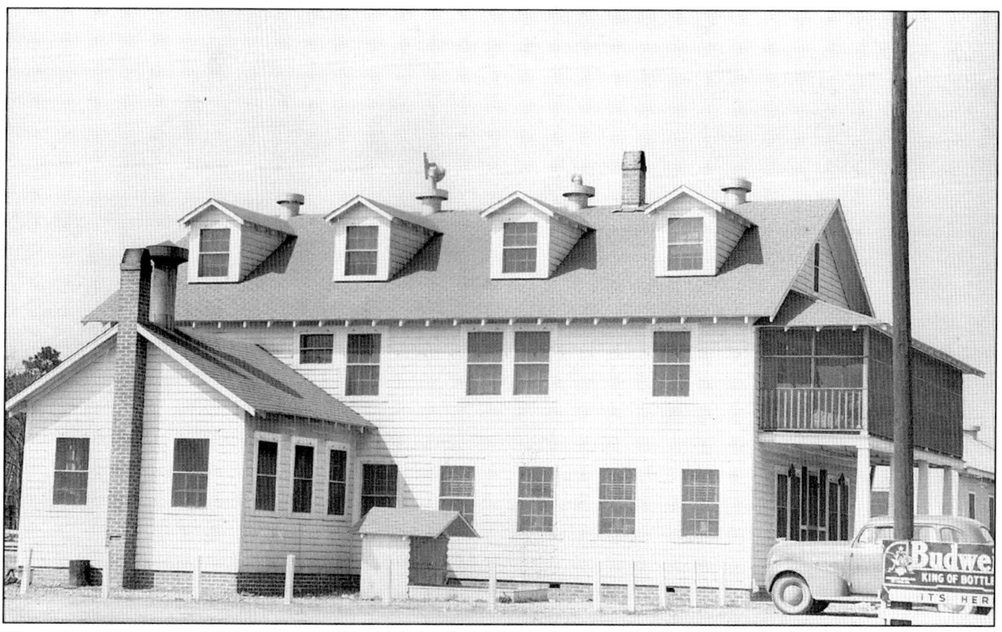

The Switch, c. 1950. In 1937, D.M. Roberson built this boarding house and restaurant mainly to serve employees of Roberson Slaughter House. It soon became a popular eating establishment in the county and continued to operate until the late 1960s. (Courtesy of the Francis Manning Room.)

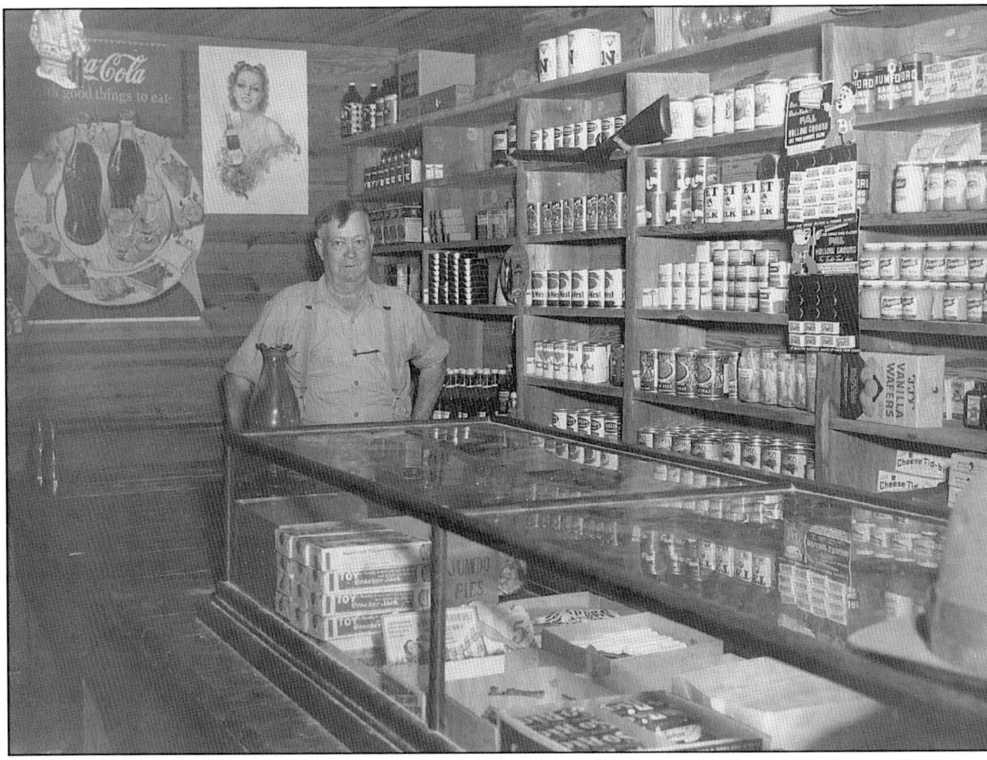

THE BIG MILL STORE IN WILLIAMS TOWNSHIP, C. 1950S. This store was part of the old Daniel and Staton Mill (later called Big Mill). The mill went out of business in the 1930s and during its early life was a popular swimming hole for Williamston folk. Members of the James family, including Mr. James (pictured), operated the store in later years. (Courtesy of the Francis Manning Room.)

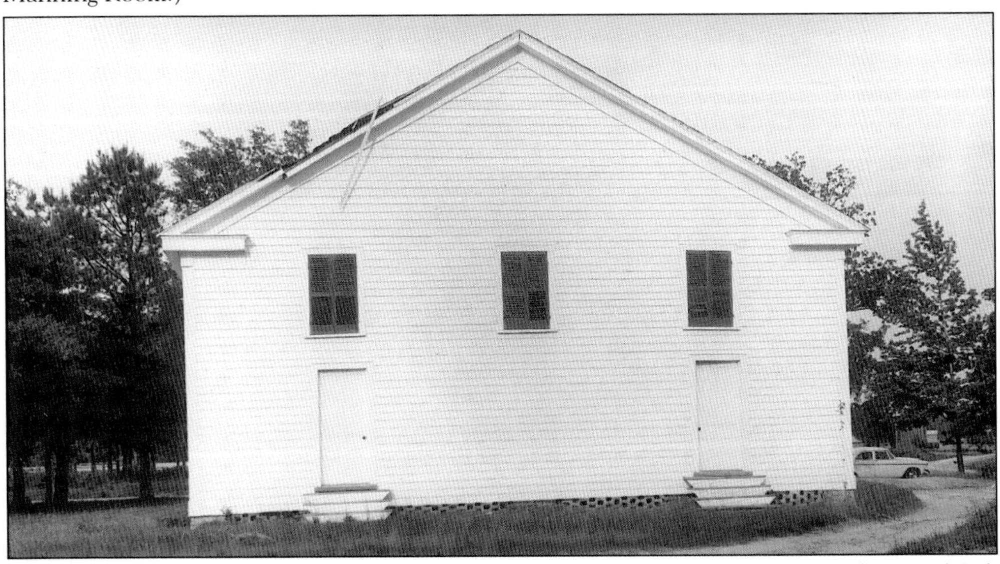

CONOHO PRIMITIVE BAPTIST CHURCH. Built c. 1850, this church was located northwest of Oak City. It was torn down sometime after 1970, when the last services were held there. (Courtesy of the Francis Manning Room.)

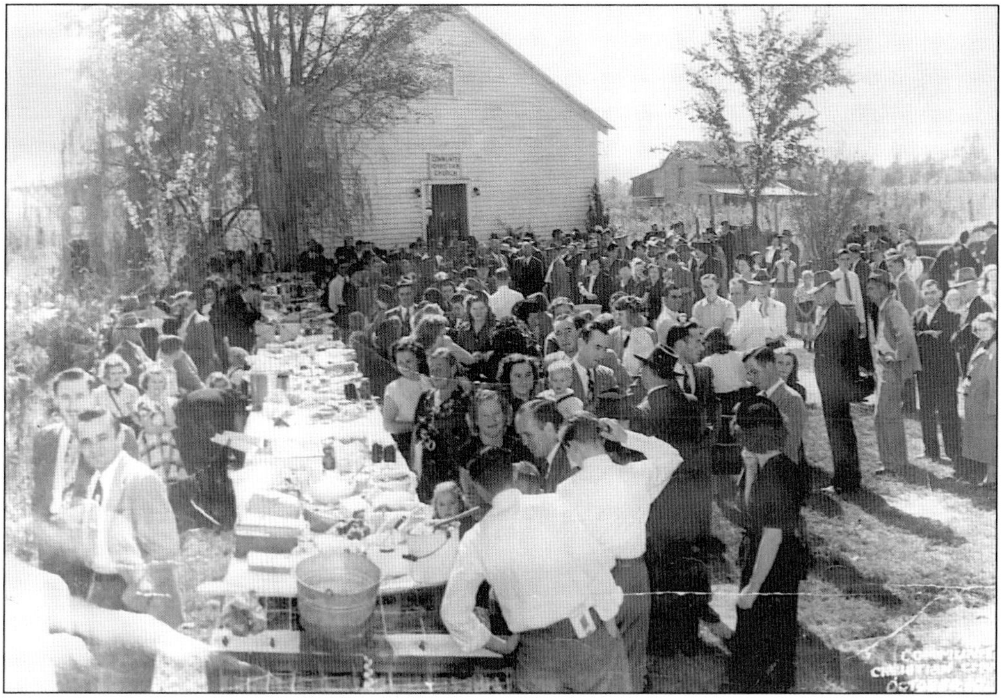

HOMECOMING AT COMMUNITY CHRISTIAN CHURCH, 1948. Located on Highway 125 between Williamston and Hamilton, this building was later enlarged in the 1950s and eventually replaced by an expansive brick structure. (Courtesy of the Francis Manning Room.)

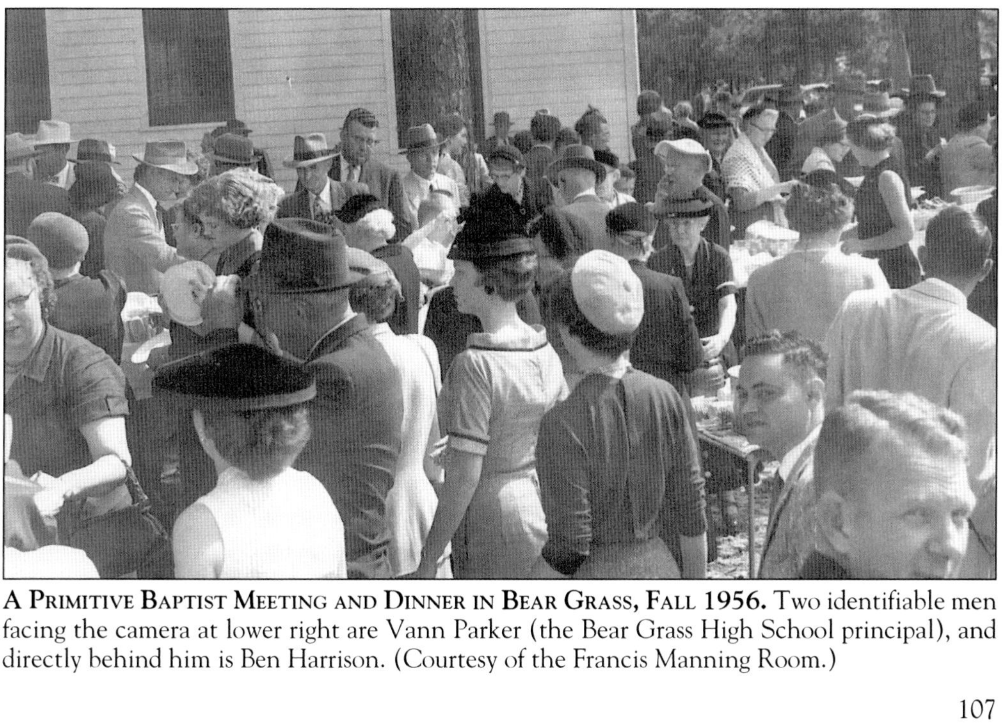

A PRIMITIVE BAPTIST MEETING AND DINNER IN BEAR GRASS, FALL 1956. Two identifiable men facing the camera at lower right are Vann Parker (the Bear Grass High School principal), and directly behind him is Ben Harrison. (Courtesy of the Francis Manning Room.)

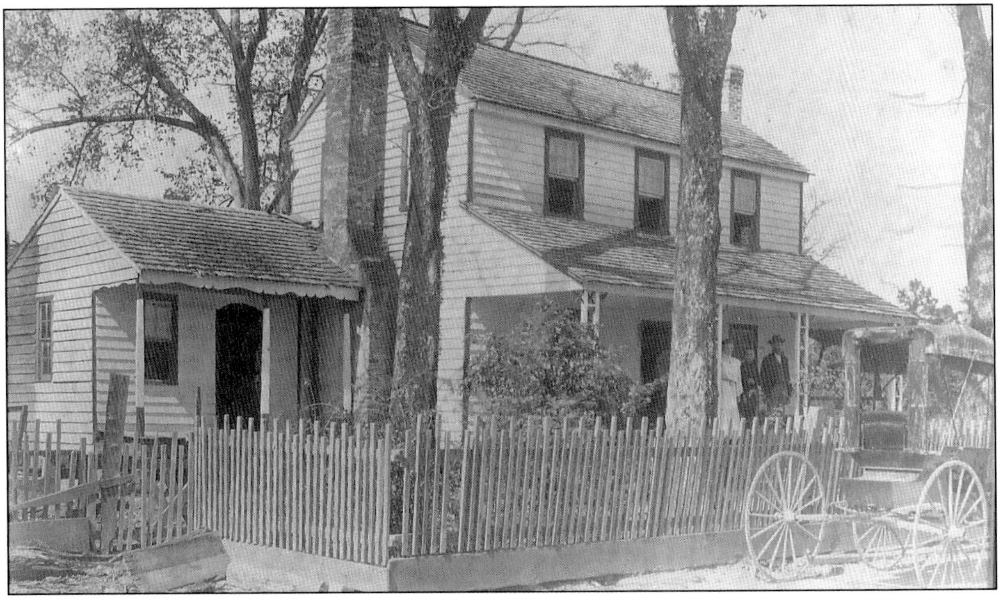

The John Gray Corey Homestead, c. 1892. Those pictured are thought to be, from left to right, Lucy Corey, Anna Corey, and John Gray Corey. (Courtesy of Chloe G. Tuttle.)

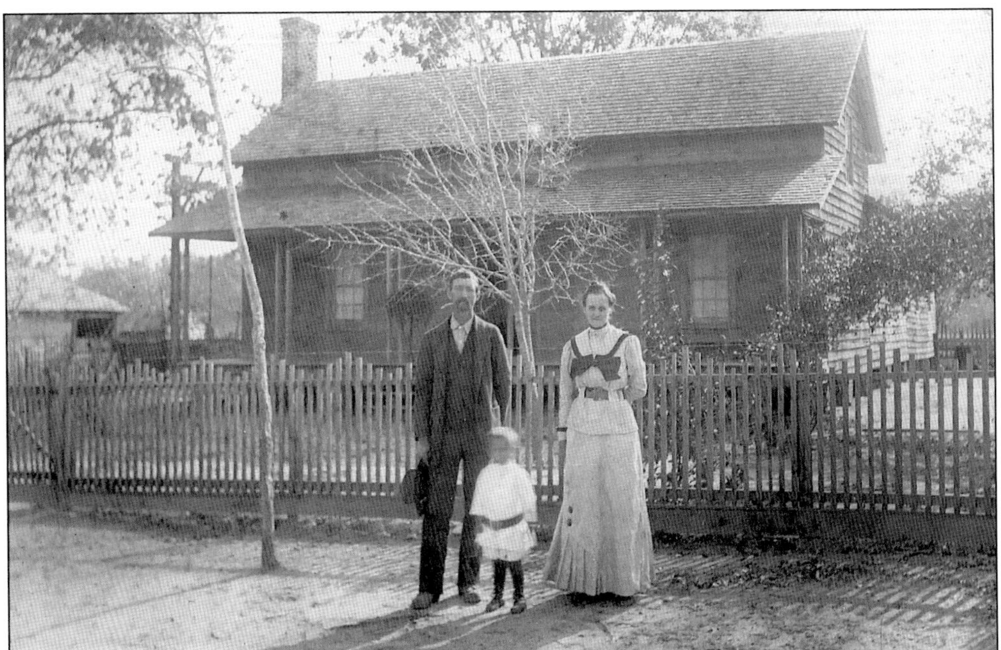

The Alfred Gray Griffin Homestead, c. 1914. Pictured here are Alfred and Sally Griffin and child. (Courtesy of Chloe G. Tuttle.)

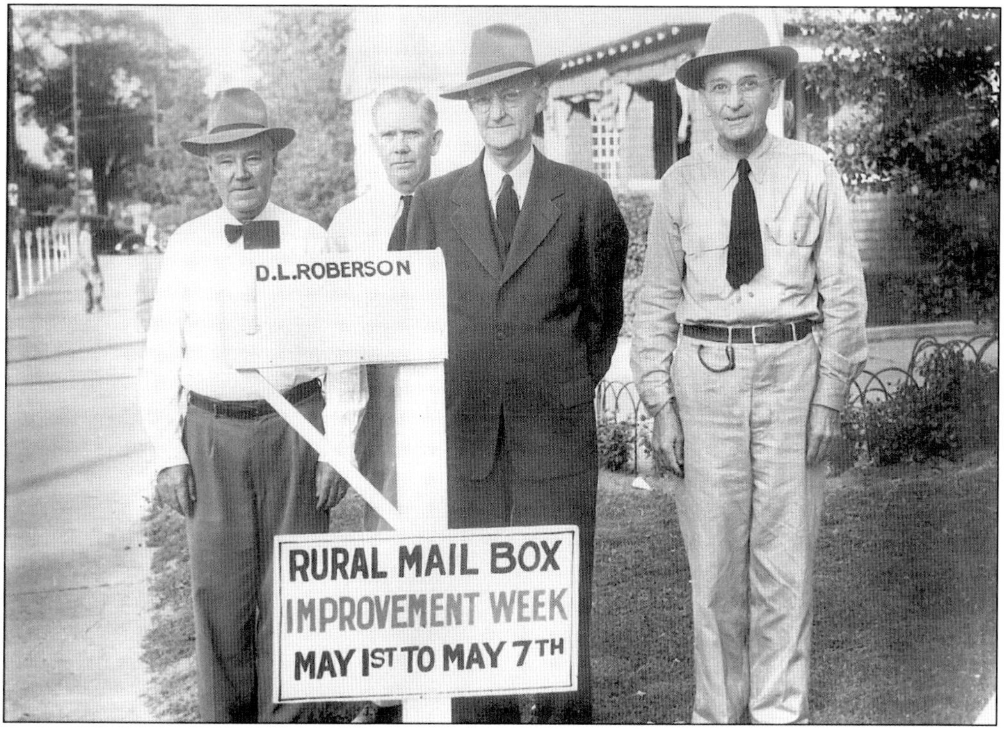

MARTIN COUNTY RURAL FREE DELIVERY (R.F.D.) CARRIERS, C. 1950S. Pictured from left to right are Arthur White, Robert Leggett, W.E. Dunn (postmaster), and John A. Ward. (Courtesy of the Francis Manning Room.)

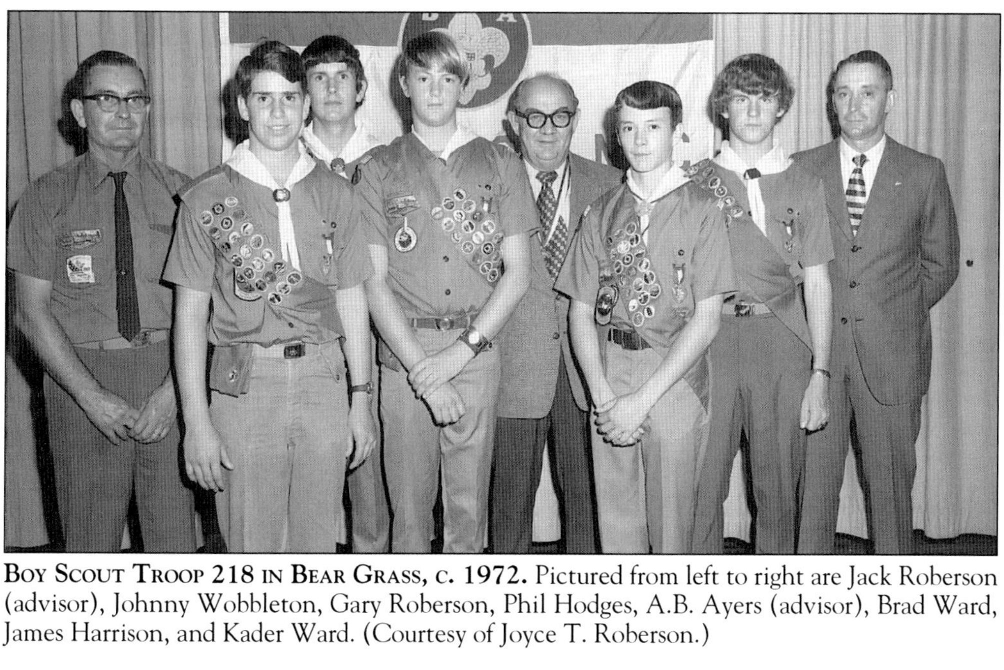

BOY SCOUT TROOP 218 IN BEAR GRASS, C. 1972. Pictured from left to right are Jack Roberson (advisor), Johnny Wobbleton, Gary Roberson, Phil Hodges, A.B. Ayers (advisor), Brad Ward, James Harrison, and Kader Ward. (Courtesy of Joyce T. Roberson.)

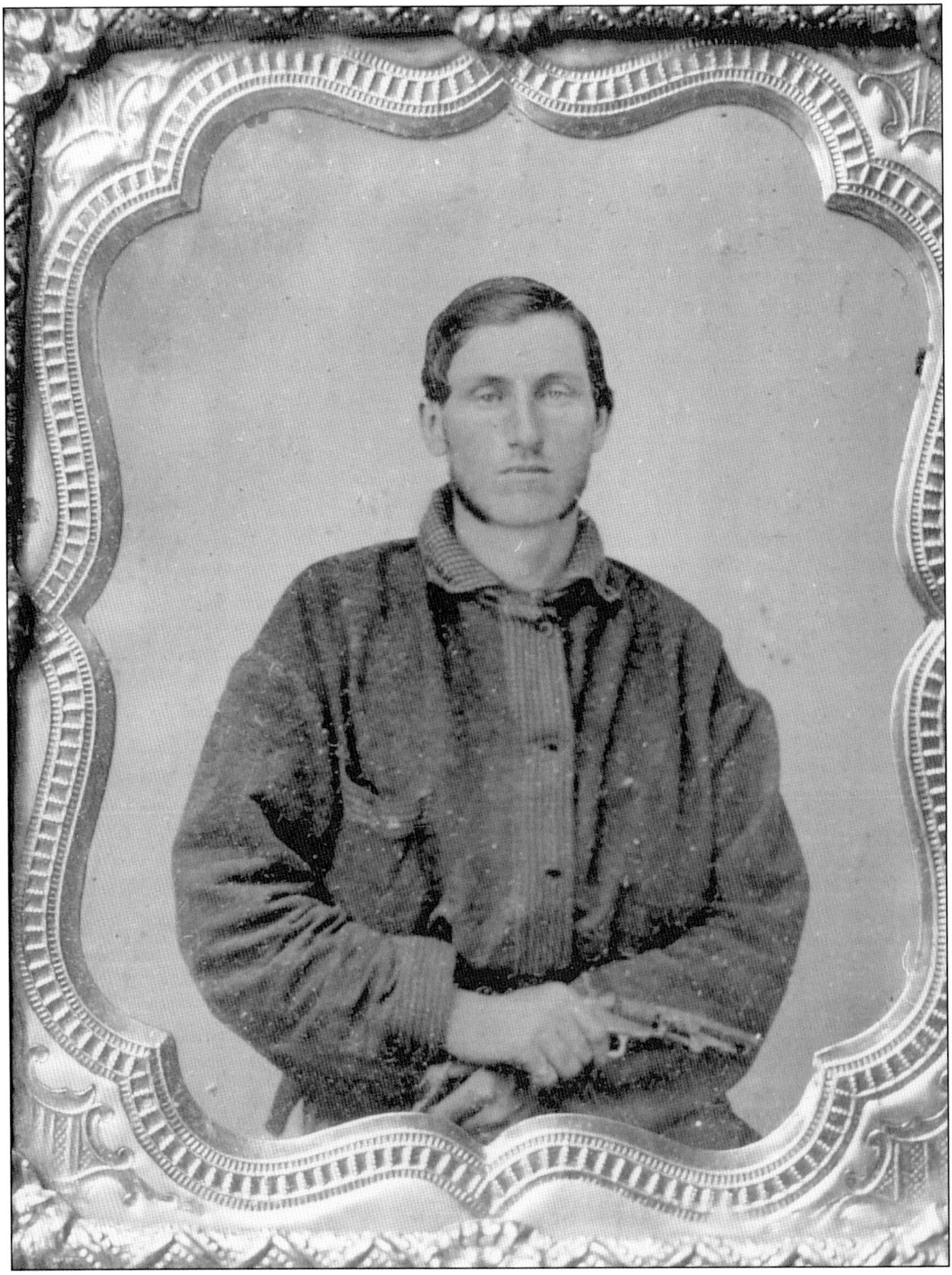

WILLIAMSTON AREA RESIDENT JOHN HARRELL IN CIVIL WAR UNIFORM, C. 1865. (Courtesy of Ann H. McKeel.)

Six

MARTIN COUNTY PEOPLE

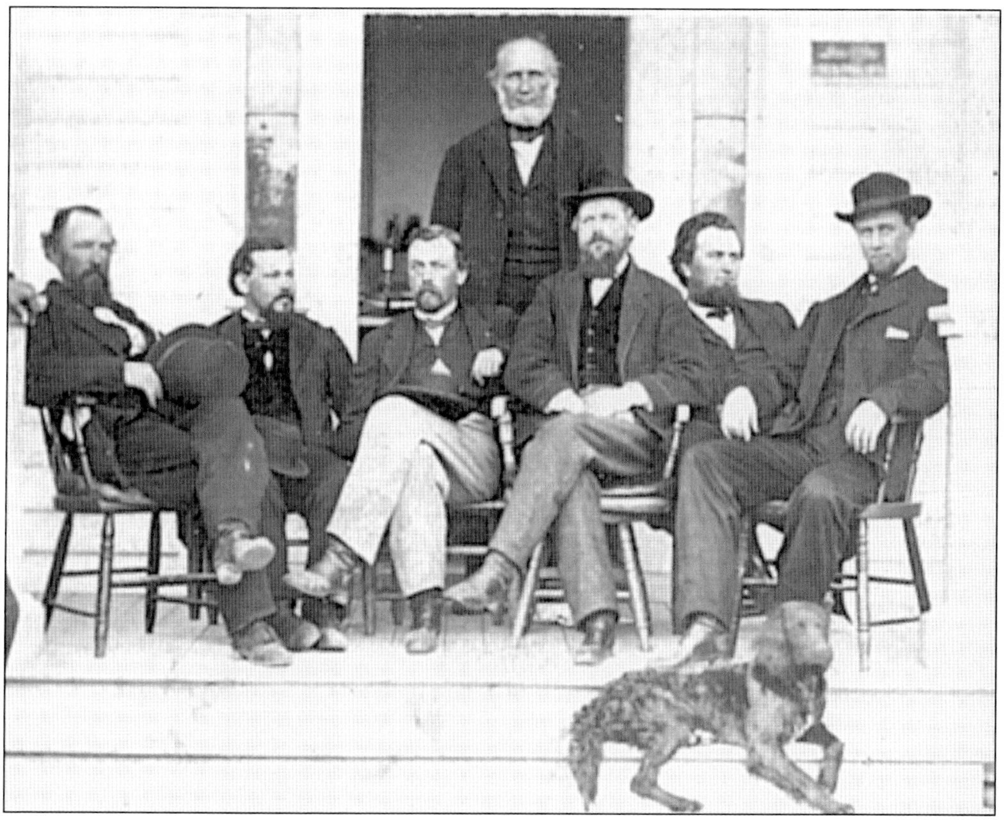

JUDGE ASA BIGGS, C. 1875. This photo was taken from the Biggs family album that is now owned by the Martin County Historical Society. Biggs is standing at center, on the porch of what is noted in the album as being the old homeplace. Biggs was a U.S. congressman and judge and later a Confederate States judge from Williamston. The political climate after the Civil War forced him to give up politics and a legal practice. Biggs turned his home in Williamston over to his daughter Cottie Biggs Crawford and moved to Norfolk, Virginia. There he spent the rest of his life as a commission merchant with his brother Kader. (Courtesy Francis Manning Room.)

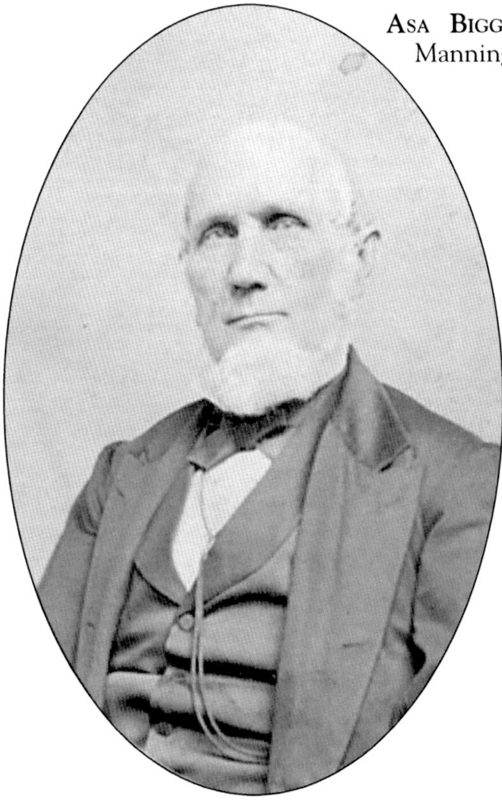

Asa Biggs (1811–1878). (Courtesy of the Francis Manning Room.)

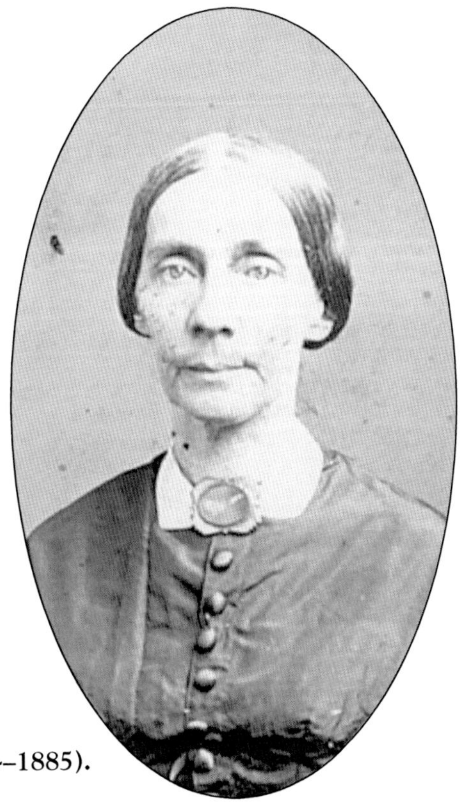

Martha A. Biggs, the Wife of Asa Biggs (1814–1885). (Courtesy of the Francis Manning Room.)

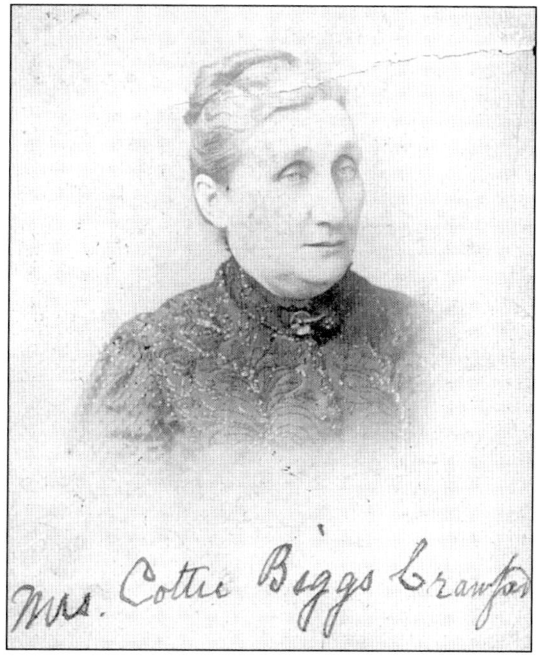

MARTHA COTTON BIGGS CRAWFORD, C. 1880. One of eight children reared by Judge Asa Biggs and his wife, Martha Andrews Biggs, Martha Cotton Biggs Crawford (or "Cottie" as she was called) inherited the family home on Church Street in Williamston. Her husband, W.T. Crawford, served as Martin County sheriff from 1860 to 1868. (Courtesy of the Francis Manning Room.)

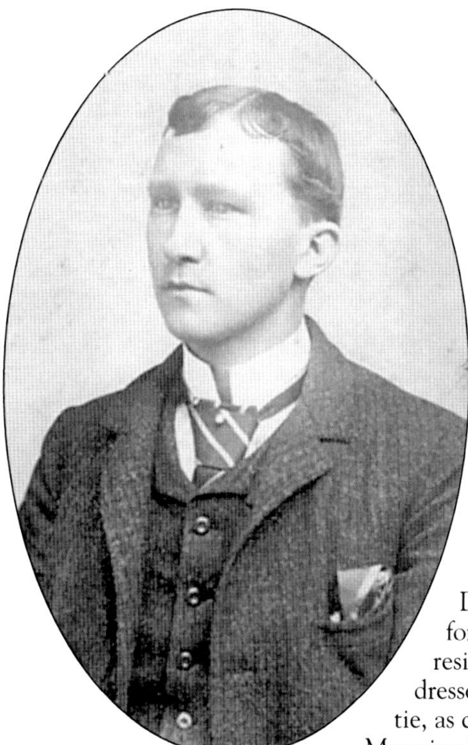

ASA TOM CRAWFORD, C. 1895. The son of W.T. and Cottie Biggs Crawford, Asa Tom Crawford married Pattie Biggs, the eldest daughter of John D. and Fannie Biggs, and became a bookkeeper for the Dennis Simmons Lumber Company. Older residents of Williamston recall him as being well dressed—he always wore a diamond stick pin on his tie, as can be seen in this photo. (Courtesy of the Francis Manning Room.)

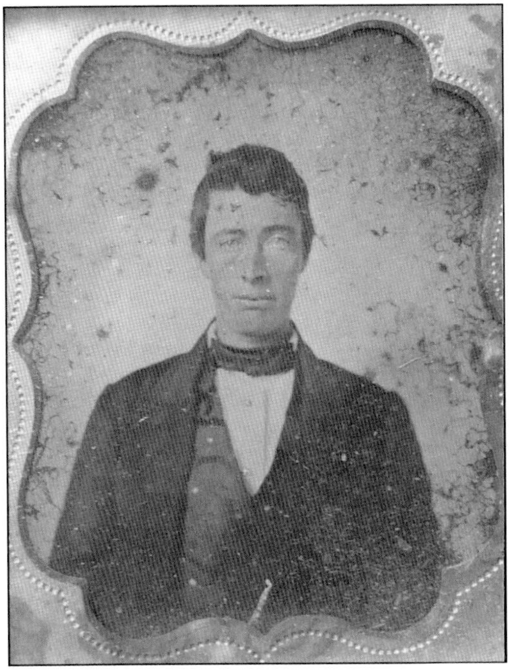

JOHN BIGGS HARRISON II (1848–1912). The son of John Biggs and Frances Biggs Harrison, John Biggs Harrison II, along with his brothers Asa and Jim, operated a family lumber and grist mill on Bear Grass Swamp. From about 1780 until 1900, this business stood as a center for trade and social gatherings in the Bear Grass community, prior to the establishment of the town of Bear Grass in 1909. The mill, referred to in later years as the Fanny Harrison or Harris Mill, was named for Harrison's mother, Frances Biggs Harrison, and continued to operate until 1911. Harrison was the grandson of James Harrison (1767–1840), an early founder of the Bear Grass community. (Courtesy of Fred W. Harrison Jr.)

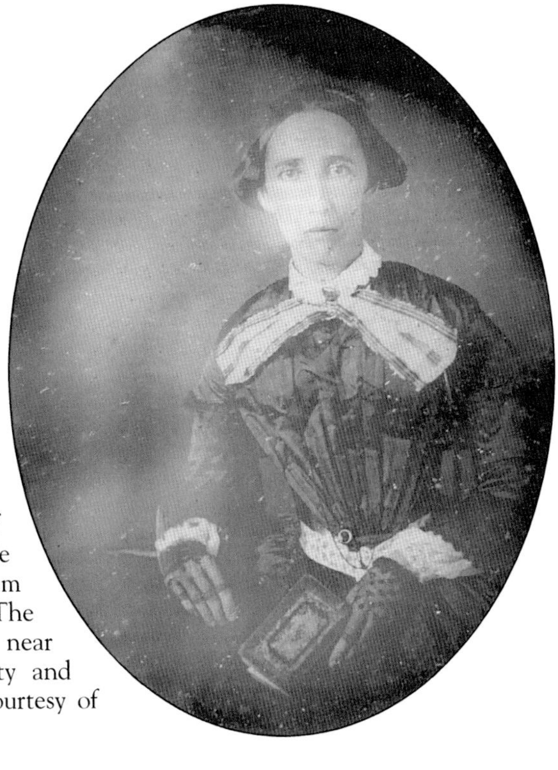

PENNY SLADE, C. 1860S. This well-dressed young woman is thought to be Fannie Penelope Slade, the daughter of William and Penelope Williams Slade and the granddaughter of Col. William Williams, the founder of Williamston. The Slades owned extensive farm interests near Williamston and were active in county and state affairs during the last century. (Courtesy of Ann H. McKeel.)

CORDELLA HASSELL SLADE, C. 1880S. The daughter of Cushing Biggs Hassell and his wife Martha Jewett, Cordella married William (Buck) Slade, a farmer and Williamston merchant. (Courtesy of the Francis Manning Room.)

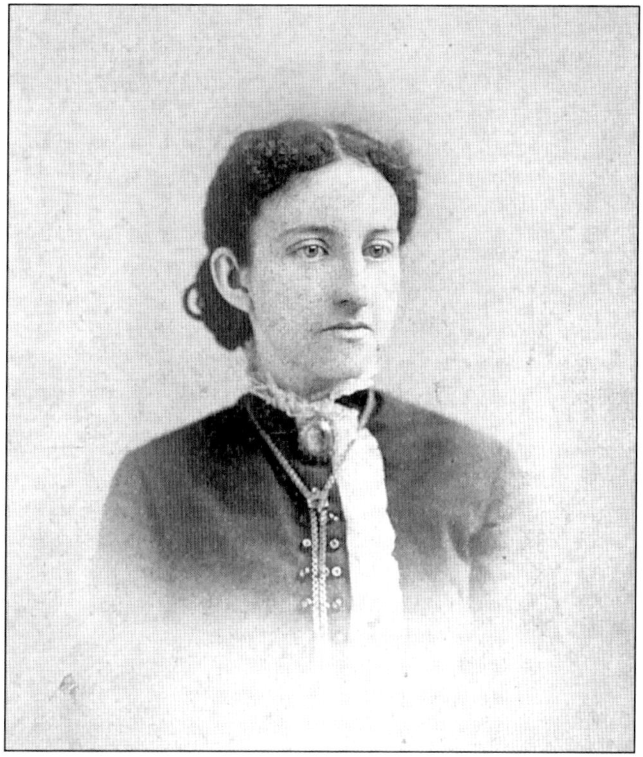

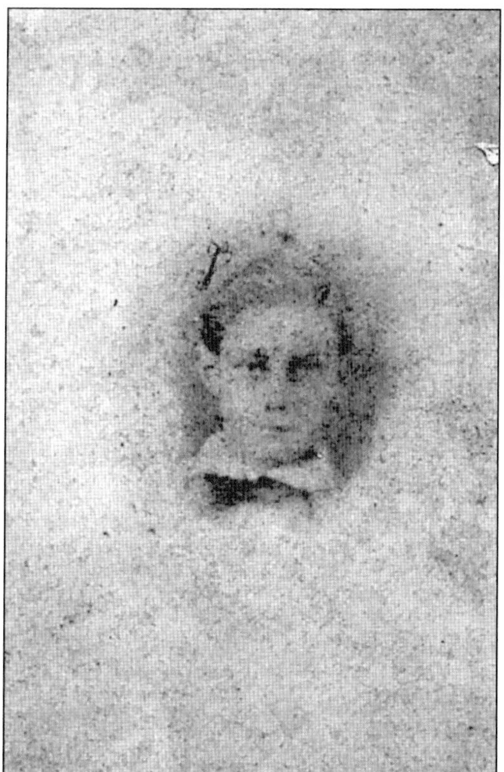

HENRY BIGGS, C. 1860S. Enlisted in the Civil War at age 17, Henry was wounded the day before Lee's surrender and later died on April 12, 1865. He was one of the two sons of Asa and Martha A. Biggs. (Courtesy of the Francis Manning Room.)

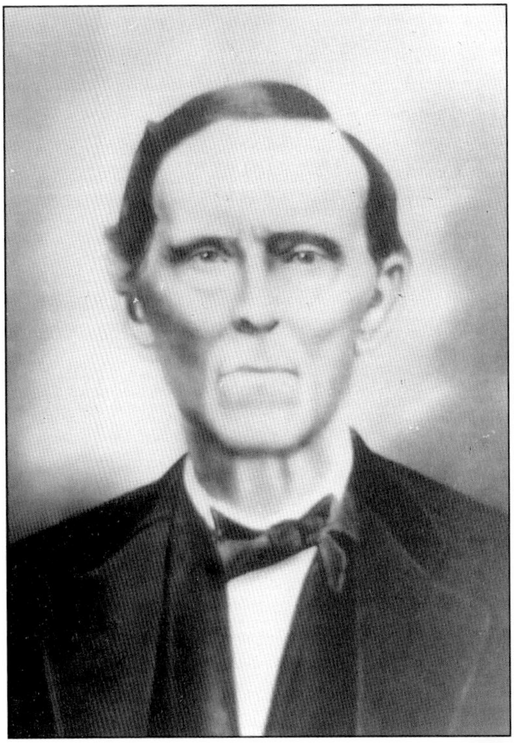

William Turner Mizelle (1847–1927). A resident of the Poplar Chapel community near Jamesville, Mizelle was the father of William Henderson Mizelle, a local educator and later founder of the *Weekly Herald* in Robersonville. (Courtesy of Fred W. Harrison Jr.)

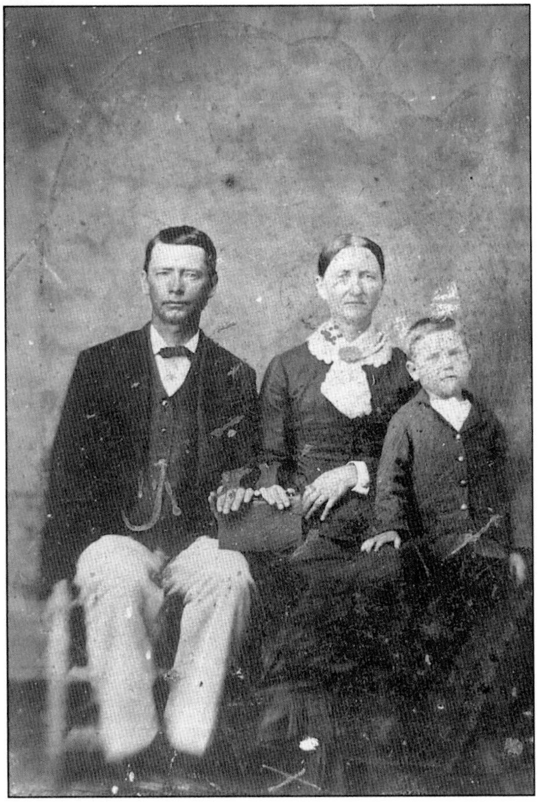

A Peal Family Portrait, Bear Grass Township, c. 1890. Pictured are William Daniel Peal (1842–1914), Sarah Frances Howell Peal (1841–1895), and their son, George Alonzo Peal. William Daniel was a highly respected farmer in the Bear Grass area. (Courtesy of Frances P. Whitley.)

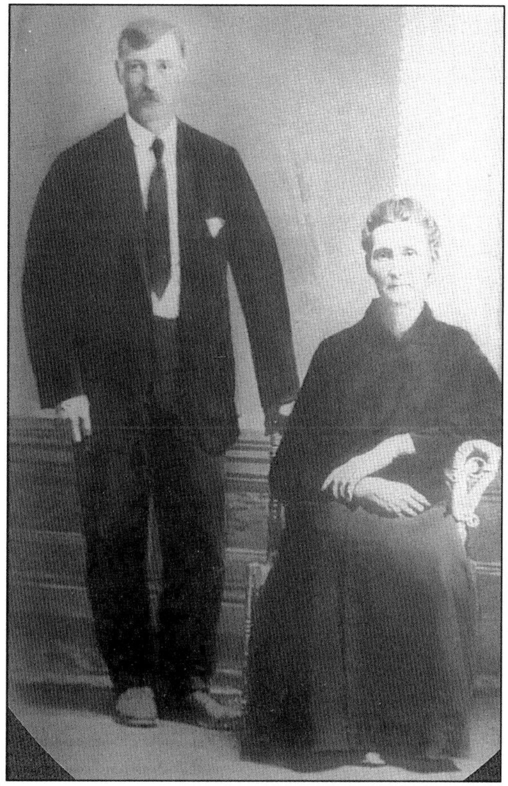

ROBERT W. AND EMMA GRIFFIN PERRY, C. 1900. A well-known building contractor, Robert (Bob) Perry temporarily left his farming interests in Martin County during the late 1890s and moved his family to a former resort hotel near Roper, North Carolina. There, he helped supervise construction of the first railroad bridge to cross the Albemarle between Roper and Edenton, North Carolina. (Courtesy of Fred W. Harrison Jr.)

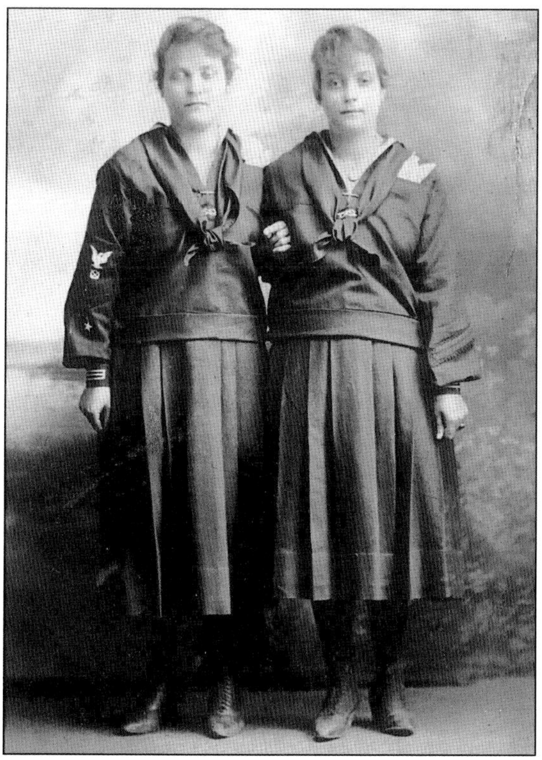

STELLA AND ZATIE ANDREWS, C. 1915. These twin sisters were the daughters of Mr. and Mrs. Sam Andrews of the Holly Spring Church community in Williams Township. (Courtesy of Clarence Pate.)

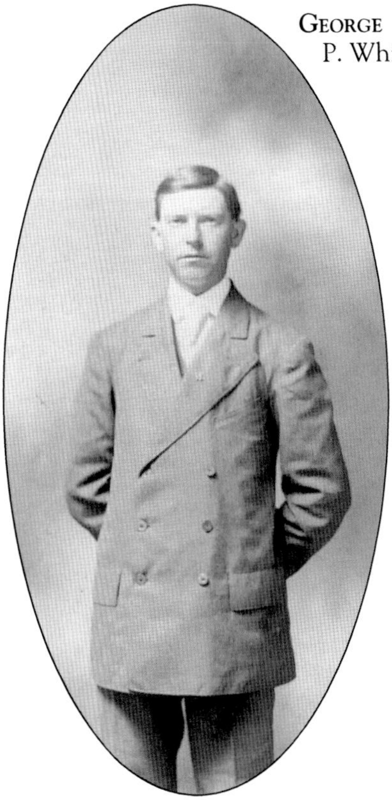

George Alonzo Peal (1878–1950). (Courtesy of Frances P. Whitley.)

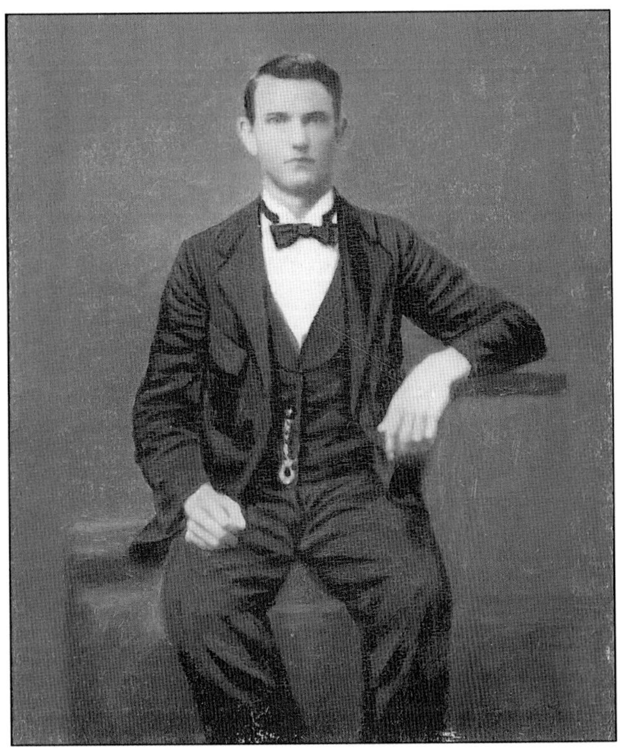

George Alonzo Williams (1875–1941). Williams resided and farmed in the "islands" section of Williams Township. (Courtesy of Sallie H. Long.)

MARY ELIZABETH ROBERSON WILLIAMS (1884–1961). Mary Williams was the wife of George A. Williams of Williams Township. (Courtesy of Sallie H. Long.)

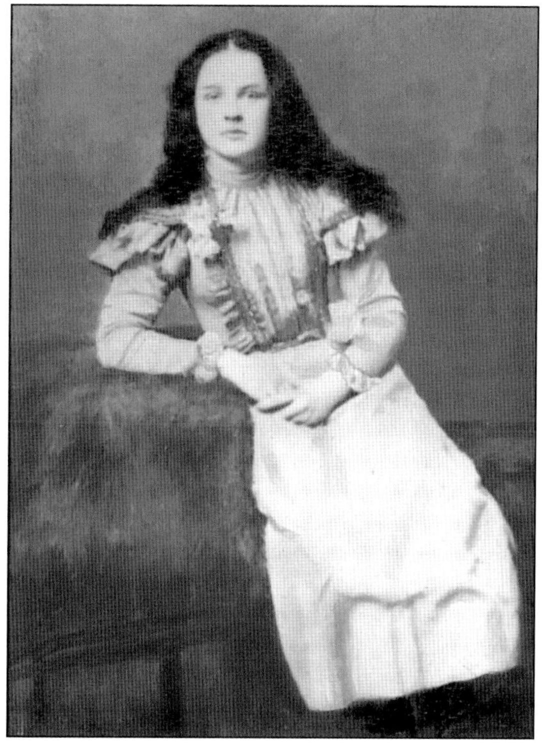

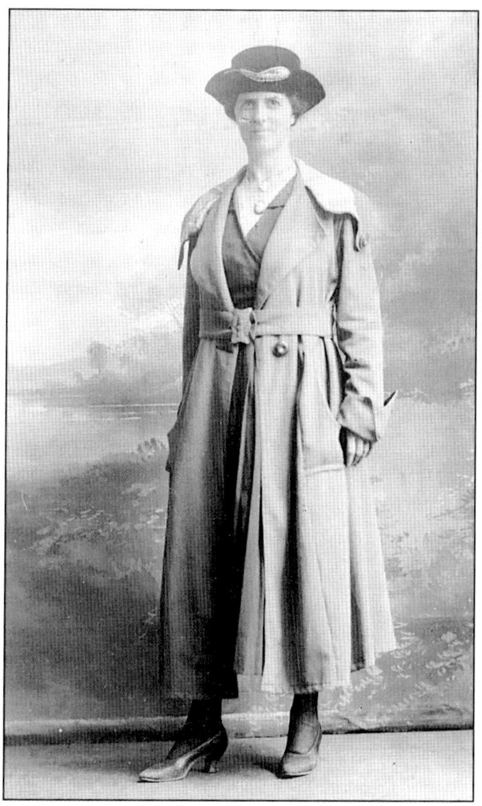

MAUDE LILLEY POWELL PEAL (1888–1958). A Bear Grass Township resident, Maude was the wife of George A. Peal and the daughter of James Allen Powell of the Gold Point community of Martin County. (Courtesy of Frances P. Whitley.)

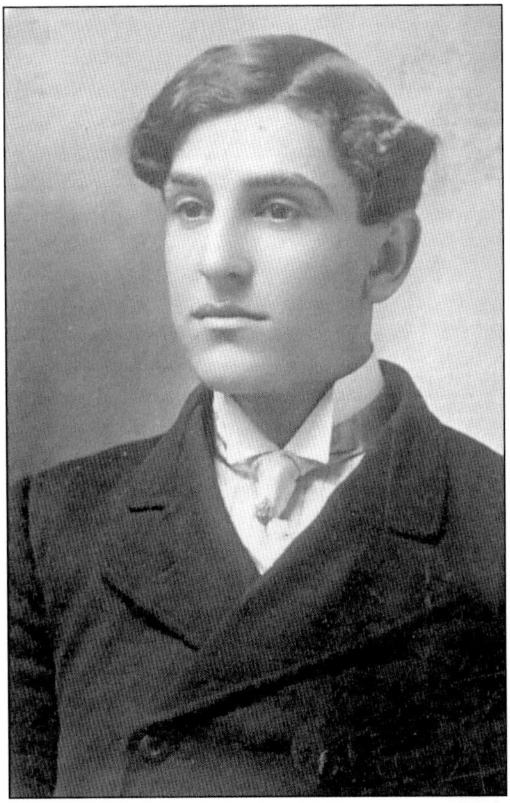

LOUIS CUSHING HARRISON (1886–1912). A bookkeeper for Harrison Brothers store in Williamston, Louis died at an early age from typhoid fever. His wife Anna maintained a business of her own for many years; it was known as the Harrison Shoppe. (Courtesy of Ann H. McKeel.)

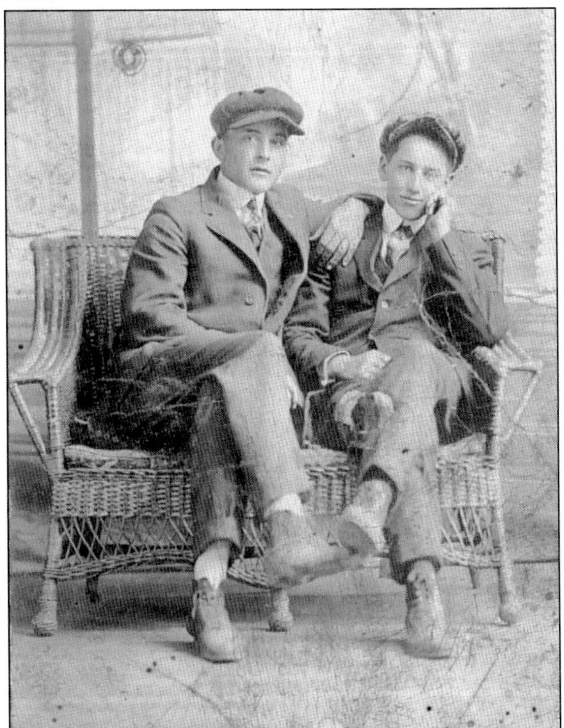

TOMMY LAWRENCE ROBERSON AND GILBERT ROGERSON, BEAR GRASS, C. 1917. Roberson was the son of Reddick Roberson, a founder of the town of Bear Grass. (Courtesy of Joyce T. Roberson.)

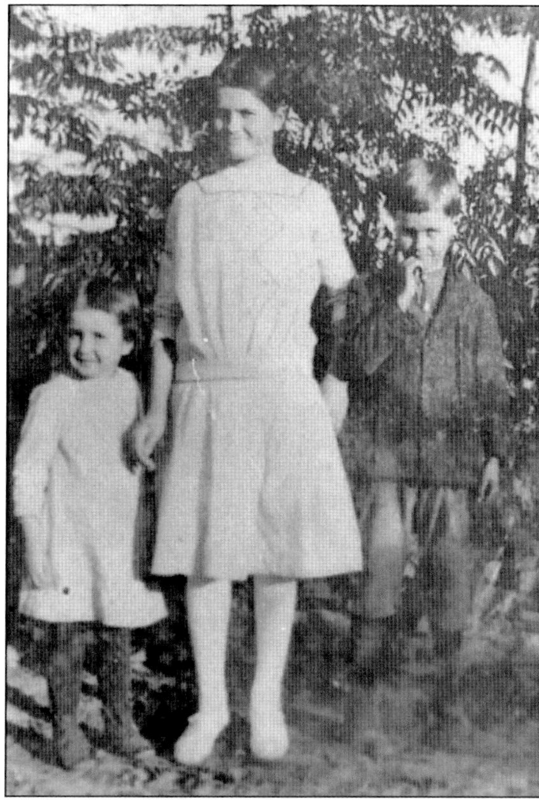

WILLARD, CREOLA, AND JOHN THOMAS HARRISON, C. 1914. The children of John Biggs and Harriet R. Harrison, these Bear Grass area youths pose for a Sunday afternoon picture, c. 1914. (Courtesy of Fred W. Harrison Jr.)

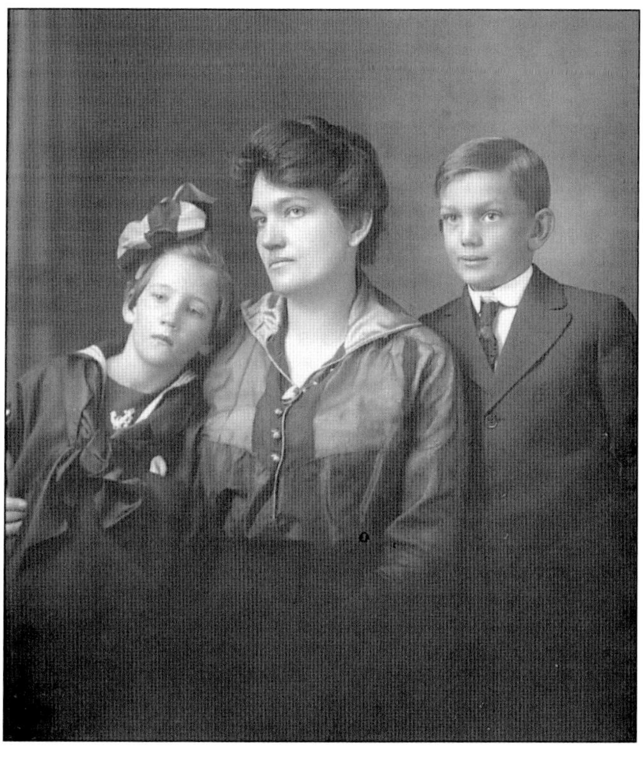

THE LOVETTE BIGGS HARRISON FAMILY OF WILLIAMSTON, C. 1915. Pictured here are Hattie Harrell Harrison and her children, Evelyn and Bill. (Courtesy of Ann H. McKeel.)

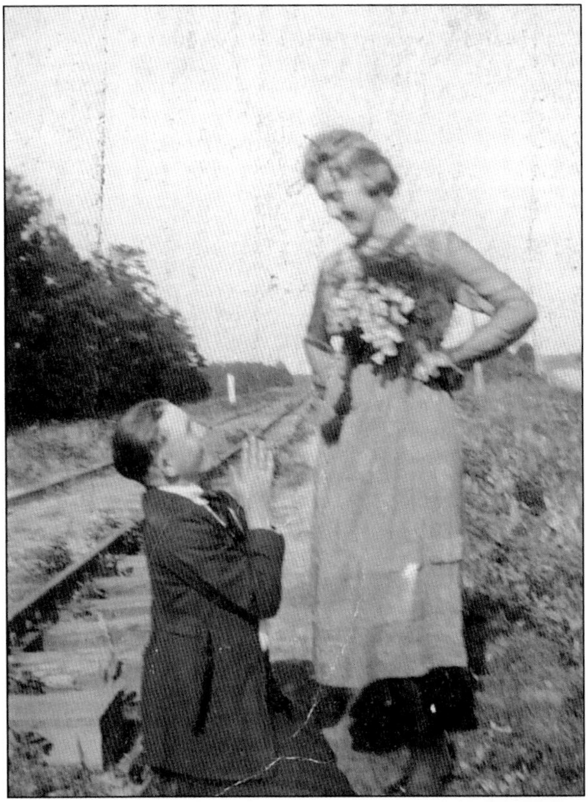

Vance L. Roberson and Myrtle Green, c. 1926. This photo is thought to have been taken of the couple sometime prior to their marriage on November 23, 1926. The area shown is possibly the railroad tracks leading to Parmele. (Courtesy of Patsy R. Miller.)

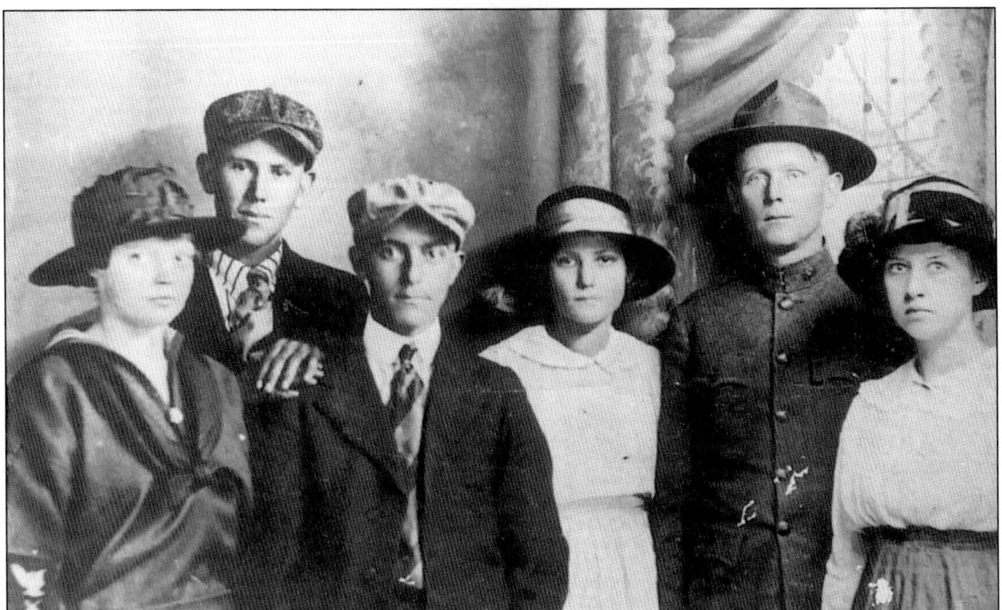

A Gathering of Friends, c. 1919. This group from the Griffins Township area poses for the camera during World War I. Pictured from left to right are Margaret Manning, Johnny Gurkin, Perlie Lilley, Callie Gurkin, Albert Gurkin, and Rosa Griffin. (Courtesy of Chloe G. Tuttle.)

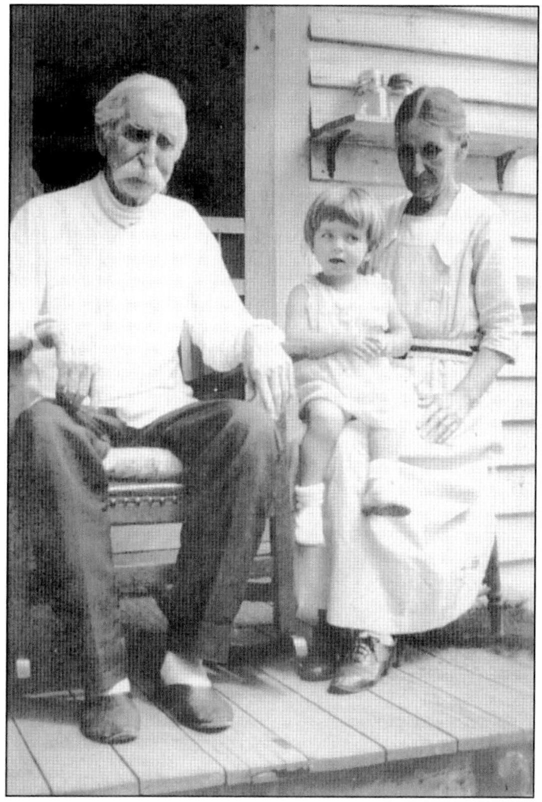

The Godwin Family of Williamston, c. Late 1920s. Pictured are Ben F. Godwin, his wife Emma, and granddaughter Mary Charles Godwin. Ben F. Godwin served several terms as the mayor of Williamston during the early 1900s. (Courtesy of Mary Charles G. Coppage.)

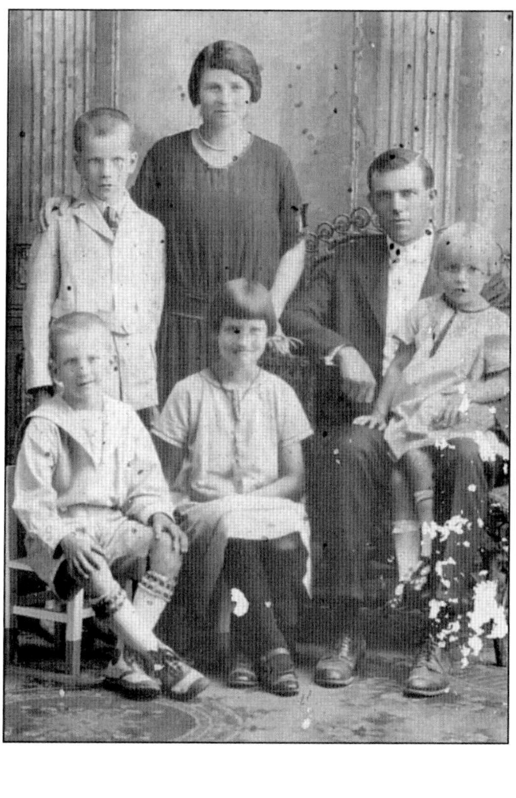

The Lee Hardison Family of the Holly Spring Community, Williams Township, c. 1925. (Courtesy of Sallie H. Long.)

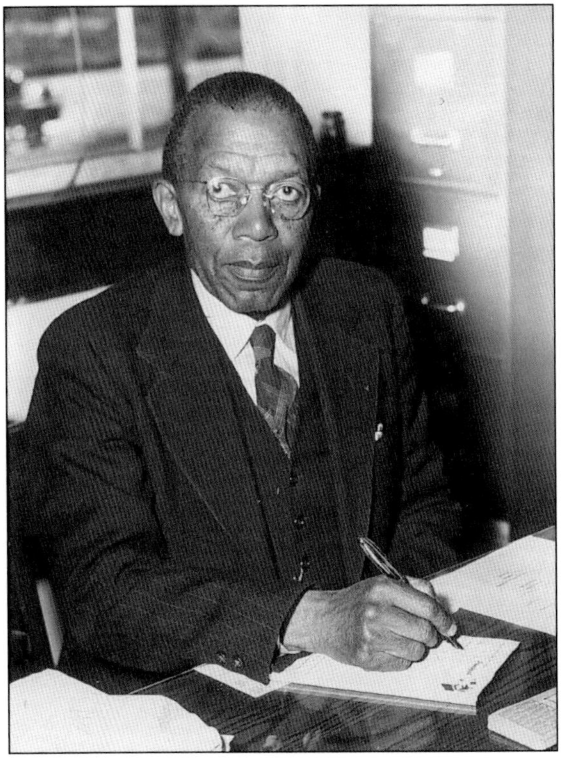

W.C. CHANCE, C. 1950. Chance was a noted Martin County educator and civic leader from the town of Parmele in Martin County. He is credited with founding what later became the W.C. Chance School. (Courtesy of the Francis Manning Room.)

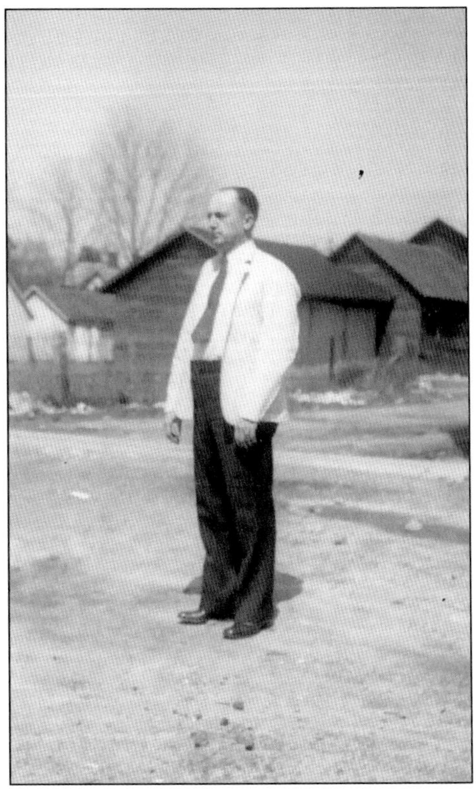

EUGENE RICE, C. 1950. Rice was a well-known photographer in Martin County and a member of the staff at Davis Pharmacy in Williamston. Many of the photographs now housed in the Francis Manning Room at Martin Community College are attributed to him. Rice is seen here at his native home in Danville, Virginia. (Courtesy of the Francis Manning Room.)

CARREY MOORE, A FORMER SLAVE, 1935. A Jamesville native, Moore was born in 1855 on the Ball Gray farm owned by Clayton Moore Sr., located just below the town of Jamesville. This photograph was featured in the local *Enterprise* and *Weekly Herald* newspapers in 1935, along with a personal account of Carrey Moore's life. (Courtesy of the Francis Manning Room.)

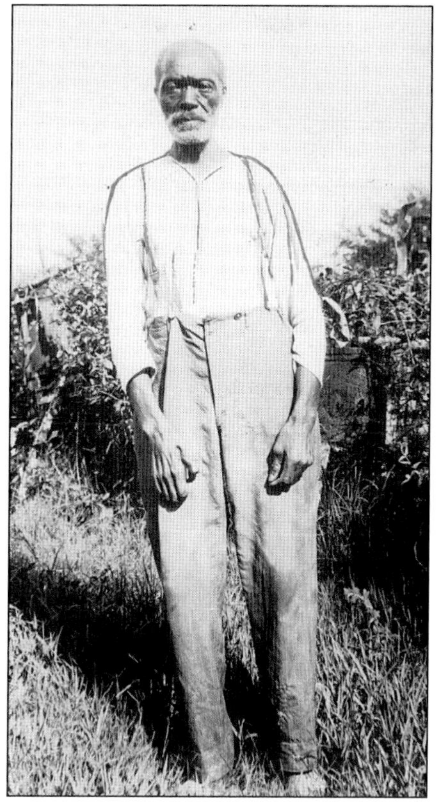

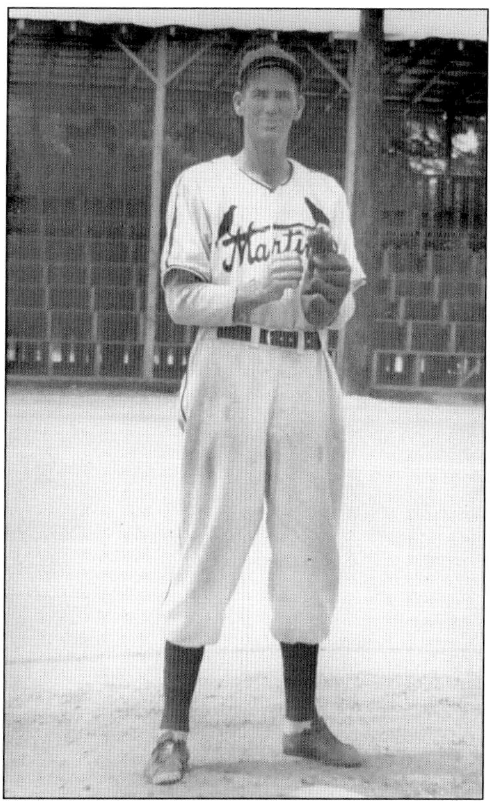

SLIM GARDNER, C. 1930s. Gardner was a star baseball player for the Williamston Martins, a semi-pro team in the Coastal Plain League during the 1930s. (Courtesy of the Francis Manning Room.)

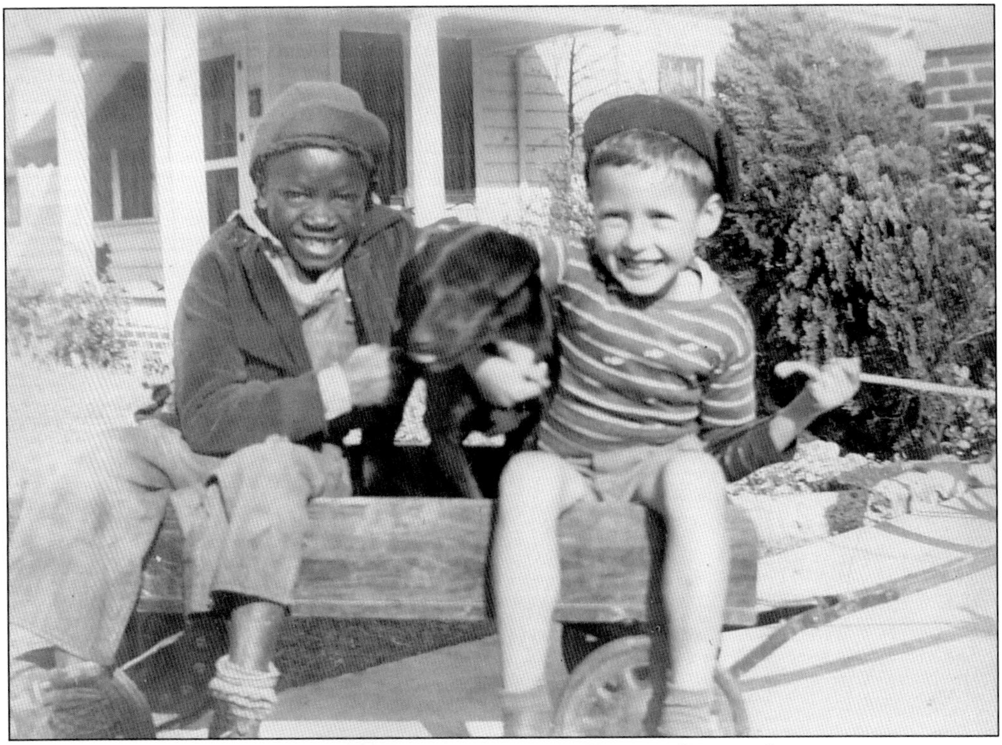

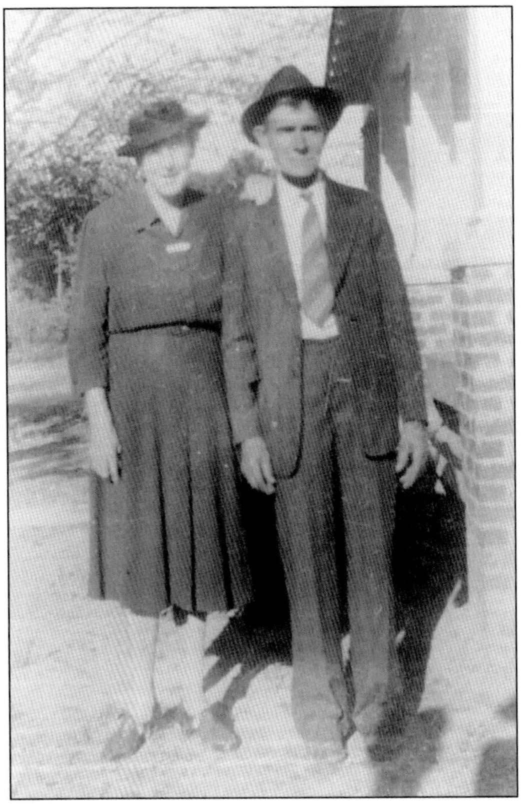

A Warren Street Scene in Williamston, c. Mid-1940s. This memorable picture taken by Elizabeth Weston Brantley shows her son Clayton Weston (at right), dog Mac, and friend Fred Hagen at play on Warren Street. (Courtesy of the Francis Manning Room.)

Mr. and Mrs. Robert D. Jones of Williams Township, c. 1945. (Courtesy of Alma J. Bailey.)

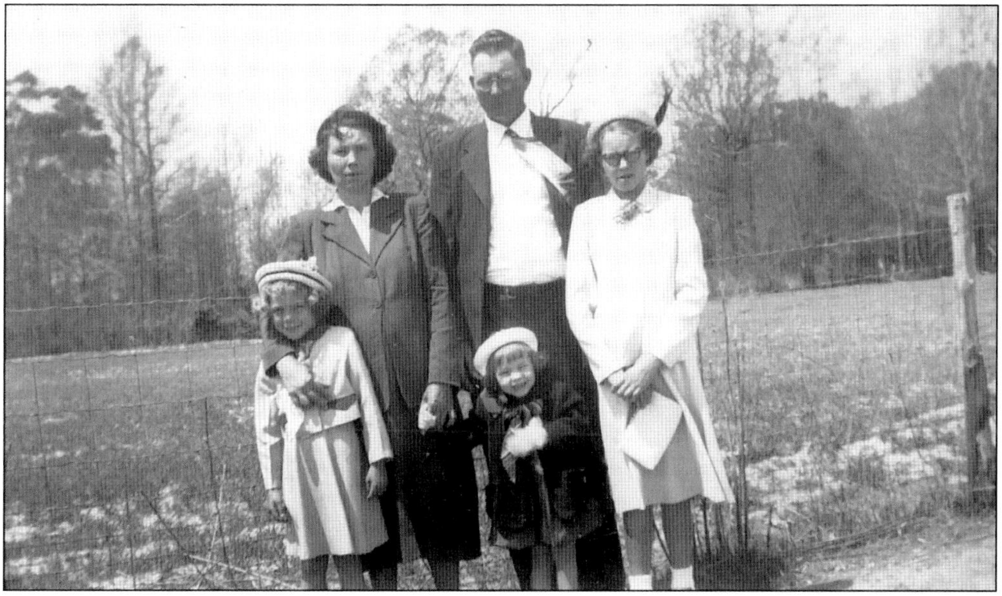

THE W.W. HOLLIDAY FAMILY, c. 1953. Pictured here are Mr. and Mrs. Woodrow W. Holliday of the Williamston area and their daughters, Judy, Nell, and Carolyn. (Courtesy of Fred W. Harrison Jr.)

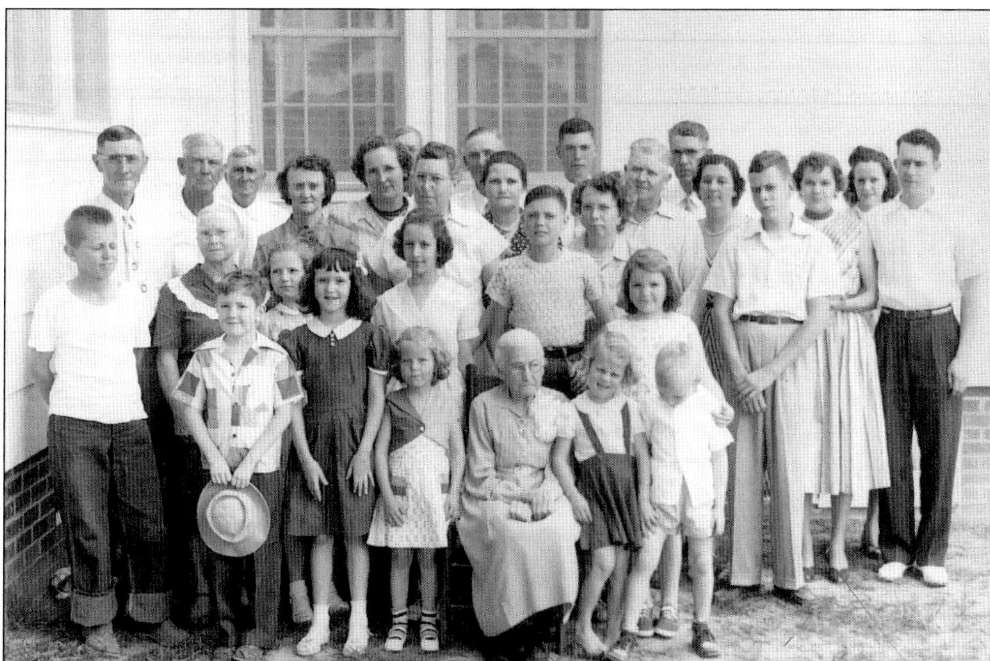

THE GURKIN FAMILY REUNION IN THE FARM LIFE AREA, c. 1955. (Courtesy of Chloe G. Tuttle.)

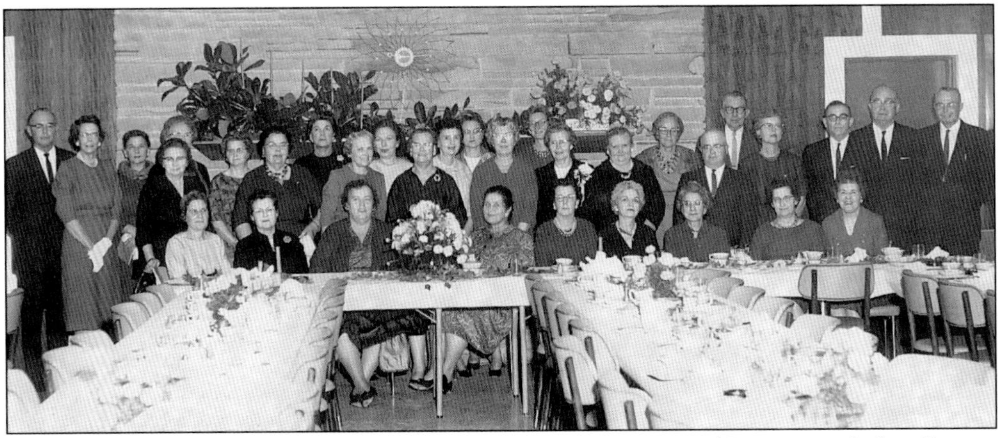

A Martin County Teachers Banquet, October 1962. (Courtesy of the Francis Manning Room.)

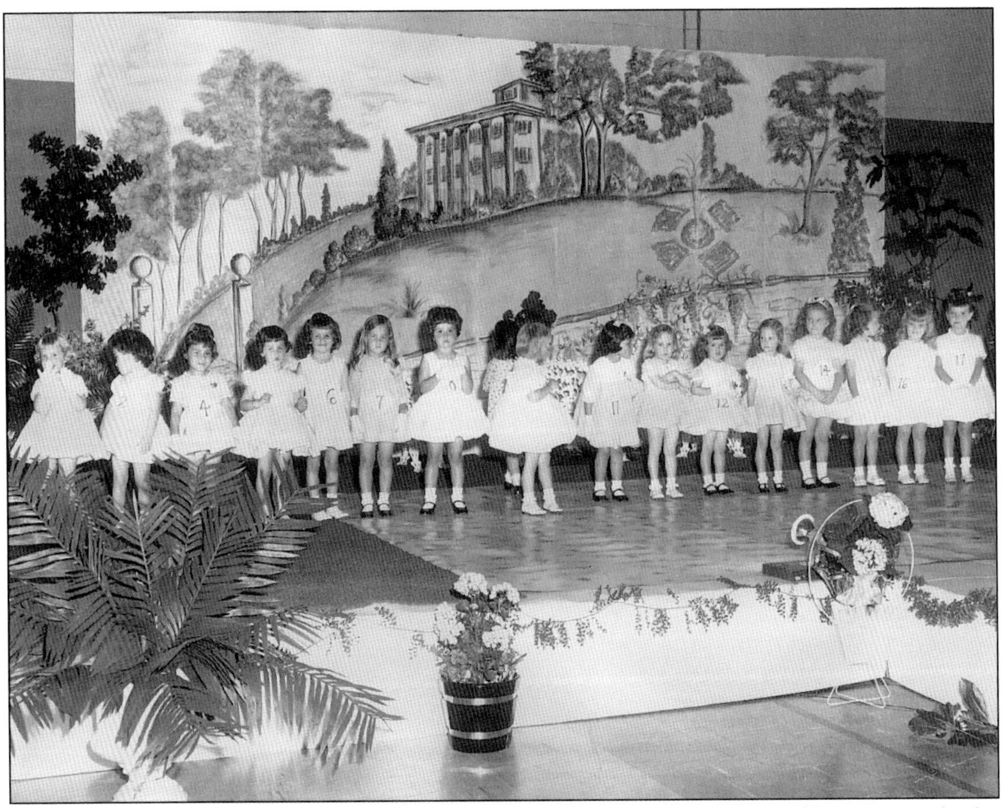

A Youth Beauty Pageant in Williamston, c. Mid-1960s. (Courtesy of the Francis Manning Room.)